I0755699

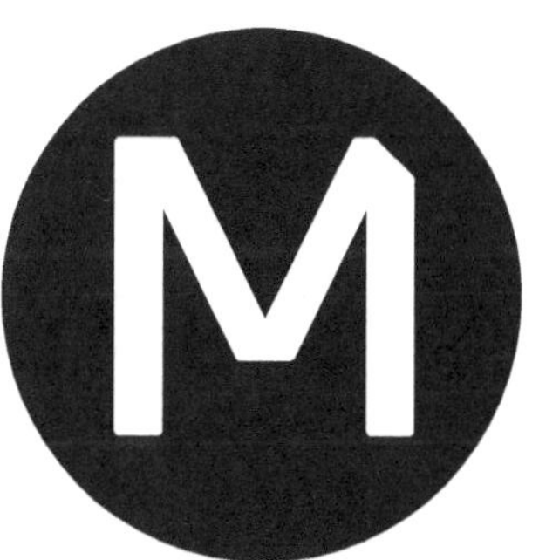
M

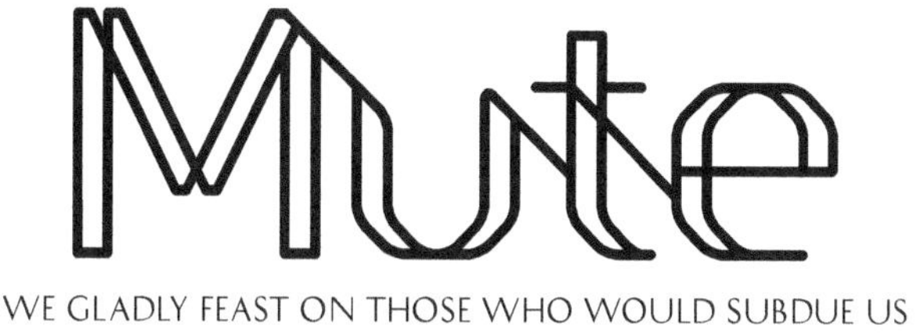

WE GLADLY FEAST ON THOSE WHO WOULD SUBDUE US

VOLUME 3 #3
BECOMING IMPERSONAL

SUMMER 2012

Published by Mute Publishing
Print colour ISBN 978-1-906496-03-6
Print POD ISBN 978-1-906496-86-9
ISSN 1356-7748-303

Also available as eBook ISBN 978-1-906496-87-6

In collaboration with Post-Media Lab, Leuphana University

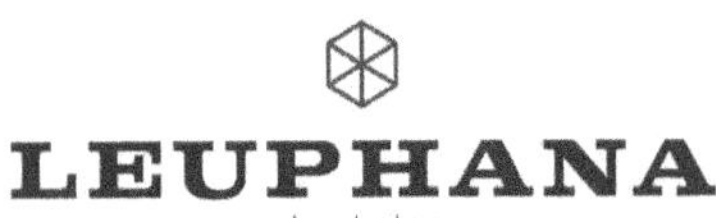

MUTE VOL 3 #3
SUMMER 2012

EDITOR
Josephine Berry Slater
<josie@metamute.org>

ASSISTANT EDITOR
Anthony Iles
<anthony@metamute.org>

EDITORIAL BOARD
Josephine Berry Slater

Omar El-Khairy
<omarelkhairy@gmail.com>

Matthew Hyland

Anthony Iles

Demetra Kotouza
<demetra@inventati.org>

Hari Kunzru
<hari@metamute.org>

Mira Mattar
<miramattar@googlemail.com>

Pauline van Mourik Broekman

Benedict Seymour
<ben@metamute.org>

Stefan Szczelkun
<stefan@szczels.plus.com>

Simon Worthington

MUTE PUBLISHING ADVISORY BOARD
Sally Jane Norman

Sukhdev Sandhu

Andrew Seto

Andrew Wilson

PUBLISHERS
Pauline van Mourik Broekman
<pauline@metamute.org>

Simon Worthington
<simon@metamute.org>

ADVERTISING & MARKETING
T: +44 (0)20 3287 9005
E: <mute@metamute.org>

WEBSITE
Metamute.org is run on Drupal FLOSS Software, with additional software services by our very own OpenMute http://openmute.org. Graphic design by Atwork, CSS by Roglok <roglok@hyperground.de>, template coding by Effusion http://effusion.co.uk

CHIEF ENGINEER
Darron Broad <darron@kewl.org>

LAYOUT DESIGN
Raquel Perez de Eulate <raquelwebs@googlemail.com>
Laura Oldenbourg <laura@metamute.org>

DESIGN TEMPLATE
Atwork http://www.atworkportfolio.co.uk

PRODUCTION MANAGER
Tom Clark <tom@metamute.org>

GENERAL MANAGER
Caroline Heron <caroline@metamute.org>

IMAGE REPROGRAPHICS
Happy Retouching <richard@happyretouching.com>

OFFICE
Mute, 46 Lexington Street, London, W1F 0LP
T: +44 (0)20 3287 9005
E: <mute@metamute.org>

SUBSCRIPTION AND DISTRIBUTION
Howard Slater
T: +44 (0)20 3287 9005
E: <howard@metamute.org>
W: http://www.metamute.org/subs

CONTRIBUTING
Mute welcomes contributions of all kinds. Email <mute@metamute.org> with your ideas. You can also publish on Mute's website [metamute.org]. Post news, text, events and comments, or upload media. The views expressed in Mute and Metamute are not necessarily those of the publishers or service providers. Mute is published in the UK by Mute publishing Ltd. and printed by OpenMute [http://metamute.org/services] print on demand [POD] book services.

COVER
Johannes Paul Raether <jpr@johannespaulraether.net>
http://www.johannespaulraether.net

SPECIAL THANKS
Thanks to Peter Cornwall

...ment — Journal for Contemporary Culture, Art and Politics

Issue 3 —
Spring/Summer 2012
€6 £5 $8

issue 3 of ...ment journal is titled F–R–A–G–... M–E–N–T (ON AUTHOR-SHIP) · 64pp

journalment.org

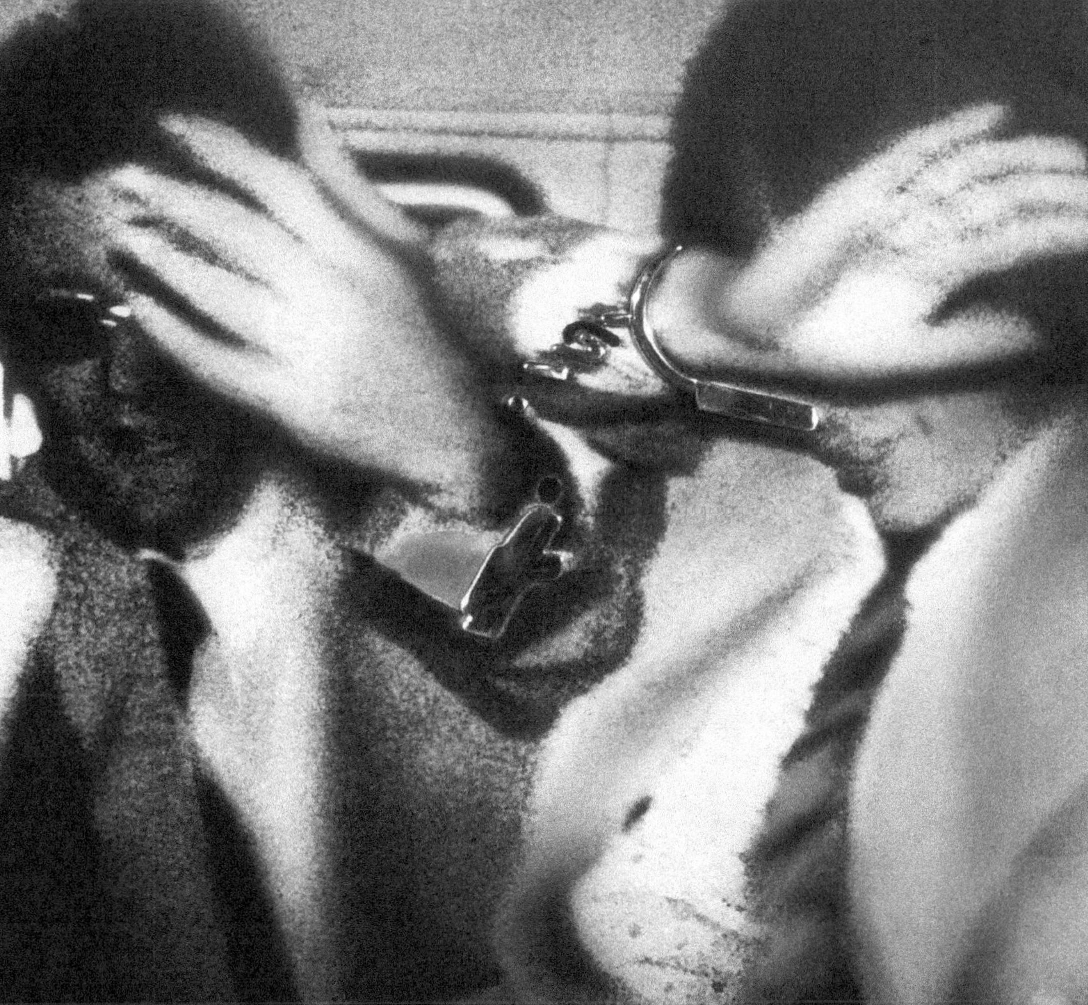

The MIT Press

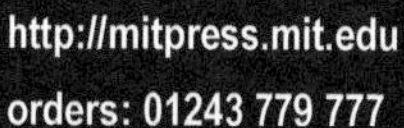

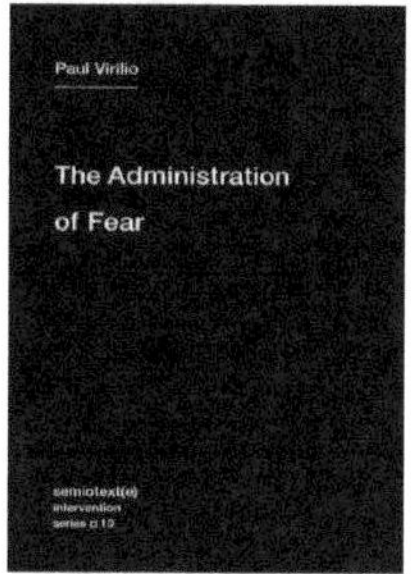

The Administration of Fear

Paul Virilio

translated by Ames Hodges

A new interview with the philosopher of speed on "how fear has become the world we live in" and how technology is utilized in synchronizing mass emotions.

£9.95 • 96 pp. • paper • 978-1-58435-105-4

Distributed for Semiotext(e)

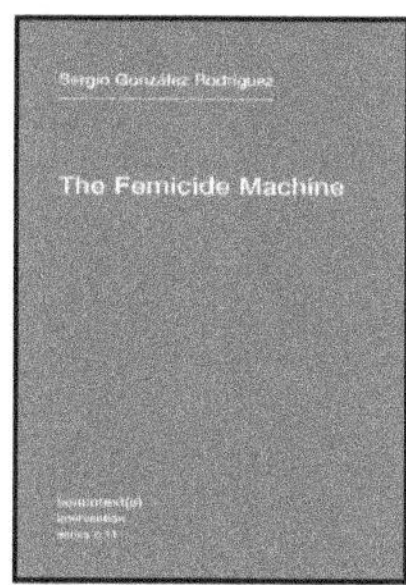

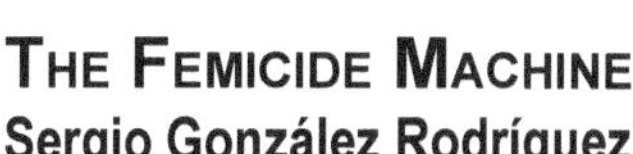

The Femicide Machine

Sergio González Rodríguez

translated by Michael Parker-Stainback

An account of the systematic rape and murder of women and girls in the Mexican border town of Ciudad Juárez, analysing the political and legal system of impunity and other "machines" that facilitated these atrocities.

£9.95 • 136 pp. • paper • 978-1-58435-110-8

Distributed for Semiotext(e)

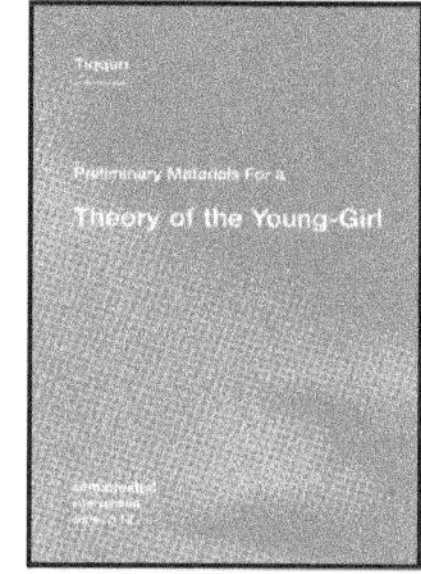

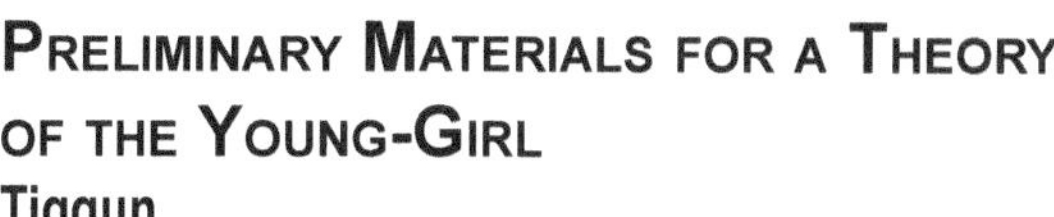

Preliminary Materials for a Theory of the Young-Girl

Tiqqun

translated by Ariana Reines

A theoretical dissection of current capitalism's degradation of the human subject and ultimate form of commodification: the living spectacle of the "Young-Girl", the consumer society's model citizen.

£9.95 • 144 pp. • paper • 978-1-58435-108-5 **August**

Distributed for Semiotext(e)

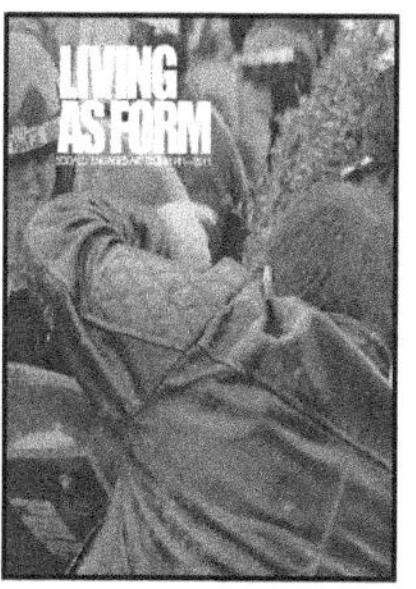

Living as Form

Twenty Years of Socially Engaged Art from 1991-2011

edited by Nato Thompson

A survey of over 100 art projects that use aesthetics to affect social dynamics. Emphasising participation, dialogue and action, these projects range from activism to theatre, from urban planning to health care, and include work from Jeremy Deller, Women on Waves and the Danish collective Superflex.

£27.95 • 280 pp. (250 colour & 50 b/w illus.) • cloth • 978-0-262-01734-3

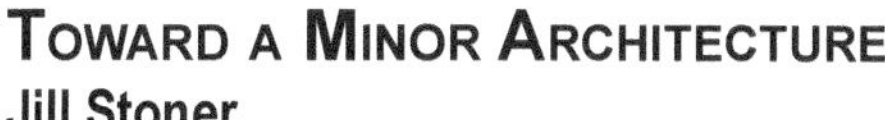

Toward a Minor Architecture

Jill Stoner

Proposing a more politicised, subversive practice of architecture and drawing on the literary theory of Deleuze and Guattari, Jill Stoner suggests that "minor" architectures, like minor literatures, can emerge from the bottom of power structures and within the language of those structures.

£13.95 • 176 pp. (25 b/w illus.) paper • 978-0-262-51764-5

VOLUME 3 #3
BECOMING IMPERSONAL
SUMMER 2012

EDITORIAL

In this issue of *Mute*, a disagreement over the politics of the 'We are the 99%' slogan emerges in articles by Clinical Wasteman and Nick Thoburn. For Thoburn, this numerical envelope binds the earth's majority into one unspecified category united in its exploitation by the remaining '1%'. Rejecting the trap of a political system which insists on the specification of demands as a means to position and ultimately neutralise dissent, Thoburn argues that the 99%, 'at once names and cuts the social relations of exploitation, among those who feel cramped by these relations, feel their intolerable pressure.' The relations of class are, by this account, identified but suspended in what is perhaps an act of nominal communism; the term invoking the inadequacy of class as a cipher of (political) identification and the hope of a classless future.

For the Wasteman though, the rhetoric of the 99% (which is not to be confused with the actions of occupiers or even Occupiers) allows its adopters to speak of 'social contradiction and crisis without reference to production, labour or class'. This observation links to his critique of David Graeber's book *Debt: the First 5000 Years* in which coin is disparaged for its impersonality, and impersonality written off as tainted with coin. Where Graeber sets up the personal, communal sociability of 'human economies' against systemic exploitation, the Wasteman insists that the two go hand in hand. Fighting against systemic exploitation by taking cover in its idealised opposite – the immediacy and mutual responsibility of community – fails to address both the personalisation of exploitation, and the nature of its global reproduction.

Elsewhere in the issue, the libertarian ideology behind Bitcoin is dissected by The Wine & Cheese Appreciation Society and Scott Lenney. The founders' dream of creating a money system that doesn't require banks or state institutions to guarantee its reliability is exposed for depending, nevertheless, on the violence monopolised by the state to enforce private property upon which Bitcoin runs. Once again, an argument is being made against the voluntarist and gestural escape from power relations – a means of consensual dreaming that, in the worst case, gives rise to likes of Time Bank; an 'autonomous' exchange system in which hipsters and creatives swap use values for sign value.

The debate certainly touches on the matter of so called symbolic protest – an overstated dichotomy, in my estimation, used to divide struggles into the effectual (non-symbolic) and the ineffectual (symbolic), while the prevailing conditions continue to darken regardless of such taxonomies, just as the reasons to tolerate them diminish. In other words, this kind of symbolic versus material political accountancy seems to sidestep the degree to which the symbolic and the material co-produce the social field. (The Diamond Jubilee as a media-Union-Jack-Tescos-workfare assemblage being just the most dumbly inescapable of recent examples).

So, what Thoburn articulates in his Deleuzian discussion of Occupy as an instance of 'minor politics' – a politics operated without the proper noun of a class-based or party guided movement, but rather by multiplying and connecting the 'cramped spaces' of privatised and scattered alienation – shouldn't be confused with an advocacy for symbolic politics alone. Although the occupations have largely targeted the (symbolic) theatres of the public sphere and not the arteries of production (with some notable exceptions, such as the shutdown of Oakland's port), they nevertheless put social reproduction at the heart of their activities. The feeding, sheltering and cultivation of the body doesn't just serve as the poster image of the movement (tents, make-shift kitchens, group deliberation over all this), it also identifies this aspect of social life, normally excluded from the public and political stage, as the site of struggle as well as of production.

In her article on the treatment of gender in communisation theory, P. Valentine considers the belated entrance of gender politics into male-dominated radical politics. While communisation theorists have sharply articulated how the production of gender, based on *some* women's ability to *sometimes* bear children, creates an underlying and *permanent* social division which underpins and sustains class relations in general, there is nevertheless an inattention to the private dimension of its enforcement, namely the use of sexual violence. Developing Valentine's argument, this obfuscation produces another outside to the legitimately political – or in biopolitical terms, another in a long series of constituent exclusions of naked life from the political.

The ways in which the personal can be grasped as political, then, seems to be an exponentially productive legacy of second wave feminism. This insistence, I think, connects the arguments made by many of the writers in this issue – from the Wasteman's emphasis of the unbearably personal experience of the impersonal pursuit of value, to Thoburn's discovery in Occupy of a collective exposure and deprivatisation of privatised hells, to P. Valentine's exposure of the social function of the private ordeal of sexual violence. The maintenance of a series of breaks or distinctions, both within the mainstream and on the left, between the personal and the impersonal, the private and the public, is exposed as actively constituent of the whole system. Johannes Paul Raether, who has made this issue's artist's project and cover, also finds in our tenderly nursed mobile phones one of the most pernicious conduits by which 'private' desires mesh with off-the-shelf subjectivities, or rather, the off-the-shelf is machined into the personal.

JOSEPHINE BERRY SLATER
<josie@metamute.org> is Editor of *Mute*

MINOR POLITICS, TERRITORY AND OCCUPY

In a talk given by NICK THOBURN *at the School of Ideas this February, some of the Occupy movement's most hopeful qualities were magnified through the lens of Deleuze and Guattari's theory*

The following is the text of a talk given at Occupy London's School of Ideas as part of a workshop called 'Deleuze and Guattari and Occupy', 25 February 2012. A little context may be instructive. Having moved from the Bank of Ideas in an occupied UBS office, the School of Ideas was situated in a spacious and attractive school building that had been left vacant for three years prior to its occupation. Two days after this talk the School of Ideas was evicted in a coordinated move with the eviction of the main Occupy London camp at St. Paul's Cathedral (at over four months, the world's longest running of the 750 camps that sprung up in the wake of Occupy Wall Street, the Spanish Indignados, and the Arab Spring).[1] Upon eviction, the School of Ideas was immediately bulldozed – a fitting emblem of the wanton destruction that characterises the current round of neoliberal restructuring and public service cuts.

Westminster local authority, just down the road from the School of Ideas, encapsulated the swagger of the new culture in its account of the implementation of cuts to housing benefit: 'To live in Westminster is a privilege, not a right'.[2] Inner London is indeed to be the class-cleansed home of the privileged; a middle class enclave serviced by a newly suburbanised and ever more precarious working class – Westminster's own figures project that 17 percent of primary school pupils could be forced to move out of the borough.[3] Meanwhile, at the other pole, March's 'millionaire's budget' cut taxation for the rich – those on incomes of £1m will benefit annually to the tune of £42,500.[4] No wonder the police and law courts have shifted up a gear in the discipline, punishment and brutalisation of student demonstrators, anti-cuts activists, and the young people involved in the August riots – a move undoubtedly driven by concern that the normalisation of this grotesque inequality can't hold indefinitely.

In repurposing the vacant UBS office and abandoned school, Occupy London has spun such critical threads as these through neoliberalism, cuts, housing and the city, and has done so in ways both analytical and practical. But the 'Bank' then 'School' of Ideas has also had a distinct *pedagogical* dimension. In Chile, California, Britain and elsewhere, direct action against neoliberal education policy has been a leading edge of the current cycle of struggles. These struggles are largely defensive, fighting for the last remnants of a model of liberal education that is far from perfect, albeit that it is vastly superior to the emerging neoliberal model of debt-financed vocationalism. But the composition of this struggle has also been characterised by new critical knowledges and solidarities, as funding cuts in tertiary and higher education, creeping privatisation of educational institutions, student debt and graduate unemployment have drawn together a diverse range of actors that have interrogated the forms, functions and possibilities of education at a new level of intensity. The School of Ideas, like other autonomous educational endeavours, has been interlaced with these developments, due not least to the circulation of participants through educational struggles and Occupy. But it was also something that 'stood up on its own', to make use of an expression I discuss below. Equal parts co-learning school, workshop, community centre, organisational base, public interface and home, one might say that the School of Ideas amplified (rather than isolated) the critical intellectual function and culture of

Occupy London. The School of Ideas has now gone; 'Occupy May' is around the corner.[5]

MINOR POLITICS

With the UK government itching to criminalise squatting, it's a real pleasure to be speaking in a building that is undergoing 'public repossession', so I'd like to thank Andy Conio for organising this workshop and the School of Ideas for hosting us. What I want to do in this talk is work through three of Deleuze and Guattari's concepts that are helpful in thinking about Occupy. What do I mean by 'helpful'? My aim is deliberately not to try and *explain* Occupy, to sew it up in a theory – that, for Deleuze, would be to negate what is inventive in a movement, but also to lose the inventive quality of *theory*, making it merely a *representation* of a state of affairs. Instead my approach will be to use theory to reflect upon certain themes or *problems* in Occupy, looking at how these problems can be approached with Deleuzian concepts in a way that might help shed light upon them and possibly aid their further development. It's a recursive relation, for reflection upon Occupy's themes or problems should also help extend Deleuzian concepts, lending them a contemporary vitality.

Given that this workshop is concerned in equal measure with bringing Deleuze and Guattari's concepts into relation with Occupy, and with offering an introduction to Deleuze and Guattari as political thinkers, I'm going to try and strike a balance between concept and Occupy, leaving space for us to expand upon the points I make about Occupy in the discussion. The concepts and problems that I address in turn are: minor politics and the 99%, territory, expression and occupation, then, fabulation and agency.

I will start with minor politics and fold in some comments about the 99% – though bear with me, the relation may not at first be apparent. Running throughout Deleuze and Guattari's philosophy is the notion that politics arises not in the fullness of an identity – a nation, a people, a collective subject – but, rather, in 'cramped spaces', 'choked passages', and 'impossible' positions, that is, among those who feel constrained by social relations.[6] This is at once a very immediate, structural experience – let's say, the experience of poverty, debt, or racism – and also something that is actively affirmed, a continual deferral of subjective plenitude that occurs when people shrug off and deny the seductions of identity and open their perception to what is 'intolerable' in social relations; for example, when they ward off the identity of the democratic citizen, the racialised majority, the entrepreneurial self.[7] So, what Deleuze and Guattari call 'major' or 'molar' politics expresses and constitutes identities that are nurtured and facilitated by a social environment, whereas 'minor politics' is a *breach* with such identities, when the social environment is experienced as constraint, as intolerable.

If this is the case, what is the *substance* of politics? Well, it can no longer be a question of self-expression, of the unfurling of a subjectivity or a people, because in this formulation there *is* no identity to unfurl, the '*people*' as Deleuze puts it, '*are missing*'.[8] Instead, minor politics is about engagement with the social relations that traverse us, the relations through which we experience life as 'cramped' and 'impossible'. By social relations I mean the whole gamut of economic structures, urban architectures, gendered divisions of labour, personal and sovereign debt, national borders, housing, policing, workfare – whatever combination

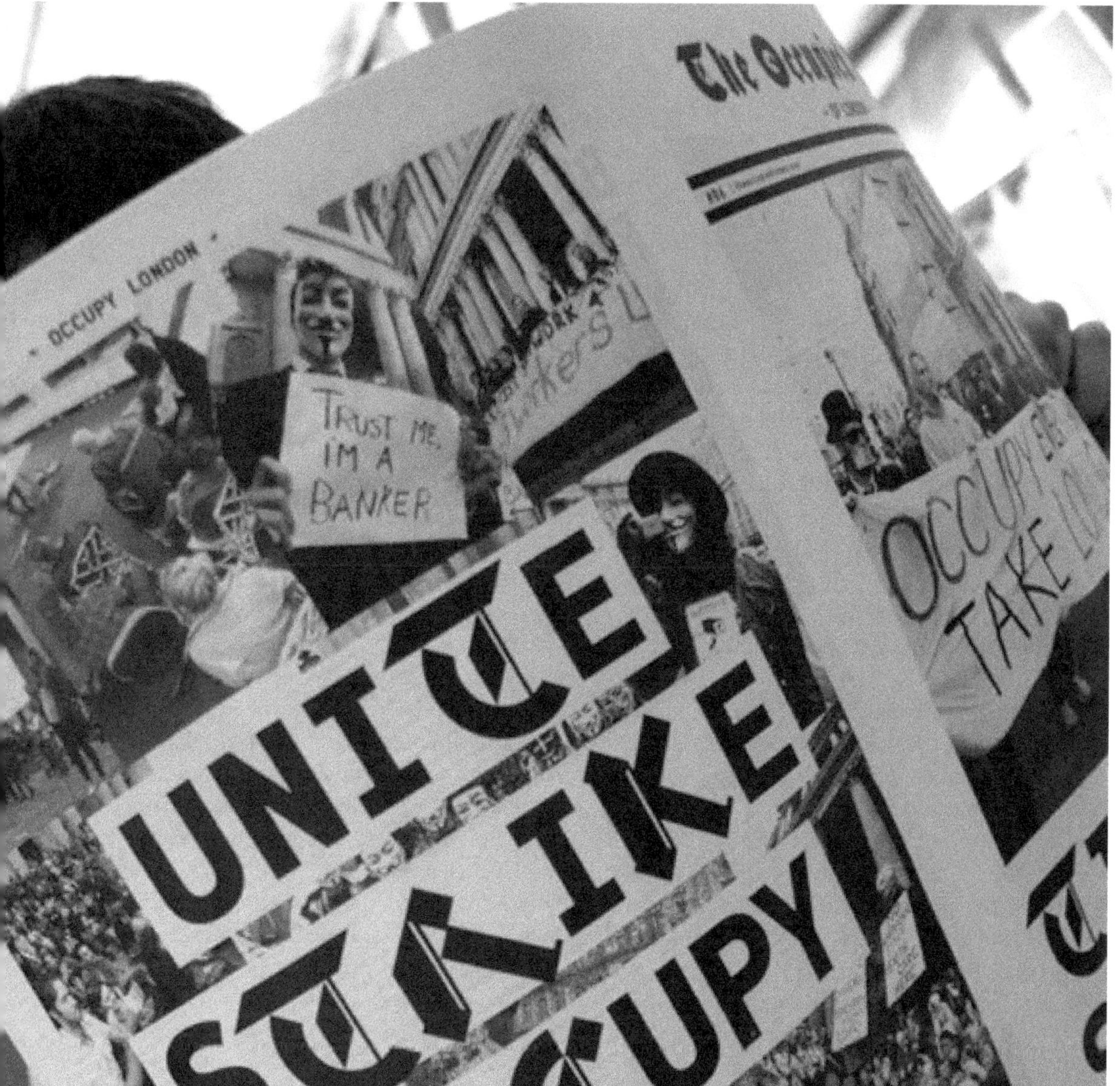

Cover of *The Occupied Times of London*, 2011

it might be in any particular situation. In this formulation, the 'individual intrigue', as Deleuze and Guattari have it, is 'immediately' political, for without an autonomous identity, even the most personal, individual situation is always already comprised of social relations, and vice versa. The deferral of identity is in no way a reduction of singularity, quite the reverse: 'The individual concern thus becomes all the more necessary, indispensable, magnified, because a whole other story is vibrating within it'.[9]

Deleuze uses an appealing image to convey this. He says that to be on the Right is to perceive the world starting with identity, with self and family, and to move outward in concentric circles, to friends, city, nation, continent, world, with diminishing affective investment in each circle, and with an abiding sense that the centre needs defending against the periphery. On the contrary, to be on the Left is to *start* one's perception on the periphery and to move *inwards*. It requires not the bolstering of the centre, but an appreciation that the centre is interlaced with the periphery, a process that undoes the distance between the two.[10]

Now, there is an important *propulsive* or *motive* aspect to this minor politics. For rather than allow the solidification of particular political and cultural routes, forms or habits, the practice of warding off identity works as a mechanism to induce continuous experimentation, drawing thought and practice back into a field of problematisation, where contestation, argument and engagement with social relations ever arises from the experience of cramped space. The constitutive sociality of this 'incessant bustle' dictates that there can be no easy demarcation between conceptual production, personal style, concrete intervention, tactical development or geopolitical events, and there is plenty of space for polemic.[11] It is a vital environment apparent in Kafka's seductive description of minor literature:

> What in great literature goes on down below, constituting a not indispensable cellar of the structure, here takes place in the full light of day, what is there a matter of passing interest for a few, here absorbs everyone no less than as a matter of life and death.[12]

I want to make one more brief point before turning to Occupy. I gestured toward a (potentially infinite) range of social relations that minor politics might arise from and engage with, but for Deleuze and Guattari there is a dynamic internal to *all* of them, the dynamic of capital. Deleuze states:

> Félix Guattari and I have remained Marxists, in our two different ways, perhaps, but both of us. You see, we think any political philosophy must turn on the analysis of capitalism and the ways it has developed. What we find most interesting in Marx is his analysis of capitalism as an immanent system that's constantly overcoming its own limitations, and then coming up against them once more in a broader form, because its fundamental limit is capital itself.[13]

As is abundantly clear in the quotation, Deleuze's assertion of 'Marxism' is not the introduction of a transcendent explanation, but an insistence that we won't understand the social field or develop effective politics without coming to grips with the contemporary modalities and dynamic structures of the capitalist mode of production, structures that set the conditions through which life is reproduced.

THE GRID OF THE 99%

A demand is a mechanism of seduction into the grid of democratic politics

What has this account of minor politics got to do with Occupy? I want to consider that question through the theme or problem expressed in the Occupy slogan 'We are the 99%'. It is a problem with a number of component parts. I'll comment on just two here. 'We are the 99%' is an assertion that the vast majority of the world's population are exploited by and for the wealth of the 1%. It names, in other words, a relationship of exploitation and inequality. And so, to refer to the point I just made about Deleuze and Guattari's Marxism, the problematisation of capitalism is central. Second, 'We are the 99%' simultaneously designates a *breach* with this relationship of exploitation and inequality. Let me stress that in neither instance does the slogan name a substantial *identity*. Rather, it at once names and cuts the *social relations* of exploitation, among those who feel cramped by these relations, feel their intolerable pressure.

This naming and breach in capital is of course very general. 'We are the 99%' is something like a 'formula' or, to use a term with more spatial connotations, a 'grid'. It lays out the abstract principle that can be taken up and extended by anyone who would embody or express it in their concrete specificity. In order to see how this grid functions, I want to compare it to one that Occupy is more or less directly opposed to, the grid of parliamentary democracy. Parliamentary democracy is, for Deleuze, a grid laid out across social space that seduces and channels political activity through its specific forms and structures:

> Elections are not a particular locale, nor a particular day in the calendar. They are more like a grid that affects the way we understand and perceive things. Everything is mapped back on this grid and gets warped as a result.[14]

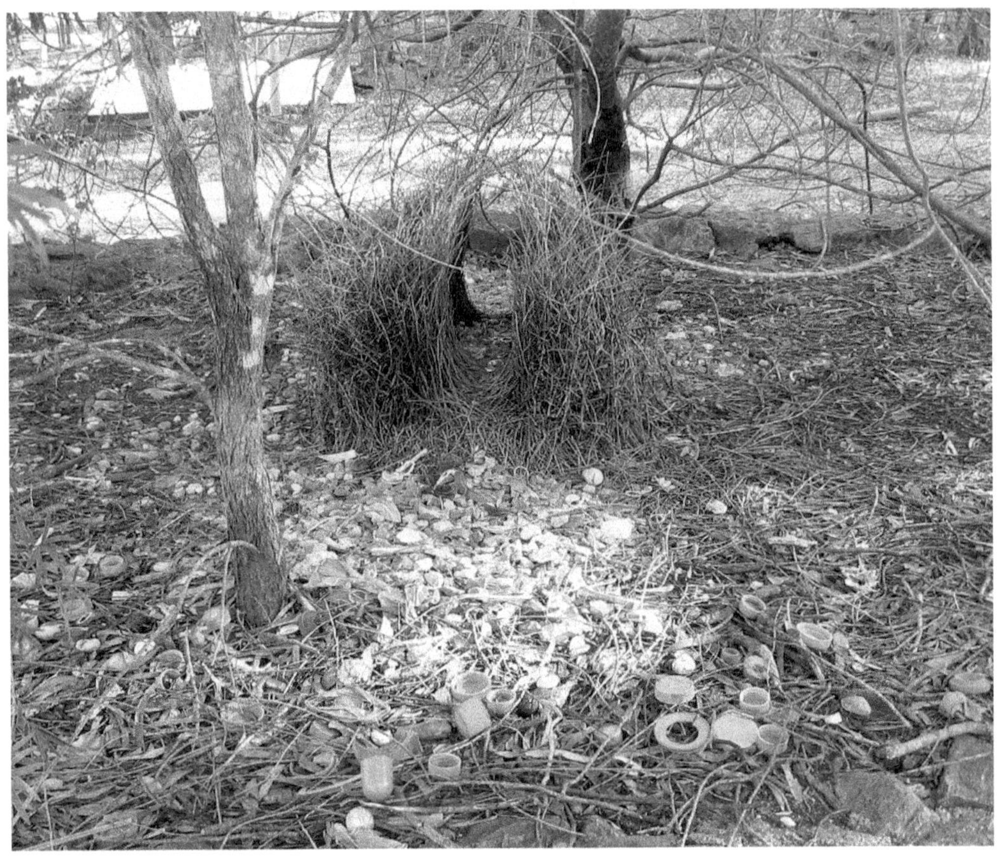

Nest of the bowerbird

Politics in this way gets 'warped' as he puts it because everything is reduced to and formatted by the status quo, to the perpetuation of that which gave rise to politics in the first place. A fundamental aspect of this warping is the filtering out of problems of inequality and exploitation from the realms of political interrogation. This was of course Marx's insight, but the condition is currently so *acute* that it has widespread, even popular recognition, as Greece and Italy have unelected technocrats imposed on the populace to force through hitherto unknown assaults on living standards, as the ConDems slice up the NHS while claiming that it matters *not 'one jot'* whether it is run by the state or private capital.[15] This is why Occupy's much remarked upon refusal to make demands is so important and so much a product of our times. A demand is a mechanism of seduction into the grid of democratic politics, a means of channelling the political breach with capital right back into the institutions that perpetuate it.

In contrast, the grid that is constituted by the slogan 'We are the 99%' is very different. Rather than a mechanism of seduction into the status quo, it is a means of *multiplying points of antagonism*, or, in more Deleuzian terms, it extends the process of perceiving the intolerable and politicising social relations. This does not occur *in general*, but from people's concrete and situated experience – it is a variegated field, where the points of problematisation are housing repossession, the laying waste of public services, privatisation of the commons, debt, police violence, workfare and so on, and the tactics range from occupying social space, through the Oakland general strike, to direct actions against eviction from foreclosed housing, non-payment of debt, the hacking activities of Anonymous, or 'public repossessions' as we have in this building. The grid is a *catalyst* across the social, not an aggregating body extending ever outwards from Zuccotti Park but a zigzag, a discontinuous and emergent process. Again, it's not a catalyst because people come to recognise themselves in it as an identity – even a *collective* identity – but because they come to embody and express its *problematic*.

Before moving on I want to directly address two points that are implicit in what I've said so far. First, it is not infrequently said by those involved in Occupy that it is in some sense creating the new world in the shell of the old. That practices of collective decision, direct action, co-operation and care, global association and so on are a kind of communism in miniature. Certainly, all of these collective practices are crucial to understanding the unfurling of Occupy, to its effectivity and affective consistency, to the complex pleasures of being a part of it. But from the perspective, of a minor politics the risk is that Occupy turns inwards, valorising its own cultural forms at the expense of self-problematisation and an ever outward engagement in social relations. Occupy's vitality lies in its extension and intensification of the problematic of the 99% through an open set of socio-political sites, in what is of course a highly segmented and stratified terrain. For it is in and through these sites that the world's population exists, and from which an unknown set of possible futures will emerge. To limit those futures to the cultural forms discovered in Occupy camps would be naïve at the least, and risks a conservative reduction of the movement's potential, a reduction to identity.

Second, refusing to make demands is not a refusal to *speak*, to formulate and express our anger, hopes and desires. On the contrary, to work through the problems of Occupy requires an incessant production of critical knowledge, knowledge that needs be circulated in the extension and development of these problems. The point is that this knowledge production is *immanent* to Occupy, not a pleading for recognition from an external power. We have seen Occupy developing slogans and concrete decisions that clearly define what the movement wants, as part of a reflection on how it's going to get it – and this, of course, is encouraging. But such formulations need to have a minor political 'efficiency', they must be adequate to the specific and mutating problems of Occupy and its world, not reproduce themselves at the level of cliché. As Guattari has it, 'either a minor language connects to minor issues [which should not be taken to mean 'small' or exclusively 'local' issues], producing particular results, or it remains isolated, vegetates, turns back on itself and produces nothing.'[16] All this knowledge production will involve critique, contestation and the development of divergent positions. Deleuze and Guattari are certainly interested in the way group consistencies emerge from distributed decision – let's say, the process of 'consensus' in Occupy's General Assemblies – but a good problem is not best extended in thought and practice by pretending *the construction of territory goes hand in hand with art which is a question of home or habitat*

that we all agree: 'The idea of a Western democratic conversation between friends has never produced a single concept'.[17]

TERRITORY AND EXPRESSION

I will move now to my second main concept and problem – on this and my third point I will be more concise. I want to look at an aspect of the tactic of *occupation*, specifically the *tent*, and explore the relation to Deleuze and Guattari's concepts of 'territory' and 'expression'.

The tent is first of all a practical object. It enables space to be taken and held for a certain duration. In this respect it has a family resemblance to the tripod as was used by Reclaim the Streets in the 1990s, an object that worked at once to cut the flow of traffic and act as a catalyst in the occupation of a road and the emergence of a street party. In Deleuzian terms, both tent and tripod play a part in 'deterritorialising' the space in which they operate – that is, in undoing the patterns of behaviour, laws, sensory structures and economic forms that determine that space as a road, stage for commerce or park. But if the tent and tripod deterritorialise in this way, they simultaneously generate a *new* territory, they *re*-territorialise into an Occupy camp or a street party.

To construct such a territory is of course difficult. It requires considerable knowledge of the territory that is to be undone: the law, movements of traffic, an intuition about likely police tactics, potential solidarities and enmities of the locale and so on. The constructed territory is thus a finely balanced constellation and can be easily botched. Things in London might have been different, for example, if Paternoster Square hadn't been barred and Occupy had not instead ended up on land owned by the Church.

But let's turn to consider the characteristics of Occupy's territory. Deleuze and Guattari make a rather intriguing argument that the construction of territory goes hand in hand with *art*, that art is a question of *home* or *habitat*: 'Perhaps art begins with the animal, at least with the animal that carves out a territory and constructs a house.' Such territory is functional, of course, but it is simultaneously sensory and expressive, that is, *artful*: 'the territory implies the emergence of pure sensory qualities, of sensibilia that cease to be merely functional and become expressive features, making possible a transformation of functions.'[18] One can see these tangled aspects of habitat and expression in the 'art' of the bowerbird.

What are the components of this constructed territory? Well, they are drawn from the environment, from existent materials – in the case of the bowerbird, twigs, berries, bottle tops – but they are also qualities and forms that emerge in the process of construction:

> This emergence of pure sensory qualities is already art, not only in the treatment of external materials but in the body's postures and colours, in the songs and cries that mark out the territory. It is an outpouring of features, colours, and sounds that are inseparable insofar as they become expressive.[19]

The St. Paul's Occupation is very much this kind of constructed territory. It comprises practical materials, the tent of course, items of furniture, cooking equipment – but also placards and signs, books, newspapers, drums, assemblies, hand signals, the people's mic, photographic images, livestreams, YouTube clips, the OccupyLSX website and Twitter feed, and so on. My point is not to proclaim that Occupy is 'art' exactly, but to suggest that alongside the *practical* tactics of occupation, the construction of territory through these functional components also includes an expressive, *sensory* quality that becomes an inseparable aspect of the Occupation.[20] This is one explanation, for instance, of the production of *newspapers* at the Occupy camps, when online production and distribution is clearly more practicable. As well as being an object of news and practical politics, the newspaper in this regard is also a *bloc of sensation*, an *aesthetic expression* of Occupy.

TENT AS MONUMENT

You might ask, 'what's the relation between this sensory or expressive quality of Occupy and its *meaning* or explicit *politics*?' For Deleuze and Guattari the two are different modalities of composition that come into a mutually sustaining encounter. They sometimes use a peculiar word for these works of art or works of territory – they call them *monuments*:

> the monument is not something commemorating a past, it is a bloc of present sensations that owe their preservation only to themselves and that *provide the event with the compound that celebrates it.* The monument's action is not memory but fabulation. [...][It] confides to the ear of the future the persistent sensations that embody the event: the constantly renewed suffering of men and women, their recreated protestations, their constantly resumed struggle.[21]

So, the monument, the bloc of sensation, *celebrates* the event of which it is a part. In our case, it celebrates the suffering and struggle that is named and enacted by the slogan or grid of the 99%.

I have mentioned the range of artefacts that constitute the work of territory, the monument, but the *tent* is a special case. It is of course a habitation, that's what distinguishes it from the tripod I mentioned earlier. As habitation it has great tactical value in the endurance of Occupy, even through the winter. But it also comes with particular sensory associations or expressive qualities. A tent pitched in the inner city conveys something of the *fragility* of life, the precariousness of existence – 'bare life', if you will, an impersonal quality of *all* life. And this impersonal, precarious life is filtered in our time through the specific condition of homelessness, as soaring rents, mortgage foreclosures, evictions, benefit and wage cuts, debt and unemployment tip the home into a state of crisis. Indeed, as we're seeing with the rise of 'tent cities' in the US, the tent has become a very real habitation for a considerable volume of displaced people – including people at Occupy St. Paul's and elsewhere: 'a part of the homeless has become Occupy London, and a part of Occupy London has become the homeless.'[22]

a tent pitched in the inner city conveys something of the fragility of life

This quality of life – fragile, impersonal, damaged – is central to the tent as monument, lifting 'suffering' to the level of aesthetic expression without losing any of its 'struggle'. Even in its expression of suffering, then, the tent is not an *abject* object. But it also conveys a rather joyous quality of mobility. At risk of playing to a cliché, it is the dwelling of the *nomad* so dear to Deleuze and Guattari, where dwelling is part of an itinerant process, tied not to land but subordinated to the journey – the production of a 'movable and moving ground' through 'pitching one's tent' (the deliberately processual quality of Occupy is plain for all to see).[23] With the tent, then, we see something of the tactical or practical aspect of Occupy interlaced with its sensory or expressive quality, a tactic and a sensory bloc – both, for Deleuze and Guattari, are constitutive of its territorial form.

The nomadic tent orients our attention to a final aspect of the territory of Occupy. As well as constituting its territory, Occupy needs also to be open to a degree of deterritorialisation of its own. What does this mean? You can think of deterritorialisation here as the spatial dimension of that opening to the social which I began with, the process of warding off identity and problematising social relations. It is a central problem for Occupy, as perfectly expressed in an editorial of *The Occupied Times*:

> [The eviction of OWS from Zuccotti Park] triggered a period of self-examination about how the Occupy movement might best move forward beyond its signature tents and into communities, enacting the movement's core message through practical action rather than symbolism. It is a journey that has seen American occupiers leave tents behind in favour of defending the homes of those about to be foreclosed. [...] Thanks to equal measures of adroitness and serendipity, Occupy London's initial encampment at St. Paul's Churchyard has now far outlived Zuccotti Park in duration. [...] It would be a bitter irony – and a failure of enormous proportions – if we allowed our comparative security to stop us seeing some of our more distinctive tactics for what they are: a tool to be employed only for as long as they remain useful. Useful tactics generate change. They inspire others to act. To do that we must look outwards.[24]

This process of deterritorialisation concerns not only the dynamics of the one territory, but also the relation or *reverberation* with other territories. The obvious example is the relation with St. Paul's itself. There's a clear sense in which Occupy subjected St. Paul's to a force of deterritorialisation, this *minor* monument undoing at the borders Wren's rather more major monument and the Church's structures of authority. Hence we witnessed Giles Fraser's resignation and Occupy's forcing of the Church to reflect upon the politics of Christianity and its relation to the City's banks. In turn, this strange reverberation between Occupy and St. Paul's had some effect on the territory of the popular imagination, if we can call it that, even on its media representation. The obvious hypocrisy of the Church in its initial dealings with Occupy seemed to lift and project the image of Occupy in the popular imagination, lending it a degree of sympathy and support that it may not have had if it had been in a straight face off with bankers and police (for, despite all that we have witnessed since 2008, when the lines are drawn between police and resistance in this way, common sense, ever re-charged by news media, unfortunately still tends to prostrate itself to the truths of authority).

fabulation is a weapon of the weak, a means of fabricating 'giants'

There are of course other points and possibilities of reverberation: other Occupy camps, the hacker cultures, precarious workers, rootless graduates, assailants of workfare, those involved in education campaigns, and so on. The aim of Deleuzian theory would be to consider the specific qualities or features of these interlaced points, all of them groping toward some sort of *patchwork* of politicised relations.

FABULATION AND AGENCY

Thus far I have worked through two sets of concepts and problems: minor politics and the 99%; and territory and occupation. I want to end now with a brief sketch of a third concept and problem. This is Deleuze and Guattari's concept of *myth* or *fabulation* and the problem of the collective *agency* of Occupy. In theory circles at the moment and in some commentary on Occupy there are indications of a return to voluntarism, with talk of the people's 'will' as driver of change. From a Deleuzian perspective, voluntarism abstracts a pure subjectivity from what are in fact multiple levels of subjective determination (economic, libidinal, semiotic, organisational, etc.), and so fails to ascertain where politics comes from or to address why subjectivity – or 'will' – tends more usually to *repress* itself. Deleuze and Guattari would counter this voluntarism with the minor political emphasis on practical problematisation that was the focus of the first part of this talk – political composition not formed of a generic quality of human being, but arisen from the specific material conditions of 'the present state of things', as Marx has it. But there is an additional aspect of Deleuzian philosophy that is helpful for getting at the issues of collective *agency* or *force* that those who appeal to the people's will are, rightly, interested in.

Concepts, problems, territories and so on are constructed by their participants in the kinds of ways that I have been discussing. But they also have a *self*-positing character – they are created by participants, and they simultaneously create *themselves*, they have a life of their own: 'Creation and self-positing mutually imply each other because what is truly created, from the living being to the work of art, thereby enjoys a self-positing of itself, or an autopoetic characteristic by which it is recognized'.[25]

This isn't easy; most created entities collapse without becoming self-positing. But if an entity *does* achieve this, if it can 'stand up on its own', as Deleuze and Guattari put it, then you have something interesting, something with an *agency* all of its own.[26] You have a revolution, an artwork, a concept, or in our case, you have the Occupy movement. What does it mean to say that Occupy is self-positing? It means that as well as being generated by the people, tactics, objects, slogans, sounds and so on that are a part of its territory, it also takes on a life of its own, a life that pulls its constituent parts along, creating *them* as parts of its event.

Now, when Deleuze and Guattari discuss this self-positing process in the context of politics, they sometimes describe it as a process of 'fabulation'. It's a word you might have noticed earlier in the quotation about the monument. Fabulation or myth-making occurs when the shock of an event - be it an earthquake, a work of art, a social upheaval - produces visions or hallucinatory images that substitute for routine patterns of perception and action and come to guide the event. In Deleuze and Guattari's reading, fabulation is a weapon of the weak, a means of fabricating 'giants', as they put it - germinal agents with real world effects in the service of political change.[27] What is perhaps most appealing in the context of Occupy is that these fabulations or myths are not so much located in individual *people* - the cults of personality, for instance, the Lenins, Maos, Churchills, what have you - but have a *desubjectified* or *anonymous* quality, generated and held in the fragmented *bits* of events, stories, medias, affects and material resources, and are associated as much with 'mediocrity' as with the grandiose.[28] In this way Deleuze describes myth as a 'monster', it *'has a life of its own:* an image that is always stitched together, patched up, continually growing along the way'.[29]

Occupy has something of this mythical quality, an agential power of its own that exists among and between us, and that pulls its particularities along. I'll end by pointing to one small (and by no means unproblematic) artefact in this myth: the Guy Fawkes mask. Think how different these two images of political myth are. Mao, a concentrated myth centred on an individual and the truth of his infallible thought. And the Guy Fawkes mask, an anonymous, distributed power - a part of the myth of Occupy, open to anyone, signifying a resistance to closure in a leader, vaguely menacing, a little bit silly, mediocre even, and pop cultural to boot. The mask's impersonal mythical power is well expressed in a cartoon in *The Occupied Times*, a cartoon that takes its words from Subcomandante Marcos and so forms a red thread across to another political myth of our time: it's not 'who we *are*' that's important, but '*what we want*', 'everything for everyone'.[30]

Nick Thoburn <N.Thoburn@Manchester.ac.uk> lectures in sociology at the University of Manchester. He is the author of *Deleuze, Marx and Politics* (Routledge, 2003) and is currently writing a book on the forms and cultures of independent media

FOOTNOTES

1 'Occupy protests around the world: full list visualised', http://linkme2.net/s7

2 Westminster council press officer quoted in Amelia Gentleman, 'Housing benefit cap forces families to leave central London or be homeless', *The*

Guardian, 16 February 2012, http://linkme2.net/s6
3 Ibid.
4 Patrick Collinson, 'Budget 2012: earning £1m? Your tax cut will pay for a Porsche', *The Guardian*, 21 March 2012, http://linkme2.net/s5
5 This article introduction was written in April 2012. See http://occupylsx.org/
6 Gilles Deleuze and Félix Guattari, *Kafka: Towards a Minor Literature*, Dana Polan (trans.), Minneapolis: University of Minnesota Press, 1986, pp.16-17; Gilles Deleuze, *Negotiations*, Martin Joughin (trans.), New York: Columbia University Press, 1999, p.133.
7 I develop this 'minor politics' at length in *Deleuze, Marx and Politics*, London: Routledge, 2003.
8 Gilles Deleuze, *Cinema 2: The Time-Image*, Hugh Tomlinson and Robert Galeta (trans.), London: Athlone, 1989, p.216.
9 Op. cit., p.17.
10 Gilles Deleuze with Claire Parnet, *Gilles Deleuze: From A to Z*, Pierre-André Boutang (dir.), Charles Stivale (trans.), Los Angeles: Semiotext(e), 2012.
11 Franz Kafka, *The Diaries of Franz Kafka: 1910-23*, Maz Brod (ed.), Joseph Kresh and Martin Greenberg (trans.), London: Penguin, 1999, p.148.
12 Kafka quoted in Deleuze and Guattari, op cit., p.17
13 Deleuze, *Negotiations*, op. cit., p.171.
14 Gilles Deleuze, *Two Regimes of Madness: Texts and Interviews 1975-1995*, David Lapoujade (ed.), Ames Hodges and Mike Taormina (trans.), Los Angeles: Semiotext(e), p.143.
15 'To be honest I don't think it should matter one jot whether a patient is looked after by a hospital or a medical professional from the public, private or charitable sector', Tory Health Minister Lord Howe, quoted in Nick Triggle, 'Private Sector Have Huge NHS Opportunity', 7 September 2011, http://www.bbc.co.uk/news/health-14821946
16 Felix Guattari, *Chaosophy*, Sylvère Lotringer (ed.), New York: Semiotext(e), 1995, p.37.
17 Gilles Deleuze and Felix Guattari, *What Is Philosophy?*, Hugh Tomlinson and Graham Burchill (trans.), London: Verso, 1994, p.6.
18 Ibid., p.183.
19 Ibid., p.184.
20 The bowerbird is certainly not the last word on 'art' in Deleuze and Guattari. Despite possible indications to the contrary here, their writing on art is not best viewed through the avant-garde lens of the subsumption of art and everyday life, for they invest considerable import in the exacting forms and techniques of modernist practice, in painting and cinema especially. See Simon O'Sullivan, *Art Encounters Deleuze and Guattari: Thought Beyond Representation*, London: Palgrave, 2006, and Stephen Zepke, *Art as Abstract Machine: Ontology and Aesthetics in Deleuze and Guattari*, London: Routledge, 2005.
21 *What Is Philosophy?*, op. cit., pp.167-8, 176-7, emphasis added.
22 'Occupy London Homelessness Statement', http://theoccupiedtimes.co.uk/?p=2594
23 *What Is Philosophy?*, ibid., p.105. Many thanks to John Bywater for pointing out this passage on the 'English' taste for camping, which helps counter any orientalism in Deleuze and Guattari's concept of nomadic dwelling.
24 *The Occupied Times* no.8, p.2, http://theoccupiedtimes.co.uk/?p=1744
25 *What Is Philosophy?*, op. cit., p.11.
26 Ibid., p.164.
27 Ibid., p.171.
28 Ibid., p.171.
29 Deleuze, *Cinema 2*, ibid., p.150; Deleuze, *Essays Critical and Clinical*, Daniel W. Smith and Michael A. Greco (trans.), Minneapolis: University of Minnesota Press, 1997, p.118.
30 *The Occupied Times* no.6, p.2, http://theoccupiedtimes.co.uk/wp-content/uploads/2011/11/OT-ISSUE-6.pdf

ORGY OF THE NON/SELF

Yayoi Kusama's recent Tate Modern retrospective provokes JOSEPHINE BERRY SLATER *to join the dots of the artist's agonising and ecstatic constellation of obliteration and multiplication*

A Yayoi Kusama can paint, I mean really paint. Her early works, displayed in the Tate Modern retrospective, would take you by surprise if you had her pegged as that dotty lady, the one whose only idea is to cover every available surface with polka dots. But the logic of the dots seems to have developed with surprising continuity from these early paintings, their rhythms and patterns, which explore accumulation as the constitutive force of the cosmos. Like Daniel Buren and his stripes, there is a tension in her later dotty work between a signature device which risks becoming a deadening calling card of identity, and the use of an accumulative gesture which generates fields, states and environments beyond the provenance of their creator. With Kusama's work, the later installations as much as the early paintings, repetitive gestures comprise a code which builds out from identity and even art, to produce patterns which throb with a cosmic pulse of creation. Her painstakingly rendered dots, which should at all costs be distinguished from those sweated out in Damian Hirst's accumulation factory, also presently on display at Tate Modern, share with the early paintings the power to reflect and induce the joyful agony of self-obliteration. 'Self-obliteration', a phrase she developed in the '60s during her Body Festival phase, is the necessary stake of her creativity, but one that always menacingly threatens a collapse into self-destruction.

Kusama's parents ran a plant nursery business in Matsumoto City, Japan, and her early paintings bear many traces of a child's micro-perception of flowers, plants, seeds and insects. From the materials she used – household paint mixed with sand and seeds, a consequence of post-war austerity – to the butterfly-winged delicacy of her paint brush as she specks and flecks the hypnotic biomorphic forms that flowed irrepressibly from her hand, her art is propelled by a vitalism, a feeling for generative life, that would carry her away were it not combined with a steadying intellect. This intellect can be seen at work in the sparse, gestural brevity of a gouache work like *Flower Bud No.6* (1952) as much as the decisiveness to carry off more epic and sustained pieces like *Accumulation of the Corpses (Prisoner Surrounded by the Curtain of Depersonalization)*, (1950). This latter work, painted some five years after the atomic attacks on Japan, depicts a tunnelled folding of intestinal cords, which sometimes burst open into vaginal lesions, drawing the eye down to a central aperture, populated by two tiny bare trees. It is a surrealistic cry of pain somehow lifted from terminal angst by the bold sensuality of its fleshiness, its sexuality.

The control, or rather, precision of these early paintings reaches a different order of magnitude in her *Infinity Net* paintings of the late '50s, undertaken as she struggled to make it as a painter on the mean streets of New York City. These entail the repetition, ad nauseum, of a 'simple act', the rendering of a tiny loop or 'O' of white oil paint, concatenated into giant nets which, on closer examination, appear to have been built up in concentric circular patches. These meshes were rendered over washes of pacific blue or grey hues, across canvases of up to 14 feet. From her diary, also titled *Infinity Net*, which I briefly perused in the gallery shop, it seems like the state in which she painted these works was often more hallucinatory than meditative. Her trance-like state was intensified by the hunger and cold she suffered during a spell of abject poverty on arrival in New York from Seattle, her point of entry into the country. The limited money she'd been allowed to bring

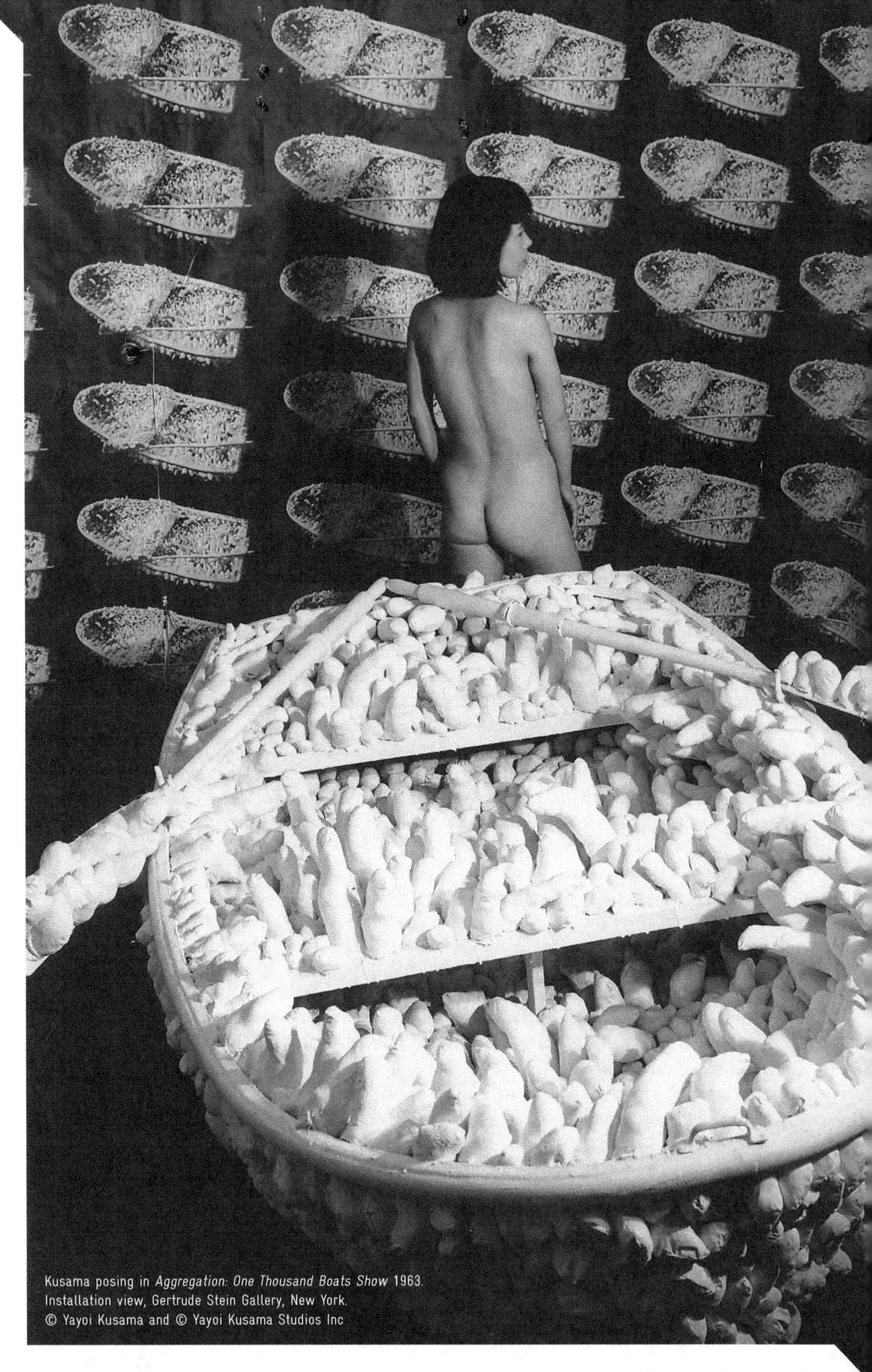

Kusama posing in *Aggregation: One Thousand Boats Show* 1963.
Installation view, Gertrude Stein Gallery, New York.

through customs, boosted as it was by the additional cash stuffed into her shoes and sewed into her clothes as well as a stack of kimonos, dwindled to nothing in the devouring city. Sleeping on a door scavenged from the street, shivering under a single blanket through the New York winter and with the heating turned off at 6pm every evening in the warehouse building where she live/worked, she drove herself from dawn to dusk, pausing only to eat a meagre meal. Painting the nets became a way to withstand this bodily ordeal. It is important to register the depth of her isolation and fragility in this stage of her life, and how it creates another 'ground' over which the net was thrown.

Later she said, 'This was my "epic", summing up all I was. And the spell of the dots and the mesh enfolded me in a magical curtain of mysterious, invisible powers.' The libidinal machine of the net paintings had a dual magic: to create a subjectless and centreless field, a field infinite enough to blot out and dematerialise the overbearing, canyon-like streets of Manhattan, the gnawing hunger, the pain of her desires, and on the other hand, to launch a guerilla attack on the machismo of the New York school painters. These paintings proved to be her meal ticket, landing her two shows first at the small artists' co-operative gallery, Brata, on Tenth St. in 1961, and then a solo show at the prestigious Stephen Radich Gallery. Against the heroics of American abstraction epitomised by Jackson Pollock – whose drip paintings attempted to thwart representation but nevertheless always courted it, as the splats and drips powerfully evoked the bodily and biographical forces which produced them – Kusama's work is 'exhaustive', as Mignon Nixon puts it. It entails a painterly drudgery that empties out identity and signification. There is an invocation of female reproductive labour that can be glimpsed in this mastery of the 'mundane' (Kusama's word), the quiet doing and re-doing of a task that self-effaces, quells the appetites, produces others, wears you out. And yet, these paintings are rendered on massive canvases and in oil, which may have seemed obligatory for anyone wanting to be taken seriously on the gallery circuit at this time; both were new departures for the painter who'd previously worked on a smallish scale, on paper and with inks, gouache or homemade concoctions. Along with many women artists of her generation, she elevates the mundanity of feminine handiwork, of craft, but it is hard to call to mind many who challenged the male avant-garde so forthrightly in its own, epic terms. How, though, should we consider this contradiction between Kusama's desire for recognition, even stardom, and her wish to self-obliterate?

The spell of the dots and the mesh enfolded me in a magic curtain of mysterious invisible powers

One answer could be that fame is itself a form of self-obliteration, since publicity is a kind of repetition compulsion spewing out reproductions of a name and image, a name, image and slogan, a name, image and slogan that equals a 'style' which, in a sense, is ownerless or at least masterless. The accumulation of publicity produces a power which confronts a self steadily overwhelmed by its own projected image. Of course it's unlikely that Kusama would have deliberately courted such a piranha attack upon herself – she talks, instead, of her blood running hot with the desire to revolutionise art – but there is a growing sense, towards the end of the '60s, that her own self-publicity machine had run out of control. Jumping on the flower power, free love bandwagon, she began staging Kusama Body-Festivals, Anatomic Explosion happenings, Kusama's Self-Obliteration events, and even launched a fashion label. What is striking about all this is her utter seriousness in the midst of what, from the looks of local headlines, was widely perceived, and enjoyed as no holds barred bohemian hedonism or free love with an Oriental twist. The obligatory self-expression of the '60s counter-culture, apparently at one with Kusama's naked orgies where everyone painted each other with dots and danced to the groovy psychedelics, is somehow sobered by the intensity of her injunction to self-obliterate. Both parties seemed to be opportunistically interested in what the other had to offer: the exhibitionists could reveal all and express their natural proclivities at her events, while Kusama dematerialised them into a field of dots. In a film titled *Kusama's Self-Obliteration*, she applies painted dots to a male participant's genitalia with an expert hand and oblivious concentration. The exhibition contains many of Kusama's flyers from this period, giving a sense of both how hard she drove herself and how serious she was about connecting to the counter-culture. One of her first Self-Obliteration events was at Woodstock in 1967, and the promotional text itself exudes something of the discomfort of this mash-up of pop and avant-gardism:

> Become one with eternity. Obliterate your personality. Become part of your environment. Forget yourself. Self-destruction is the only way out! On your trip take along one of our live bikini models.

It's easy to discern echoes of pop irony in Kusama's adoption of marketing spiel and, as it turns out, Kusama was both an anticipator and glancing collaborator in the movement. Her 1963 installation *Aggregation: One Thousand Boats Show*, pre-empted Andy Warhol's use of wallpaper by several years as a means of environmentalising two dimensional images and estranging them through repetition. This work, which preceded the self-obliteration festivals, came in the midst of her accumulation sculpture period, which are reminiscent of the slapdash, prosaic plaster objects in Claes Oldenburg's shop. Kusama relentlessly covered household objects, shoes and clothing in monochrome protuberances, often referred to by critics as 'phalli', though they are equally reminiscent of the tentacles of sea anemones, pebbles on a beach or animal droppings, as my kids pointed out. The boat installation, while sharing the use of industrial repetition with pop, belongs most of all to the surrealist phylum. A rowing boat, with oars resting along its sides, is covered in biomorphic tentacles and spray-gunned white. It sits, spotlit, in a room entirely covered with black wallpaper printed over with a photographic image of the boat that forms its focus. This romantic escape vessel, which makes you think of the Lady of Shalott's doomed pursuit of Lancelot, has passed from the epic's production of solitude into the desiring-production of the unconscious as it proliferates a-signifying flows. The boat has been perverted, and this perversion is also cinematic; the wallpaper's photographic repetition of the image also alludes to the cinema's production of movement through the repetition of frames. But the boat is grounded for now, and its absent steersman is no matinee idol running on the tracks of narrative, but the accumulative force of the libido whose byproducts silt up the world, clogging up the cogs of all our projection machines until they shudder to a stop.

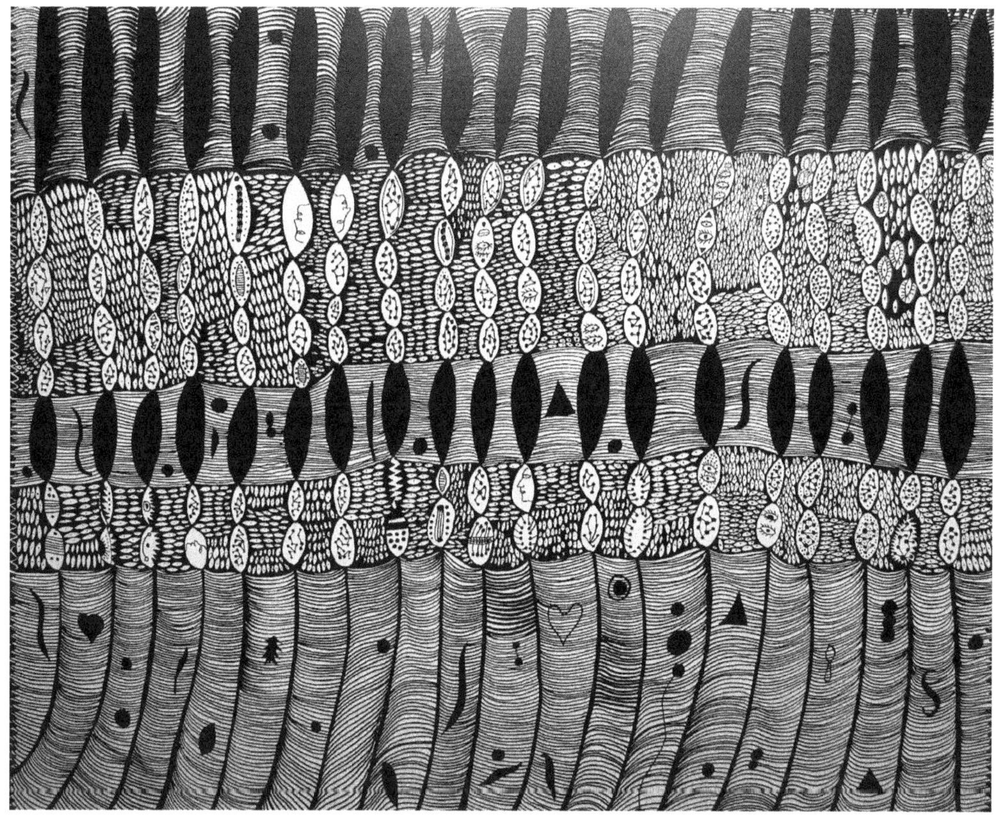

Yayoi Kusama, *Guidepost to Youth [HOTQOX]*, 2007

A work which might seem to reduce the dramatisation of her immigrant and female vulnerability to the level of farce is *Walking Piece*, 1966; a series of photographic slides taken by Eiko Hosoe projected onto a wall which document her walking around some of the industrial and poor neighbourhoods of New York in pink kimono, gold slippers, plaited hair and an umbrella covered in flowers. We see Kusama pose for photos amidst what can only be described as the toxic brutality of New York, her flower-like delicacy offsetting the filth of the gum stained pavements, the vulgarity of signage ('Banquet Meat Pies 2.35'), the ambient pollution (in several slides she dabs her eyes with her sleeve, as if cleaning out grit), and the lie of the American dream (in one slide she strides away from the Manhattan skyline, the Empire State appearing as a distant fantasy; in another, a poor white woman sits on chair in the street, watching the artist go by, in a further one she inspects a homeless man asleep under a tree). If anything, these images seem to dramatise the bankruptcy of what might be inadequately called industrial capitalism or the American way of life; her delicacy isn't fey, for her expression is wise, her gestures highly conscious. She seems to represent an alien consciousness making observations which will be ported back to a more evolved life form, or a witness of all these sorrows. Both her choice of locations as well as the insertion of her kimono'd form bring forth the 'masculine' side of the city – its smokestacks, main arteries, silos, its crushing labour – not as a way of dramatising *her* vulnerability, I think, but in order to bring its crushing, productive logic to the fore.

This is one of Kusama's few detours into representation, even documentary, and it certainly strikes a different note to the vitalist positivity of much of her other work. But, if we consider some of the early Holocaust inflected images and their titles (*Corpses*, *Accumulation of the Corpses*, etc.), it is possible to see how her exodus from representation as much as identity is consistently connected to a civilisational horror, a recognition of the abyss of humanity's attempts to master nature and substitute it with something better. Or, as with the resemblance her paintings evoke between flowers and planets, she likewise registers the multiple scales of brutality, finding it at the heart of innocuous domestic objects as much as in industry, science and, indeed, art. The accumulation sculptures of the early '60s erupt the apparent homeliness of domesticity, revealing a lurking perversity – sofas and armchairs are ready to mindlessly violate their sitters and enjoyment itself is understood as something structural, endemic to muted and naturalised power relations. In *The Man*, 1963, she covers a canvas in phallic feelers, and suspends a kettle from the longest one, seemingly urging some handmaiden to put the kettle on. This connection of the canvas to an endemic sexism brings to mind the concluding lines of beat poet Diane di Prima's *The Quarrel* from 1961:

> Hey hon Mark yelled at me from the living room.
> It says here Picasso produces fourteen hours a day.

Kusama is an unlikely feminist, as well an unlikely negator of capitalism. She seems, in many ways, too complicit with the system, both the art world and the seduction industry. The photo on the cover of the Tate catalogue is a perfect example of the problem. She lies on her back in a field of stuffed and spotted biomorphs, her eyes blackened with '60s eye makeup, hair spread out and her dress pushed up passed her knickers, kicking one leg up. This slightly awkward self-presentation as 'babe' isn't a one off. She famously posed naked but for a pair of black high heels and covered in dots on her sculpture *Accumulation No.2*, a phallus encrusted white sofa. Much ink has been spilt by Amelia Jones, in her book *Body Art*, on deciphering this image, connecting it, as she does to the second wave feminist strategy of foregrounding and acting out the obscured and occluded nature of (sexual) desire which stratifies the field of art. In this image, Jones sees Kusama as making explicit the western desire and fascination for the body of the exotic Other predicated on the apparent modesty and supplication of Oriental women. The artist seems to deny this cliché of the appetitive subordination of (Oriental) women to men – she lies on a phallic field of her own making, she is the mistress of her own jouissance – but the image is also seductive. She can still be enjoyed by an audience who is nevertheless approached and arrested by the usual friction of titillation. Is this just a consumer revolt in the shopping mall of the spectacle, a soft subversion of the status quo?

There's a haunting image of Kusama on her arrival in Seattle in 1957 with the gallerist Zoe Dusanne. Both are dressed 'Japanese style', in kimonos, in what appears to be Dusanne's apartment, or a back room of her gallery. The walls are hung with Miro-esque paintings, which could possibly be Kusama's own work.

Kusama looks out like an unwilling accomplice, as her ghoulish patroness apes the Geisha style of makeup, her waspish pearl necklace and earrings offsetting the masque. In the letters displayed in the exhibition, Dusanne's offer to Kusama of her first show in the States is fleshed out into full mise-en-scene, almost a diplomatic mission of cultural exchange. Having patronisingly suggested that the show should be in spring because her very Japanese patio will be in bloom, she remarks, 'I have many Japanese friends who would be very happy to wear costumes and serve Japanese tea at the opening.' With friends like this, no wonder Kusama wanted to self-obliterate! This image registers the length of the journey Kusama had to undertake from such a servile entry into the American art world to her glorious, titillating provocations a decade later. If nothing else, this is a story of admirable self-empowerment, and possibly liberation. What is worth noting, with regards to her use of her own image as 'babe', but also as psychedelic priestess or bizarrely wooden fashion model for her own 'fashion brand', is the certain indifference which she always expresses. There is a touch of Robert Bresson's use of actors as blank mannequins, but turned around into a self-use. This indifference is expressed in the title of the show's penultimate installation (a living room covered in coloured stickers and illuminated with ultra-violet fluorescent strips), *I'm Here, but Nothing*. In fact the strange dimensional effect of the UV light which only picks up the stickers (think teeth in a night club), thereby throwing the rest of room and its conventionality into semi-darkness, seems an apt metaphor for Kusama's speculative realism, to abuse a neologism.

'Consensus reality' is a ground over which Kusama throws her magic net, but this ground needs to be there to bring her net to life. Her art shifts the focus back and forth between the dematerialisation, or cosmic relativisation of the brutal or banal social field – the domestic space or the city, the orgy or the gallery, the fashion industry or the seduction industry – and its sharpened articulation. It seems to come forward and show its face at the same moment that she makes it recede. Her early '60s accumulation canvases of air mail stickers and fake money work in just this way; without labouring the point, they attest not only to the repetition-disorder of capitalism, but show how there are other repetitive and accumulative dynamics at play, which underpin but also ultimately dwarf it: those of the libido and the procreant urge of the world. In the words of the great Walt Whitman:

> I have heard what the talkers were talking,
> the talk of the
> beginning and the end,
> But I do not talk of the beginning or the end.
> There was never any more inception than there is now,
> Nor any more youth or age than there is now,
> And will never be any more perfection than there is now,
> Nor any more heaven or hell than there is now.
> Urge and urge and urge,
> Always the procreant urge of the world.
>
> – 'Song of Myself'

Josephine Berry Slater <josie@metamute.org> is editor of Mute and co-author, with Anthony Iles, of the book *No Room to Move: Radical Art and the Regenerate City*

INFO

Yayoi Kusama's exhibition was at the Tate Modern 9 February – 5 June 2012

NO INTEREST BUT THE INTEREST OF BREATHING

This is not in any normal sense a review of David Graeber's book, which is erudite yet non-specialist, often brilliant and always fiercely devoted to the overthrow of present social relations. The scope of Graeber's historical, anthropological and theoretical reference makes it impossible to gloss the whole thing here. In what follows,* CLINICAL WASTEMAN *picks up on the author's 5,000-year survey at the point where it intersects with nascent capital, in order to suggest that any thought of overthrowing capital as such may require quite a different standpoint, in which impersonality is not the enemy*

When I tell any Truth it is not for the sake of Convincing those who do not know it, but for the sake of defending those who do.

– William Blake

This book by an anarchist anthropologist was covered excitedly by the *Frankfurter Allgemeine Zeitung* and plugged several times by *Financial Times* US editor (and ex-anthropologist) Gillian Tett, along with more conventional praise in the culture sections of what pass for serious bourgeois newspapers. Why this should be so is a question worth asking, because Graeber conscientiously avoids the usual shortcuts to liberal embrace of leftist polemics: the book is neither a catalogue of under-analysed moral outrages nor a scholarly survey keeping tactful silence on present-day social antagonism. Not only is Graeber's formidable scholarship free of the positivistic manner that cripples peer-reviewed Human Sciences, his writing bristles with hostility to capitalism, or at least to the social order around him as he sees it, which may not be quite the same thing. A clue to the reasons for the book's reception in the *FT* and *FAZ* may lie in Graeber's willingness to claim authorship of the worst political slogan in recent memory. Rather than fleeing blame for 'We are the 99%', he has robustly defended his association with it. Of course the actual practices making up the 'Occupy movement' are not to be dismissed lightly or even assimilated into a single 'politics' at all; but actual practices were not the concern of the commentators who lavished earnest analysis both on the public statements made in the name of 'Occupy' and on Graeber's book. These journalists – or some of them anyway – are not fools. Technical knowledge of debt crisis makes it hard for them to ignore the contradictions of debt, the uncontainable scope of crisis and the social confrontation involved. In slightly different ways, the Occupy statements and the Graeber book offer the Experts an irresistible opportunity, inviting them to talk all they want about social contradiction and crisis without reference to production, labour or class. The notion of the 'unsustainability' of capitalism slips easily into capitalist media when everything specific to capital as such is left out of the question.

All this may or may not go some way towards explaining Graeber's popularity with respectable explainers, but it doesn't make him liable for anything they say. To denounce

* Anyone who has not read the book and wants to see its themes articulated in Graeber's own terms should turn to this interview (http://tinyurl.com/3k9dbsf) and this article (http://tinyurl.com/bocmupz).

Graeber wants to sweep aside all of western political economy

a non-Marxist author for neglect of Marxist categories would be vanity worthy of tenure track. Even a book aimed straight at a niche in the ideology market (as this one is not) may carry some descriptive or critical power: Graeber's sometime source Michael Hudson, who rather more forthrightly sets out to save capital from itself, is a good example. If some parts of *Debt, the First 5,000 Years* are alarming, it's not because they might appeal to 'reformist' columnists, but because the most radically 'anti-capitalist' moments call forth a lower-case 'communism' barely distinguishable from 'community', i.e. the currently favoured excuse for the social policing the author quite sincerely deplores.

Graeber is not engaged in sectarian point scoring. He wants to sweep aside all of western political economy (in his view of which Marx features only as a minor irritant) and set something else up in its place. Thus, towards the end of a convincing rebuttal of the 'barter myth' in general, and Adam Smith's use of it in particular, he asks in passing why that myth wasn't simply dumped by later economists along with other obviously embarrassing parts of Smith's thought: for example, *the labour theory of value*. This one-liner is allowed to sink in over several ethnographic and ancient-historical chapters before the author confirms that yes, he does mean it, and will try to back it up. But the backup doesn't involve any further discussion of labour in relation to debt, money or value. What is attacked instead is the whole materialist categorical framework in which anything like a labour theory of value could arise.

The strongest part of the book is a two-chapter description of the reciprocal determination of forms of money, state and religion/ideology across Asia, Europe and parts of Africa between 800 BC and 1450 AD, or the

'Axial Age' and 'Middle Ages'. This section not only contributes to a correction of the Eurocentrism common to orthodox economic history and much of Marxism, it approaches the best materialist history in its treatment of the economic formation of culture and the cultural articulation of economies. Graeber wouldn't like to be called a materialist though, and he'd be right. First because his economic perspective, from before 800 BC to the present, is almost all about exchange or circulation: not a trivial category, but not one that can be detached from production and made to stand by itself for material life as such. And then because all his attention to the detail of social conjunction and upheaval across many centuries and much of the geographical world is subordinated to a single transhistorical structure, in which the 'Cycles of History' everywhere deliver eternally recurring alternation between economies (or rather circulation systems) of personal 'credit' and impersonal 'coin'.[1]

The detailed description in these chapters is made to serve an explicit attack on 'materialism', in which the latter appears as an atrophied scientism of a kind surpassed in Graeber's own semi-materialist historical passages. The so-called materialism which the author finds flourishing during 'coin economy' periods from the Axial Age onwards – associated with quantification of inert objects for sale – is rightly identified as one side of a crude matter-spirit dualism, each side of which always entails the other, whether the ideal complement is a theological construction or the 'objective' eye/I of the empirical observer (e.g. a social anthropologist). Graeber's way of conveying this is at least original: instead of drawing attention to the idealism of positive science (an unfinished project with which any help would be welcome), he discovers the scandal of the secret materialism of Axial Age spirituality! Rhetorical surprises aside though, it's disingenuous to label as 'materialism' the metaphysical dualism of academic, commercial and political rationality. Materialist thought and gesture has negated this dualism in its scientific and spiritual forms since before Newton or Kant and ever after (Spinoza, Milton, Marx, Iggy Pop...), shadowed by a dialectical idealism that strains to enfold rather than expel the worldly (Bruno, Hegel, Blake, John Coltrane... and Graeber?) The problem with materialism is not that it has anything to do with the technical priestcraft and spiritual accountancy that give capital its metaphysics and common sense; rather, materialist negation languishes as a culturally tolerated curiosity while the corresponding social *practices* of negation remain provisionally held down.

If it's remembered throughout that what Graeber calls materialism is actually the matter/spirit dualism negated by materialists from monist scholastics to dialectical rioters, the story of this depleted science as it emerged and re-emerged along with more or less mercantile social conditions is useful. But the insistence on 'materialism' as a name for the ideological component of 'cash economies' can't help but evoke a vernacular meaning (actually less a part of any spoken idiom than a fixture of newspaper sermons): materialism as unseemly preoccupation with mere commodities, or simply 'greed'. As in: 'bankers/gangsta rappers/ *we* western consumers are *shallow and materialistic* and must be retrained in spiritual/community values'. Unlike the professional and amateur ideologists who actually say that sort of thing, Graeber is not preaching spiritual renewal as a *substitute* for satisfaction of material needs. But he clearly disapproves of materialism in the 'vulgar' sense to which he restricts the word:

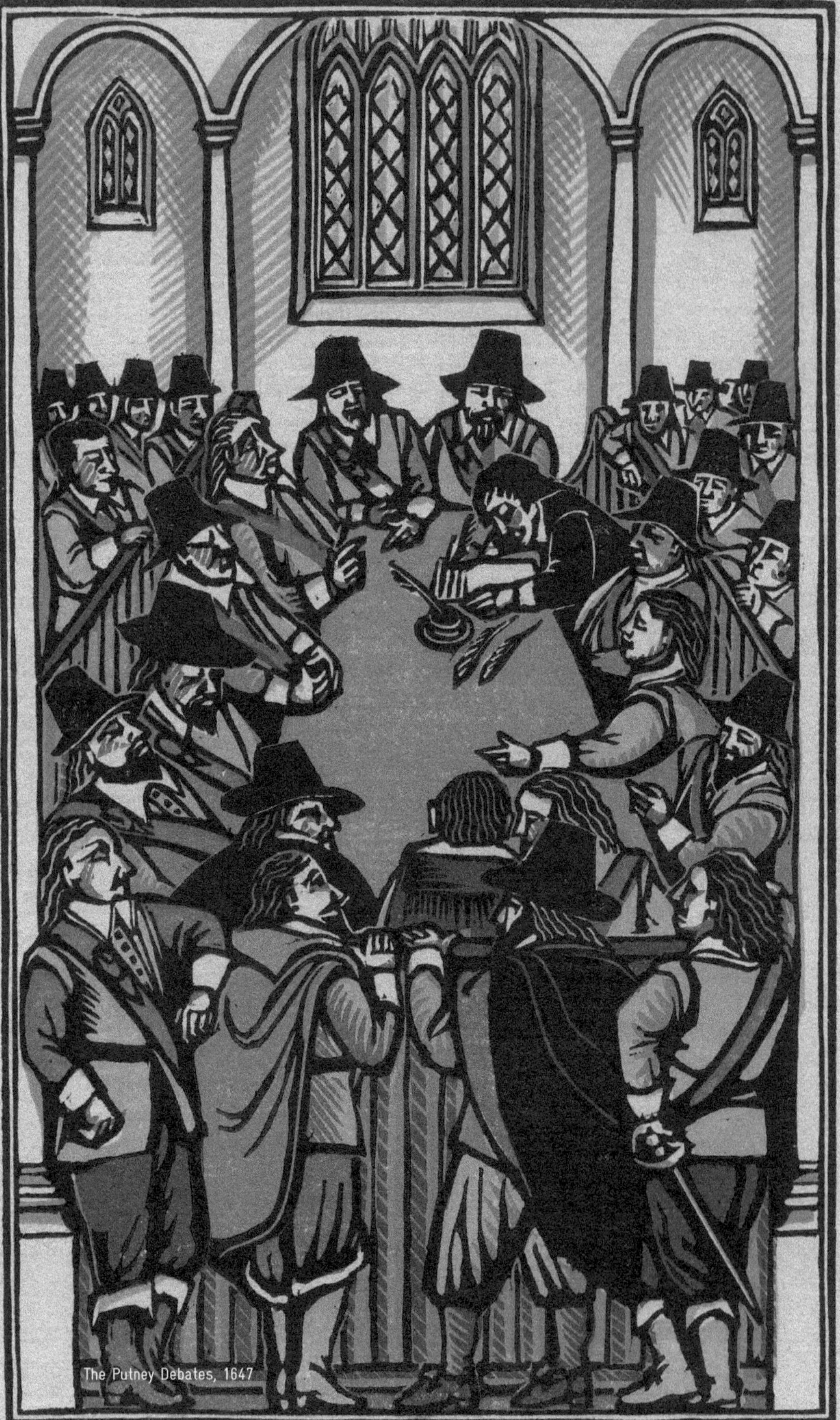
The Putney Debates, 1647

no sympathy at all for the elementary principle that *proletarian greed is good.*

Disdain for 'merely' material satisfaction aligns Graeber with many post-situationists and some (not all) theorists of 'communisation', who likewise presume that any revolution must be anthropological first: a collective self-curing of psychological 'alienation', with alienation of labour in the commodity to melt away as a second-order effect. One of the best answers to such thinking was pre-emptive, coming from a satiated bourgeois professor almost 30 years before cultural 'liberation' was first packaged with material retrenchment in response to 'the events of 1968'. 'There is tenderness only in the coarsest demand: that no-one shall go hungry any more'. Only 'a mankind which no longer knows want will begin to have an inkling of the delusory, futile nature of all arrangements hitherto made in order to escape want, which used wealth to reproduce want on a larger scale'.[2]

The stakes of the polemic against 'materialism' become clearer when the same treatment is visited shortly afterwards on 'interest/s' (as in 'self-interest'), probably a target with fewer defenders to begin with. Graeber starts from 'self-interest' in Hobbes, notes the etymology of *interesse*, as in interest on a debt, and thereafter sticks to a definition so narrow that any supply-side/rational markets theorist would approve. 'Self' is strictly a single individual, untroubled by contradictory desires and unbound by outside attachments. 'Interest' is not susceptibility in general to pain and pleasure or destruction and perpetuation, but strictly 'the continual pursuit of profit'. This giddyingly reductive formula serves the purpose of blanket moral condemnation, but as in the case of materialism, it either excludes or slanders most of what the word in question stands for.

Graeber's point is that the personal cost-benefit calculation called 'self-interest' in a tradition running from Hobbes to present day econometrics in no way resembles the entanglement of needs, impulses and constraints that really determines human social interaction. This much is true, but there's no reason in the first place to accept a Hobbesian/Chicago School reduction of the scope of subjective (including collective) interests to a simple profit-loss ledger kept by simple individuals. Once the caricature is admitted, then certainly almost everything lies outside it, but *how is this large remainder to be understood?* Graeber suggests 'love and amity, but also envy, spite, devotion, pity, lust, embarrassment, torpor, indignation and pride' as real human 'motivations'. The list is not supposed to be exhaustive, but its exclusively psychological and individual content is still striking. A few pages later Adam Smith is accused of ignoring 'the role of both benevolence *and* malevolence in economic affairs'. Thus a sphere of narrow, competitive individual 'interest' is counterposed to a disinterested sphere containing all the rest of personal morality. Such are the analytical and strategic materials left to anyone hoping to understand and change the world without attention to the contradictory, shifting, mediated interests that constitute, animate and rupture social subjects.

A dynamic conception of impersonal interests is not something peculiar to Marxism or otherwise eccentric: bourgeois political ascendancy would not have got far without it, any more than the ascendant class could have done without a world of personal morality for the edification of the lower orders. Graeber notes the transfer of 'interest' from bookkeeping to social philosophy in Hobbes (Leviathan, published 1651), but this was by no means an 'opening salvo' as he claims. The word was well established in English political vocabulary by the mid-17th century, most definitely as part of proprietor ideology, but not in anything like so narrow a sense as a 'penalty for late payment on a loan'. Rather, foreshadowing an argument repeated against franchise extension down to the 19th century, property owners would assert – against arbitrary royal power and feckless, landless rabble alike – their interest in the country. 'Interest' here combines today's financial and vernacular senses of exposure, with the second sense derived from the first. Ownership of land and/or mercantile capital amounts to something at stake, something to lose, in the political course of the state, and as such justifies the claim to a say in government. This doctrine, which contributed so much to bourgeois political legitimacy, simultaneously released the germ of its overthrow. The contradiction bursts forth in the voice of Oliver Cromwell at the Putney debates of 1647 (four years before *Leviathan*), where more than one future momentarily seemed within reach. 'Where is there any bound or limit set', he asked, if elections are opened to 'men who have no interest but the interest of breathing?'[3] The 'interest of breathing' is not an ironic rhetorical flourish: every successful bourgeois power since the 1640s has followed the example of Cromwell's Major-Generals in taking the merely-breathing interest seriously enough to plan some combination of its repression, division and corruption in advance.

Without a sense of the contradictory, indistinct, unstable interests of self-contradictory, indistinct, unstable 'subjects', it's impossible to understand endless warfare *between* the merely-breathing, and therefore impossible to think of overcoming it, unless you expect this to be achieved by some supreme effort of moral will. Hence the anathema early in this article against the '99%' slogan. Giving its proponents the benefit of the doubt that the percentage in question is intended as global rather than national, not 99 but 100 percent of the world's population share an abstract interest – or a concrete interest infinitely mediated – in the abolition of a value-form tending ultimately towards human annihilation. But the 99-1 breakdown disallows any innocuous dreaming of such things. It asserts a definite opposition – something that sounds like a class conflict, even – and names the sides. Yet these two sides are not really classes at all: they are not defined in terms of their material interaction, but demographically, i.e. by *personal identities:* whatever number (70 million, or 1 percent of 7 billion?) of the wealthiest individuals against everyone else in the world. Sophisticated supporters will object that 'the 99%' is just a slogan, neither meant as analysis nor subject to it, but when a slogan is repeated so often it's worth considering what the exact words imply. Which in this case is, if not perfect identity of all interests within the respective '99%' and '1%' groups, at least relegation of internal conflicts on either side to secondary, unimportant status. So that, for example, the difference between a London lawyer with a big mortgaged house (still 99 percent) and a hedge fund billionaire with a property portfolio (1) is fundamental in a way that the difference between the lawyer and a childcarer she employs on a semi-indentured temporary visa is not. And the conflict between immigrant African workers in South African townships and the local African workers who slaughtered them in the pogroms of 2008 must all have been a tragic misunderstanding, unless it was false consciousness or an explosion of individual sin. And likewise unreal is the contradiction lived by a low-paid specialist in

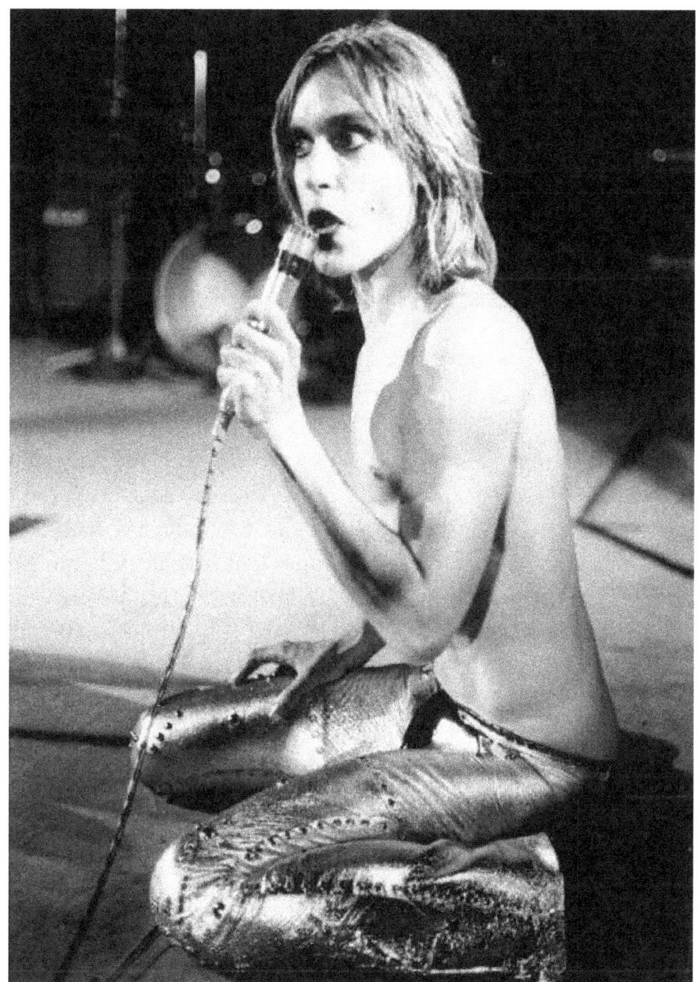

Materialist gesture (Iggy Pop)

violent enforcement – employed, say, by G4S in an outsourced policing role or by a 'criminal' organisation – as a proletarian and punisher of proletarians.

Once again, the point here is *not* to criticise the practices associated with the '99%' slogan (and obviously not to propose its adjustment to 75-25, 50-50 percent or any other ratio). The simple mindedness of slogans dividing the world into identity groups (whether 99-vs-1 percent, nationalities or 'classes' as hallucinated in cultural terms) is emphasised only because what it occludes is precisely the way contradictory interests cut across all such groupings. Only a dynamic conception of interests – one extending far beyond Graeber's 'pursuit of profit' definition, all the way in fact to his 'love, spite, pity, torpor' etc., *as mediated by the crudest material need* – allows some understanding of the contradictory needs, stakes or exposures intersecting in any subject position *and* the relations of dependence binding these contradictory elements together.

Nor is attention to interests in any way pessimistic. Graeber is relentlessly hostile to 'impersonality', which he finds gestating throughout 'coin economy' episodes in world history until it becomes the defining characteristic of 'capitalist empires'. But he fails to see why the impersonality of interests – and of the classes comprised by them – holds out the only possibility of overcoming intra-class warfare, even as the depth of conflicting dependencies makes the attempt so traumatic. A subject does not *belong to* its interests in the way a person is imagined (for as long as the superstition holds) to belong to categories of identity: kinship, caste, feudal station, nationality, psychological profile, etc. These latter categories *also* represent interests with coercive social weight of their own, of course, but once they are recognised as such – or secularised – the spell is broken. An interest bespeaks a *relation*, a situation, rather than an innate personal attribute. As such it may be contradicted by other relations or interests binding the same subject. And as such, unlike personal properties, *it is susceptible to change*, repudiation, or, in the language of identity so often superimposed on interests, *betrayal*.

Repudiation of interests is not a matter of inner conversion but of changing 'external' relations, as a consequence of which a subject position composed of interests may change. Again, this is not some outlying Marxist notion. A conception of contingent, interest-bound, internally contradictory subject positions is implied in the *Realpolitik* practised by the factions administering bits of capital in their dealings with each other and their private discussion of the merely-breathing-and-working class. Identity superstitions are only introduced when the administrators address their inferiors, who are welcome to maul one another in the name of 'competition' or 'community' but can't be trusted not to turn a realistic image of contradictory interests into the wrong kind of social explosive.

A collective interest is possible in a way that a collective identity is not, because an interest doesn't fully account for the bodies involved: it describes *one* shared relation to the social totality, leaving all other contradictions raging. Solidarity in a collective interest must overpower the contradictory interests of the *same* subjects if it is not to be destroyed by the contradictions (as, for example, in a strike defeated by the immediate threat to the strikers' means of survival). *Self-betrayal* for the sake of collective or expanded self-interest may be merely momentary (as in the 'gang truce' reported during last year's London riots), or otherwise slow, uneven and perpetually reversible (as in the ordeals of class formation through history). Its generalised, irreversible form is as yet unseen: Marx called it the self-abolition of the proletariat.

'Capitalist empires' get a dedicated chapter towards the end of the book, followed by a conclusion on the post-Bretton Woods period, somewhat surprisingly partitioned given the multi-millennial perspective. Something new is acknowledged to have happened since a 'baseline date' of 1700, but it amounts at most to a radical reshuffling of elements of the earlier 'cycles of history'. A distinct mode of *production* would be 'outside', as academics like to say, 'the scope of this study'.

A section of the 'capitalist empires' chapter is headed 'So what is capitalism anyway?', although it's not quite clear whether the answer on the next page is meant as a general definition or a narrower description of a moment known elsewhere as 'primitive accumulation'. 'What we see at the dawn of modern capitalism is a gigantic financial apparatus of credit and debt that operates – in practical effect – to pump more and more labor out of just about everyone with whom it comes into contact, and as a result produces an endlessly expanding volume of material goods'. Earlier on Graeber dismissed the labour theory of value from Adam Smith onwards in a casual quip. Now it's spelled out more or less theoretically that the extraction of labour is a secondary consequence of the 'financial apparatus of credit and debt': the content of the credit and debt must be something else, even if the apparatus of collection extorts prodigious toil from the indebted. Then there's the 'endlessly expanding volume of material goods': not necessarily untrue, but put that way it sounds more like overabundance of consumer stuff than accumulation of dead labour as capital for reinvestment. Graeber is free of the anti-consumption moralism that usually accompanies the myth of overabundance, but the relation between expansion of 'material goods' (as *cause*) and the pumping of more labour (as *effect*, then cause again, and so on) remains unexplained.

unwaged or incompletely waged labour is named as 'the secret scandal of capitalism'

The expansion of capital is misconstrued again a few pages later when unwaged or incompletely waged labour is named as 'the secret scandal of capitalism'. (Examples given are chattel slavery, indentured/debt servitude, the truck system[4] and informal appropriation in kind; housework is omitted for some reason.) The enormous amount of wageless work converted into capital can probably never be emphasised enough, but the attempt to use it as evidence that capital has never 'been organised primarily around free labor' amounts almost to a statement of the opposite. If a social relation 'organised around' commodified abstract labour existed only in enclaves of formally free wage work, the incorporation of foreign bodies into capital would be incomprehensible except as a series of discrete miracles, and most of the world would not be capitalist today. Graeber illustrates the 'secret scandal' revelation with references to Peter Linebaugh's *The London Hanged*, but Linebaugh's great book is all about the way capital 'organised around' formally free labour draws in and feeds on extraneous social practices, with or without full assimilation into the 'free' wage system. The idea that the organisation of capital reaches only as far as its formal perfection curiously mirrors the most factory-centric workerism. The scandal of capital's perpetual unwaged component is much like that of Apple's failure to build physical computers in an enlarged Palo Alto garage, or a mafia boss who declines to shoot people personally.

None of this means Graeber reduces capitalism to credit and debt as usual. That would be highly unlikely, given that he strongly disapproves of capital but *not* necessarily of credit. Because *inter-personal* debt, as every 16th century 'English or French peasant' (and since then various ethnographically observed villagers) knew, is what 'ties communities together'. The 'origins of capitalism', in which this communal binding frayed, are located in 'the story of how an economy of credit was converted into an economy of interest; of the gradual transformation of moral networks by the intrusion of the impersonal - and often vindictive - power of the state'. This is not some claim about a 'statist' coup: one strength of the book is its insistence throughout on the interdependence of military/state consolidation and private accumulation. In this particular passage, the key words are 'impersonal' and 'intrusion'. Throughout the '5,000 years' of the title, regimes of impersonal coin are said to have *alternated* with 'human economies' of personal credit. But here 'intrusion' and 'conversion' mean something more like takeover than simple substitution: the cycles of history spin off their axes (or the spokes of the wheels are at least reordered) when the impersonality hitherto associated with instant cash transactions acquires the temporal elasticity and, under new military-state forms, the socially binding power, otherwise assigned to 'moral networks' of personal liability.

This impersonality is what qualifies as specifically 'financial' the 'gigantic apparatus of credit and debt' seen in capital, in contrast to earlier non-cash credit structures. Graeber insists uncontroversially that the financial apparatus chronologically precedes full scale industrial commodity production. More surprisingly, he finds in this sequence a 'paradox' and 'a genuine challenge to familiar ways of thinking'. Because: 'We like to think of the factories and workshops as the "real economy", and the rest as superstructure,

inter-personal debt is what 'ties communities together'

constructed on top of it. But if this were really so, then how could it be that the superstructure came first? Can the dreams of the system create its body?' Apart from caricaturing all talk of capitalist *production* as dumb base-superstructure dualism, he propounds here a shockingly simplistic theory of history, in which chronological equals ontological priority. If the financial apparatus appears earlier than other phenomena associated with 'capitalism', it must contain the latter's essence. By this logic the truth of capitalism might equally be sought in feudal agriculture, absolute monarchy or the first Atlantic slave raids, as the book's own examples show. In fact Graeber's own account of the persistence and transformation of 'pre-capitalist' social forms through the 18th, 19th and 20th centuries already almost answers his pseudo-paradox, describing many elements of the historical dialectic his theory rejects, i.e. the way a pre-existing 'apparatus' contributes to an emerging mode of production in which that apparatus will itself be changed and messily subordinated.

Some such transformation, anyway, must be implied if the impersonality of cash/interest economies, traced in discrete local episodes back to Babylon, is supposed to have become a World System of impersonality from 1700 onwards. But Graeber's reticence on the content of the second, 'gigantic' impersonality – or his reluctance to acknowledge the capitalisation of labour as more than incidental to the astonishing leap – leads to new kinds of confusion. A brilliant insight into the historical *interaction* between wage labour and modern slavery ('most of the scientific management techniques applied in factories in the industrial revolution can be traced back to the sugar plantations'), gives way to speculation on an abstract 'affinity': both wage work and slavery are 'in principle impersonal'. The 'affinity', however, is wholly spurious. While waged employment may be called 'impersonal' *in theory* (despite the recent intensification of the drive to deepen or *personalise* discipline, which goes back at least to Henry Ford), the word applies to chattel slavery only in the context of the slave *market*. The slave is a fungible commodity with a cash equivalent – like an hour of anybody else's labour time – in the process of wholesale purchase, transportation, retail sale and any subsequent resale. But the relation between the working slave and the owner who may or may not name, feed and house or rape and kill her is strictly *personal*: the owner's absolute legal rights over the slave's person do not apply to the slave of another, nor does any other proprietor share the same rights over that particular slave. Still less, of course, could one slave slated for torture or for manumission change places with another. The structure of slavery as a function of *personal identity* is perhaps best explicated in Mark Twain's *Pudd'nhead Wilson*, a work of compressed but violent rage that plays out the legal and logical consequences in full.

Chattel slavery, in fact, perfectly embodies one of two defining features of the 'human economies' which Graeber wishes to oppose to 'commercial economies – or market economies as we now like to call them'. These 'human economies' are 'concerned not with the accumulation of wealth, but with *the creation, destruction and rearranging of human beings*'. The plantations of the Old South and the colonial Caribbean miss out on full membership of the set inasmuch as they certainly accumulated wealth (until they began to haemorrhage it), but they stand out as radiantly 'human' in their direct practice of 'the creation, destruction and rearranging' of living, *personal* bodies.

The most obvious problem with this second criterion is that it excludes nothing. Graeber doesn't use the word 'direct'; he seems simply to believe that some economies 'create, destroy and rearrange human beings' while some others, somewhere, do not. (And this latter kind, remember, is supposed to be the norm today.) Of course Graeber is not obliged to accept the definition of the commodity as a form that mediates *a relation between humans*, but unless

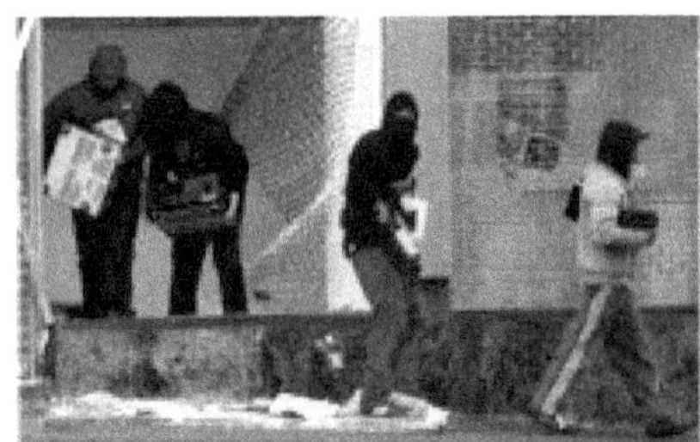

Greed is Good

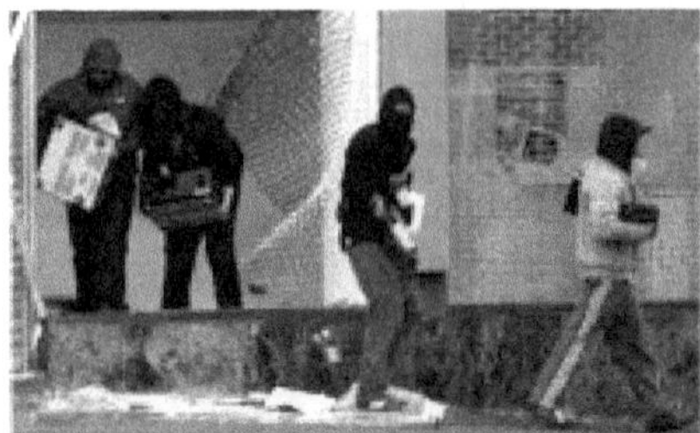

Greed is Good

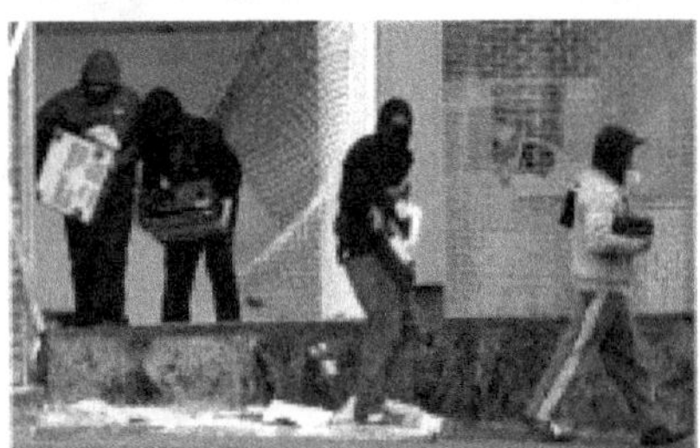

Greed is Good

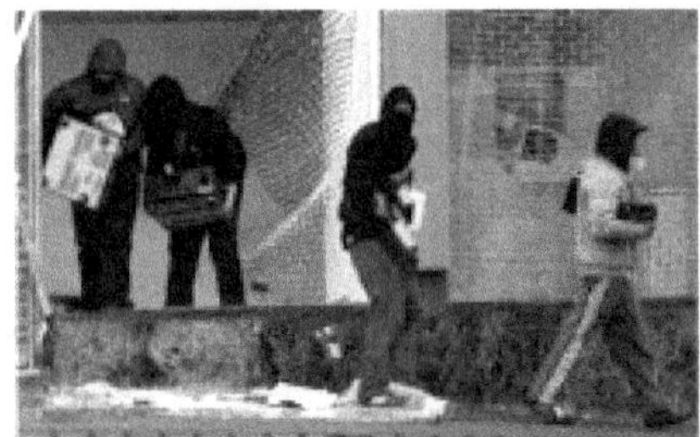

Greed is Good

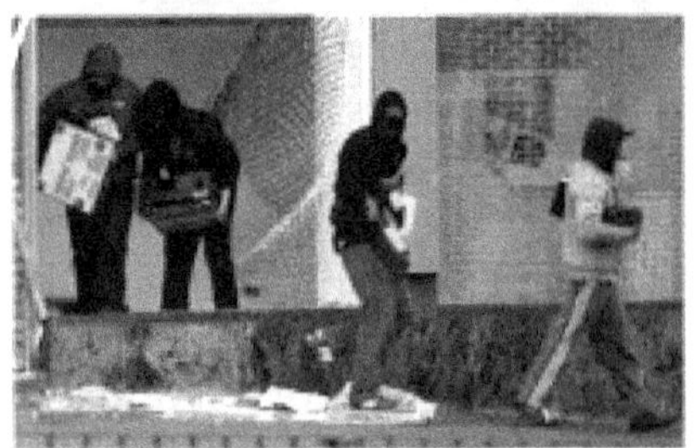

Greed is Good

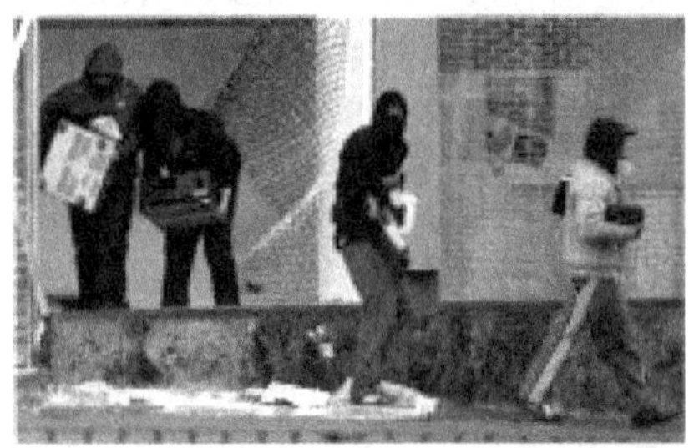

Greed is Good

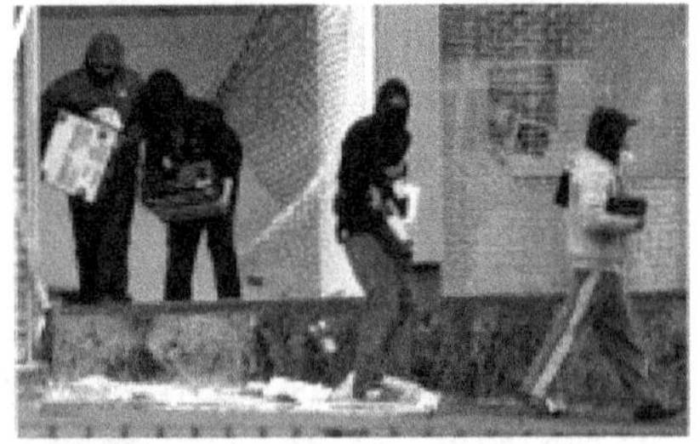

Greed is Good

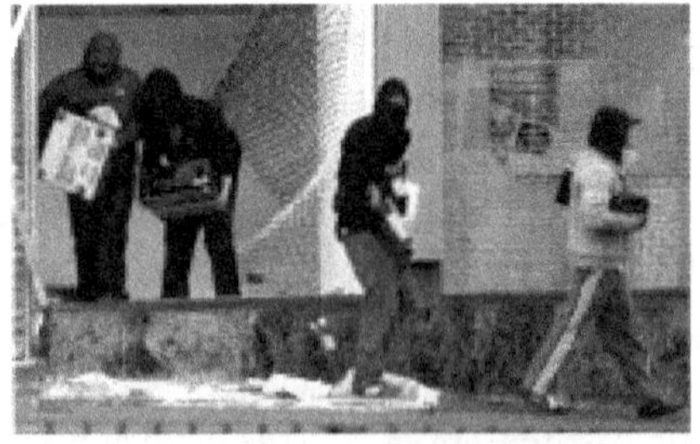

Greed is Good

Arts Against Cuts 'Greed is Good' poster, created for anti-cuts demonstrations, November 2010 he forgot all about it he seems to regard it as beneath his contempt, for in the course of 453 pages it merits not even the kind of glib one-liner bestowed on the labour theory of value.

As for the non-accumulation of wealth, this is not the place to rehearse the case against 'primitivism', but it's telling that Graeber's examples of human economies, drawing on centuries of ethnographic and historical research, are all shadowed to some extent by the accumulation of *poverty*. One commonplace is perhaps worth repeating here: the attempt to abolish accumulation in its present form, i.e. that of capital, does not necessarily mean rejection of the *social* accumulation of use-values, or material 'wealth'. However much they may enjoy camping, despisers of social accumulation should be careful what they wish for, especially when they wish on others' behalf.

Graeber doesn't automatically endorse every economy counted as 'human': he admits as soon as he introduces the category that some such systems 'are quite humane; others extraordinarily brutal'. 'Human economy' qualities seem rather to be regarded as necessary but not sufficient for any desirable form of social life. Despite the all-inclusiveness of the 'creation/destruction/rearranging of human beings' definition as it's actually worded, it's fairly clear what kind of qualities are meant. 'Codes of honor, trust, and ultimately community and mutual aid' are identified as 'typical of human economies' the last time the terms appears in the book; these elements of *sustained* interaction between individuals personally known to one another are also essential components of the informal 'communism' and finally 'love' which the author would rescue from degradation into 'numbers' and the 'morality of debt'.

It should be noted at this late stage that Graeber's attacks on punitive debt-morality, especially in the concluding chapter, are often more powerful than any number of clumsy forays based on orthodox materialist theories of capital. In what looks at first like a casual aside on student debt, the disastrous fetish of 'fairness' – apparently ineradicable on the left in the Britain, where Graeber now lives and works – is properly reassigned to its prison-building role: writing off existing loans would be 'unfair' to previous payers to the same extent that 'it would be "unfair" to a mugging victim not to mug their [sic] neighbors too'. More counter-consensually still, Graeber repudiates the obscene idea that anyone could ever owe a 'debt to society' – the slur in which economic and criminal punishment converge – along with its subsidiary monster, 'our debt to nature'. And here he finds exactly the right words: 'What could possibly be more presumptuous, or more ridiculous, than to think it would be possible to negotiate with the grounds of one's existence?' He ends the book with a slightly timid defence of 'the non-industrious poor' ('at least they aren't hurting anyone'), in a section called 'Perhaps [?!] the world really does owe you a living'. These political intentions are consistent throughout, and the welcome rejection of the 'morality of debt' is not diminished by the objections belaboured in the present article. Rather, the book is criticised here in order to *defend* the thread of urgent and rarely stated truth running through it from annexation to a communitarian vision of 'communism', or a

Perhaps [?!] the world really does owe you a living

world whose local 'networks of honour' replace crude mathematical debt with acutely personal perpetual bonds.

In a *Mute* article a few years back, also called Debt, the first 5,000 years, Graeber stood out as a rare leftist writer willing to recognise the one truth Margaret Thatcher ever told: there is no such thing as society.[5] In that short article the use of 'society' as a euphemism for 'state' is slapped down resoundingly, and the feat is repeated in the book in case anyone missed it the first time. But a complication that hardly seemed to matter in the shorter format is more troubling here. While the myth of 'society' undoubtedly serves to moralise the police powers of states, it also extends the same morality – i.e. discipline in the name of identity, disavowal of disruptive interests – beyond the reach of the law, deep into informal, everyday material life. At this point (or more often long before it, given the rise of unlegislated, personal policing) the word 'society' becomes interchangeable with 'community', as in community values, leaders, service, punishment.

Graeber is quite sparing in his use of the actual word 'community'. Far from concealing or apologising for the patriarchy and coercive violence of particular human/communal economies, he draws attention to these aspects where they occur, distinguishing his argument from a certain kind of uncritical, romantic primitivism. But whether named as such or not, something like 'community' is the *precondition* underlying almost every case of the 'communistic' social interaction held up in the book as hopeful or desirable.

'Communism', as Graeber uses the term, refers neither to some hypothetical social structure nor to anything like a 'real movement abolishing the present state of things'. Instead it names a 'bedrock' habit of sociable, co-operative personal interaction, including immediate, face-to-face sharing of material things (work tools, a village feast, etc.). This 'foundation of all human sociability', which 'makes society possible', is overlaid with equally transhistorical structures of 'exchange' (defined in terms of 'impersonality' and 'equivalence', as if one always entailed the other) and 'hierarchy' (in which 'formal equality' and 'reciprocity' are non-existent, and onto which the disasters of identity are conveniently displaced). These 'baseline' elements of social life are apparently eternal, or at least continuous through 5,000 years, but the relation between them is treated as something subject to change. Although the book is not set up as a platform for concrete proposals, a broad political problematic emerges early on and is deepened in the course of the trans/historical survey.[6] Something like: how can the role of baseline communism in social life be expanded so that it displaces exchange and hierarchy as far as possible?

But alas, the question is unanswerable, because *behavioural* communism, or communitarianism, cannot, by definition, be expanded. The only example given of 'communistic' behaviour between *strangers* is that of a lighter or cigarette offered by a smoker to a passer-by who asks for it. Even here direct personal contact is required, and this is the absolute lower-limit baseline.

In large, impersonal urban communities, such a standard may go no further than asking for a light or directions.[7] This might not seem like much, but it founds the possibility of larger social relations. In smaller, less impersonal communities – especially those not divided into social classes – the same logic will extend much further: for example, it is often effectively impossible to refuse a request not just for tobacco, but for food – sometimes even from a stranger; certainly from anyone considered to belong to the community.

In other words, the more intimate the community relationship, the more communistic the behaviour. Ongoing mutual acquaintance is repeatedly invoked as a prophylactic against exploitation; polite anonymous encounters belong to the world of cash, slavery and war.

Sustained interpersonal intimacy is presented as the condition of 'communism' through a series of loaded examples rather than a programmatic statement, but the premise is no less stubbornly clung to for that. The extension of 'communism' to a larger-than-local - and therefore necessarily impersonal - scale could surely have been broached if the author saw the question as valid. But wherever the contingencies of the future rather than the cycles of the past are concerned, something like microeconomic fundamentalism 'from below' forbids any suprapersonal, *universal* standpoint. A larger scale is just a lot of relationships between individuals; no other perspective is human enough.

Right from the start, Graeber identifies 'communism' with the axiom 'from each according to their [sic] abilities, to each according to their needs'. There's nothing wrong with this kind of rhetorical borrowing as such, but there is something crushing in the way the meaning is trivialised, the stakes reduced from total social upheaval to *behaviour change* in personal encounters. The power of individuals to decide on the taking or giving of anything - according to ability or need or otherwise - remains objectively pitiful all the way up to the wealthiest charity donor. If the logic of 'need and ability' is ever to overthrow that of Return On Equity, it must impose itself globally, i.e. far beyond the reach of friendly sociability, and collectively, i.e. *impersonally*.

The Clinical Wasteman nurses an animus

FOOTNOTES

1 No, Giambattista Vico is mentioned neither in the text nor in the copious bibliography.

2 Theodor Adorno, 'Sur l'eau', *Minima Moralia: Reflexionen aus dem beschädigten Leben*, 1951.

3 Christopher Hill, *God's Englishman*, London: Penguin, 1970.

4 Token wages, effectively spendable only in exorbitant and pestilential company stores.

5 David Graeber, 'Debt: The First 5000 Years', *Mute* Vol 2 #12, 2009 http://www.metamute.org/editorial/articles/debt-first-five-thousand-years

6 The one exception is a call at the end of the book for a total debt 'jubilee', seconding similar, though politically disparate, proposals from Michael Hudson and writers associated with *Midnight Notes* and later *The Commoner*. Graeber's relation to *Midnight Notes* is ambivalent. In his account of the non-waged component of capital he draws heavily on Peter Linebaugh's book and on other (uncredited) work by the collective, but a mean-spirited footnote chides them for an 'economistic' fixation on the reproduction of labour power, missing the point that they are talking about something specific to capital, even if he is not.

7 The reference to 'directions' pertains not to a second case of inter-stranger communism, but to an incident in which the anthropologist E.E. Evans-Pritchard was given *false* directions by Nuer pastoralists in southern Sudan, for the very good reason that he was an agent of the British government.

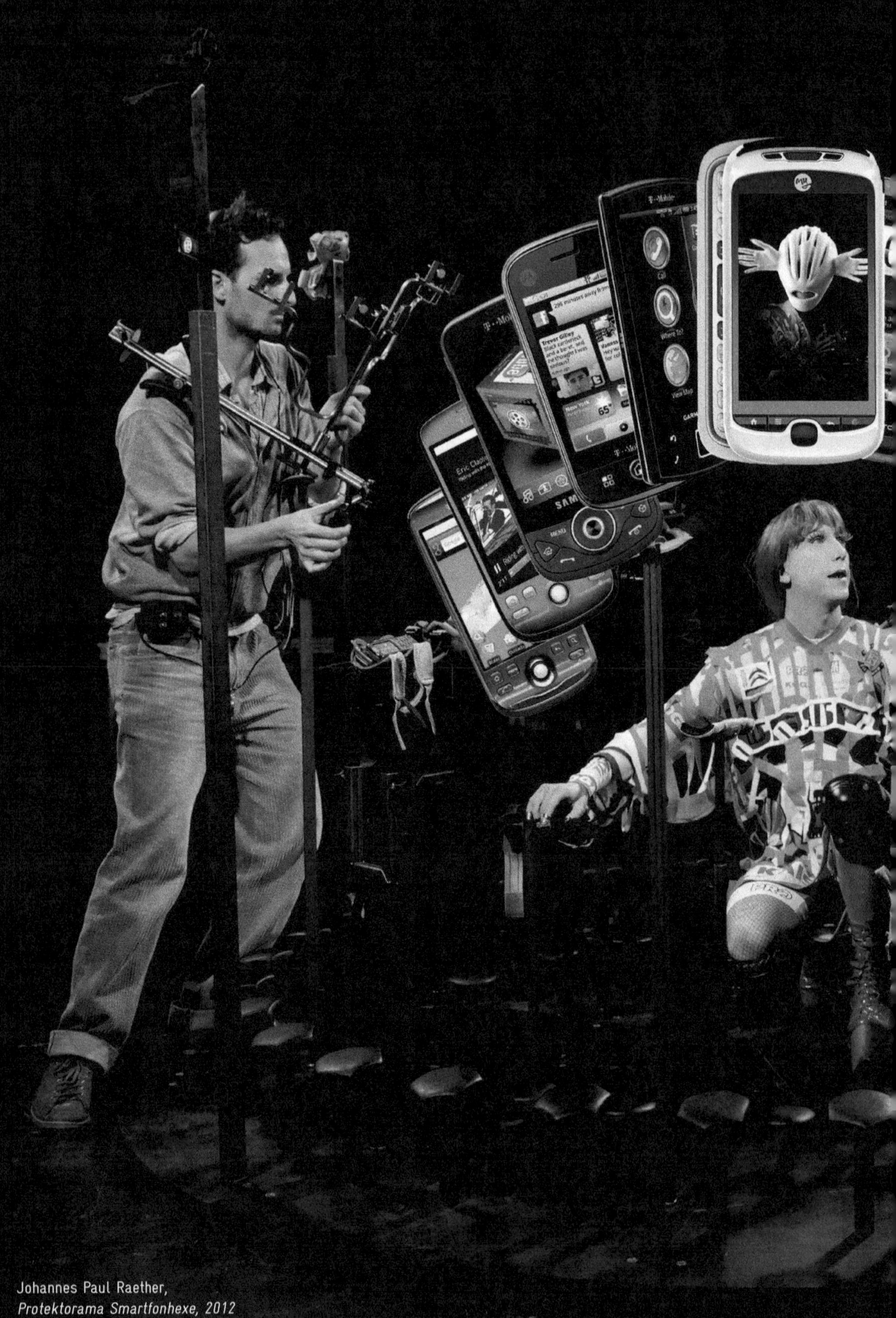

Johannes Paul Raether,
Protektorama Smartfonhexe, 2012

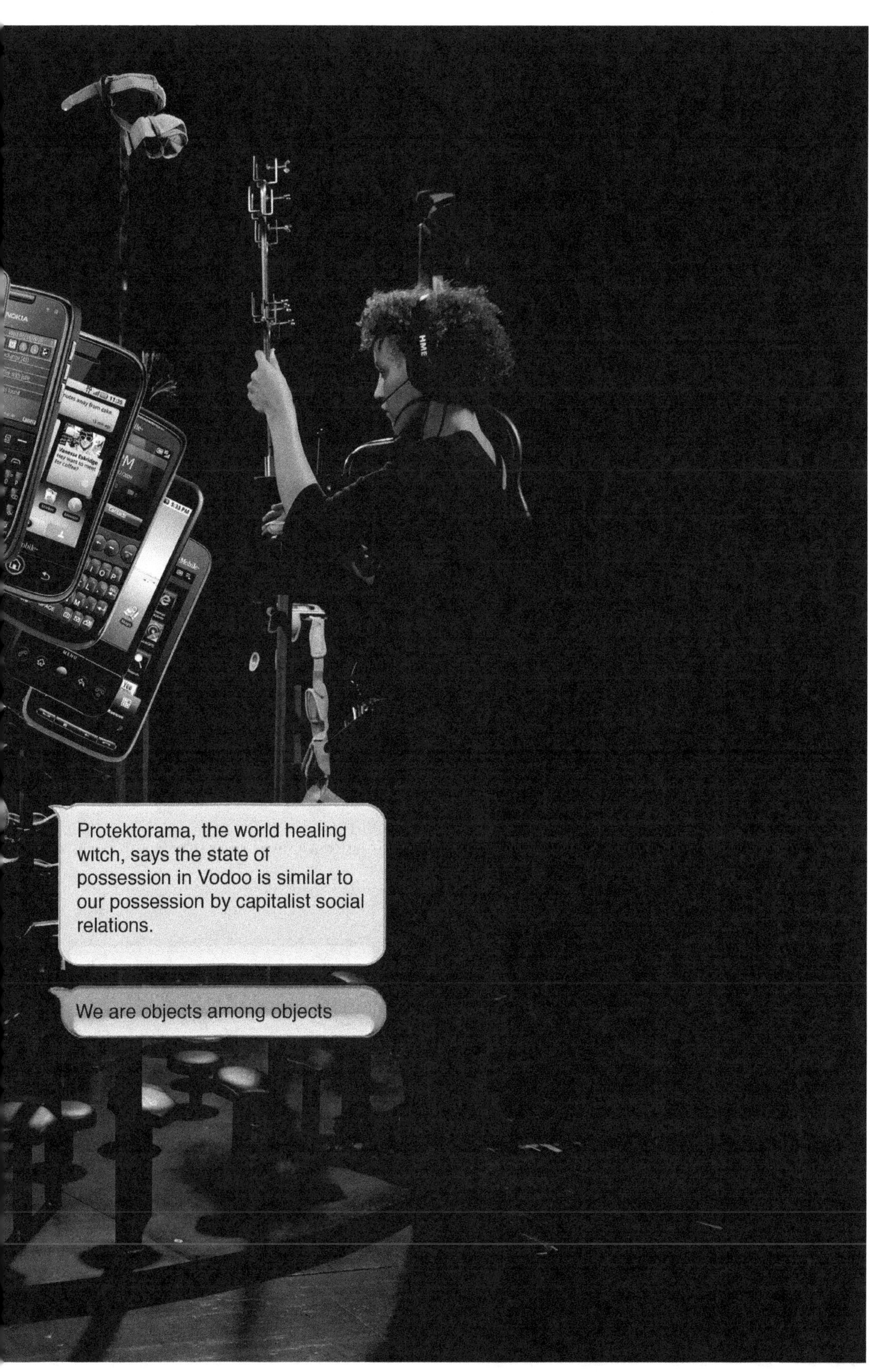
Protektorama, the world healing witch, says the state of possession in Vodoo is similar to our possession by capitalist social relations.
We are objects among objects

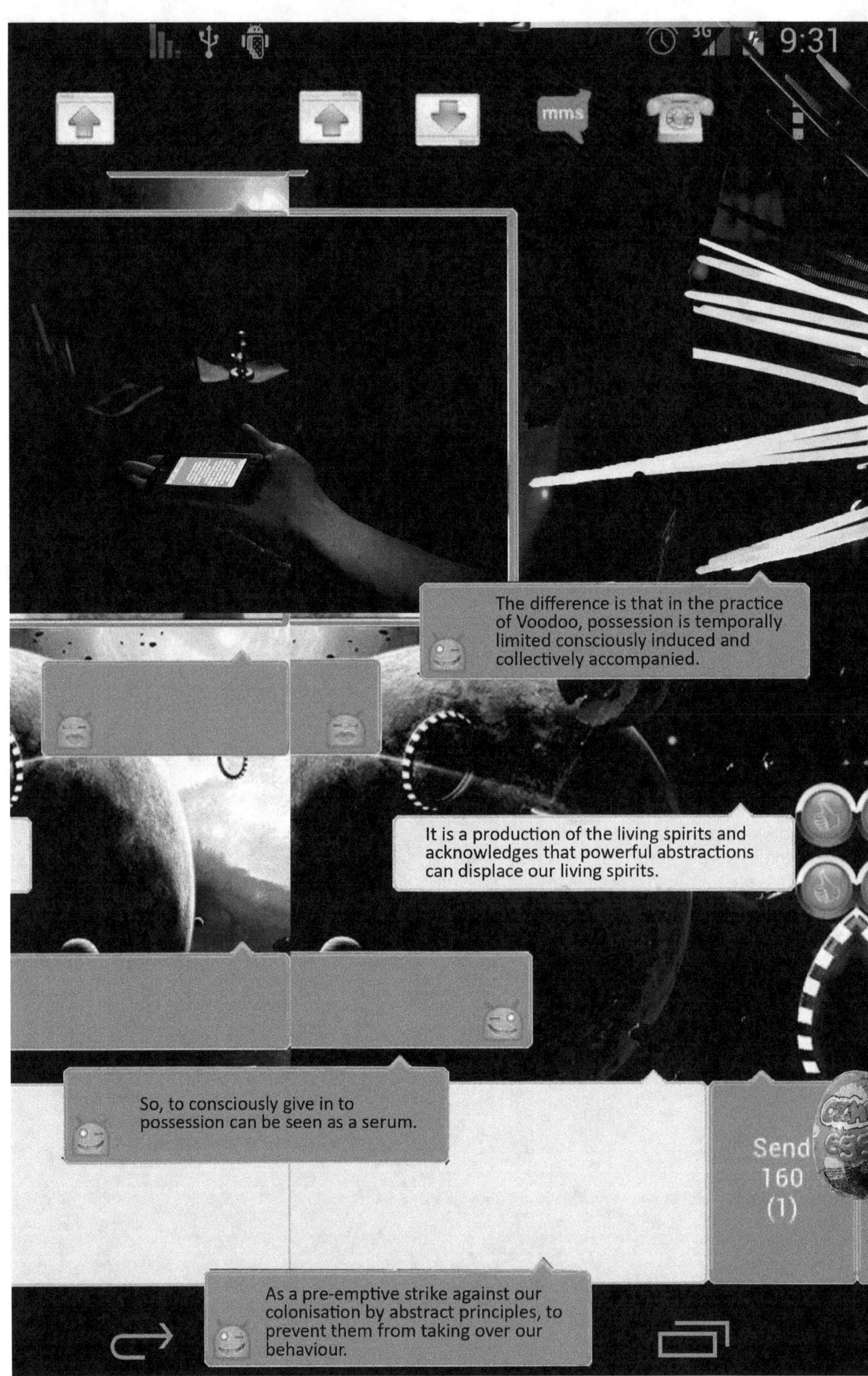
9:31
mms
The difference is that in the practice of Voodoo, possession is temporally limited consciously induced and collectively accompanied.
It is a production of the living spirits and acknowledges that powerful abstractions can displace our living spirits.
So, to consciously give in to possession can be seen as a serum.
Send 160 (1)
As a pre-emptive strike against our colonisation by abstract principles, to prevent them from taking over our behaviour.

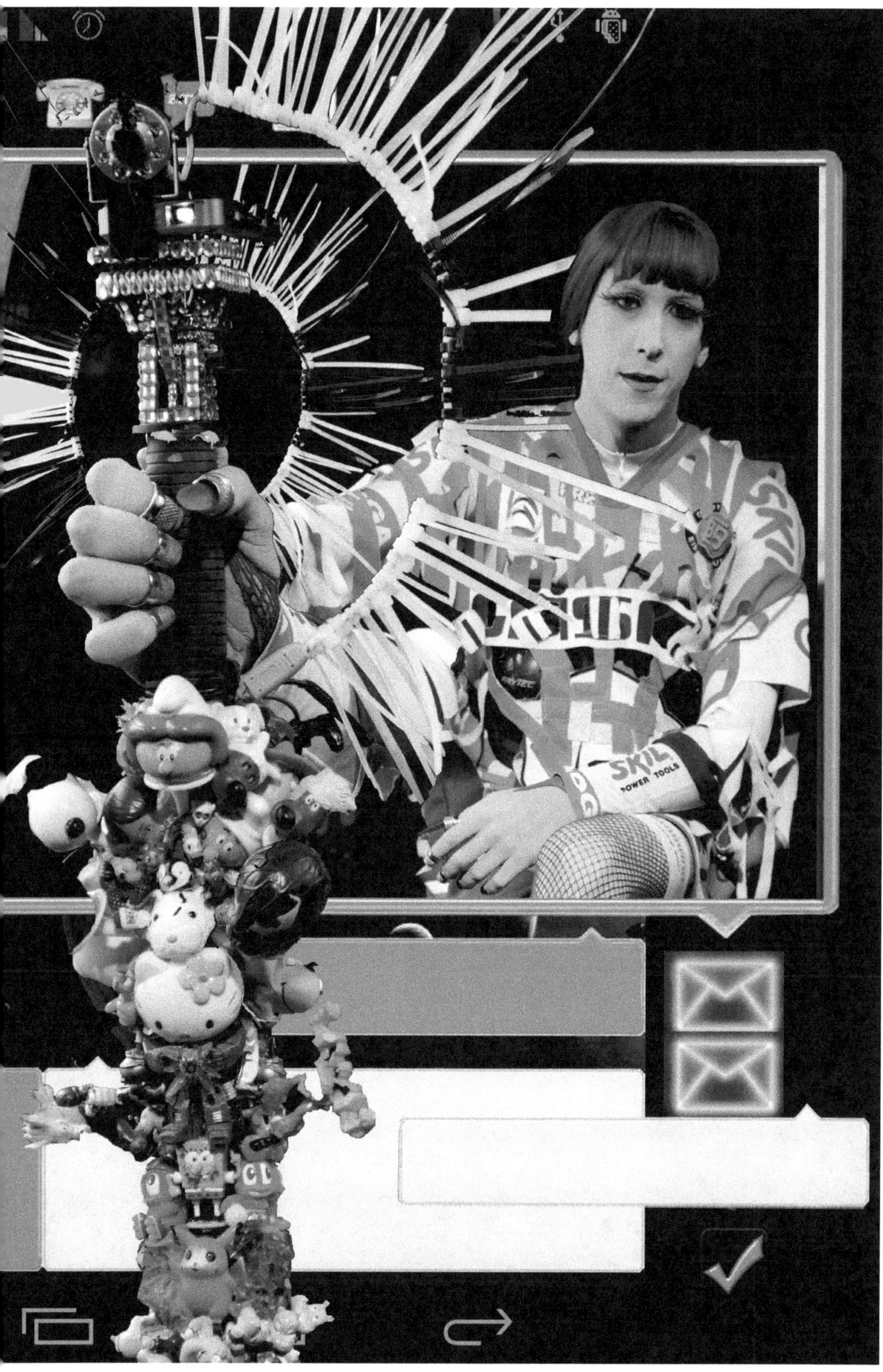
SKIL
POWER TOOLS

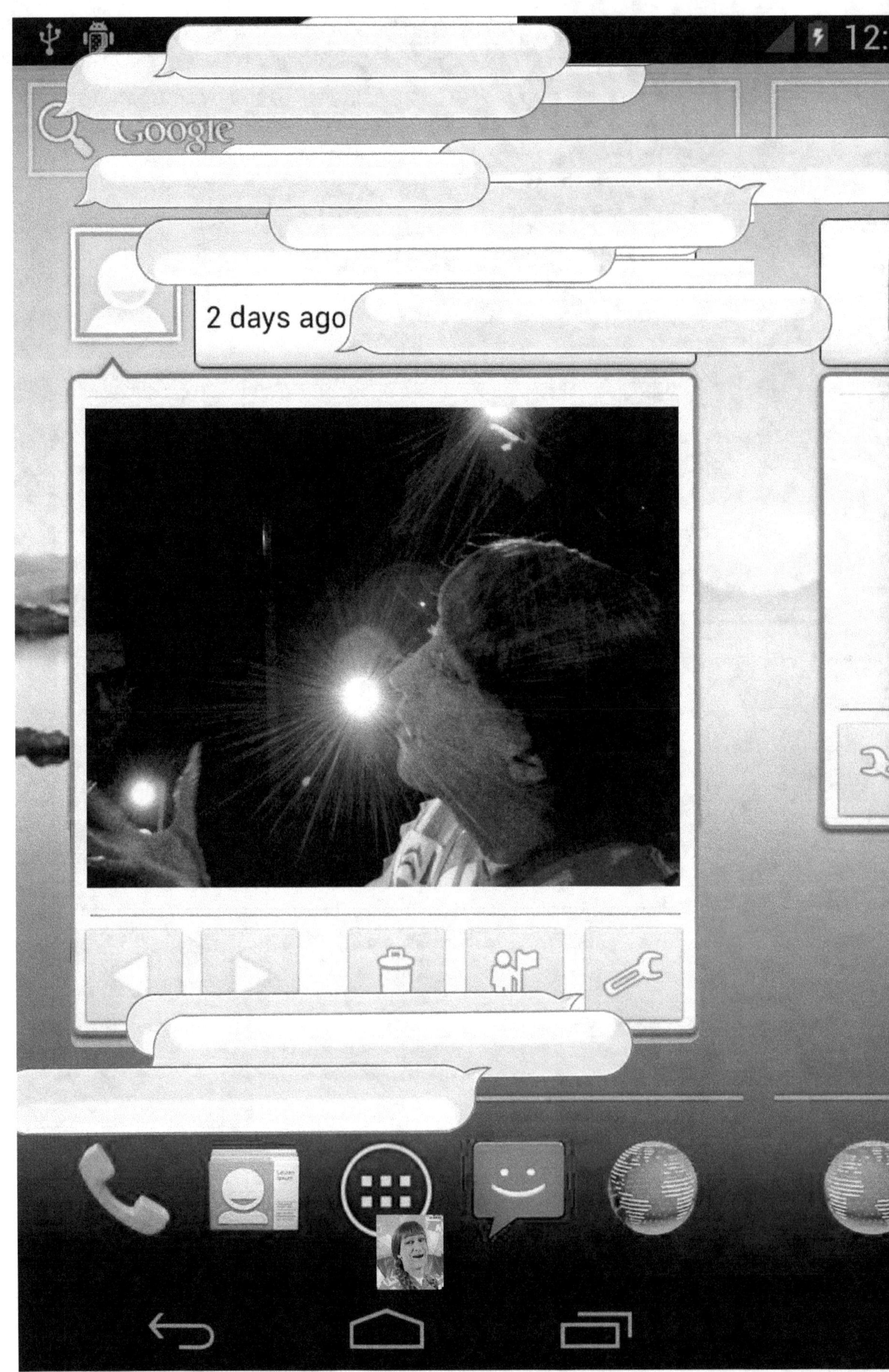
Google
2 days ago

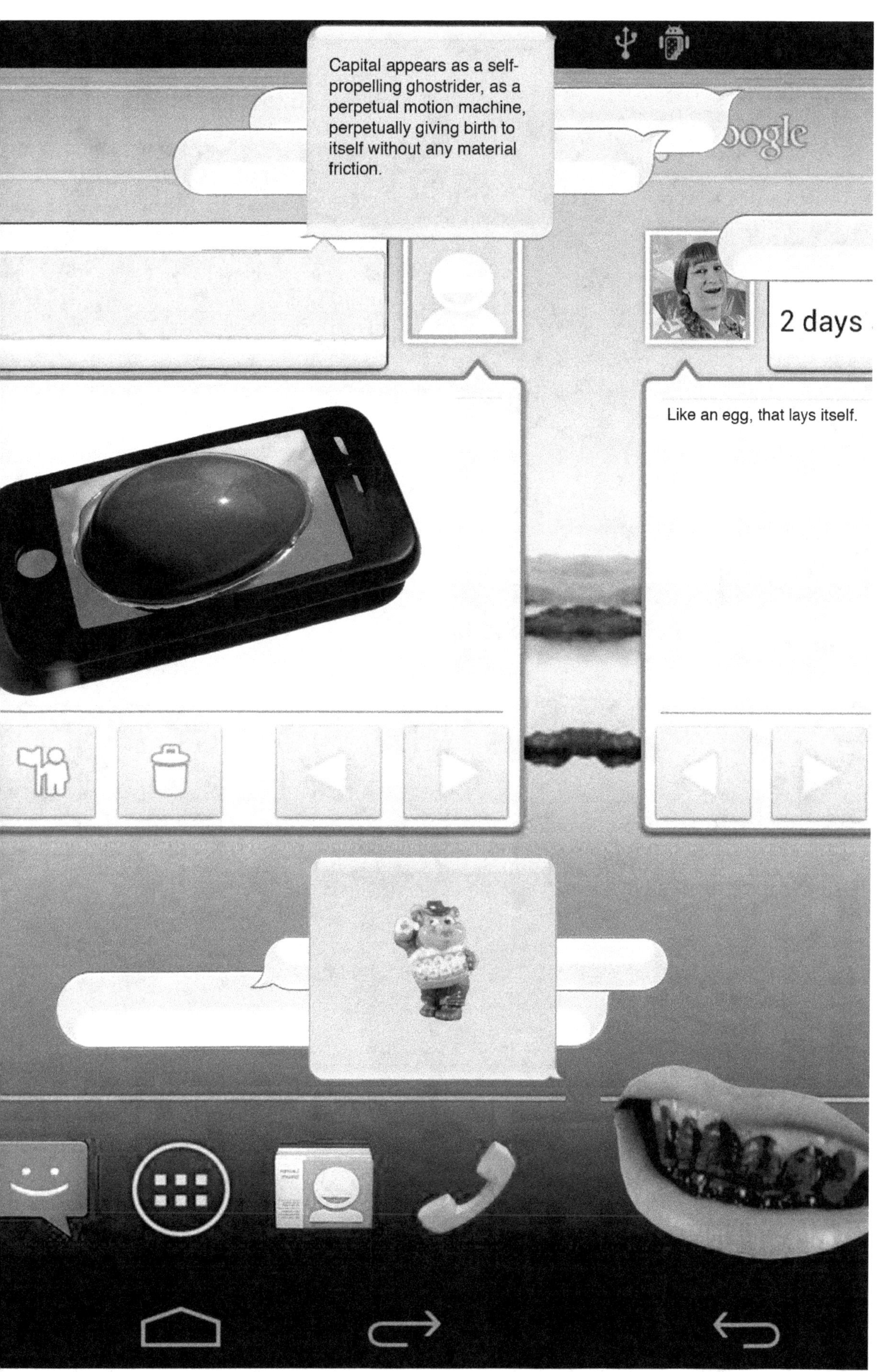
Capital appears as a self-propelling ghostrider, as a perpetual motion machine, perpetually giving birth to itself without any material friction.
2 days
Like an egg, that lays itself.

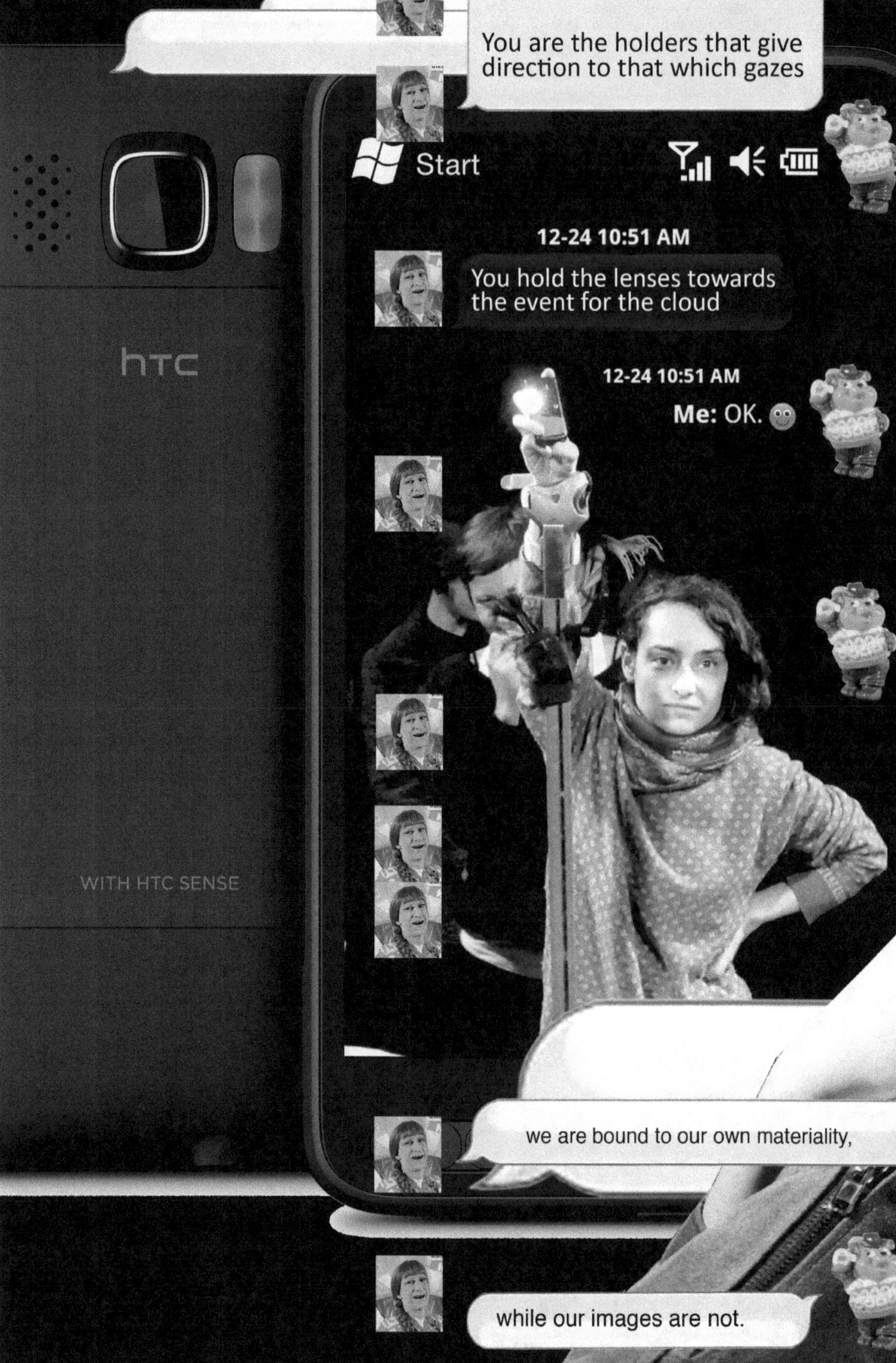
You are the holders that give direction to that which gazes
Start
12-24 10:51 AM
You hold the lenses towards the event for the cloud
12-24 10:51 AM
Me: OK.
htc
WITH HTC SENSE
we are bound to our own materiality,
while our images are not.

OZMO
egg
OZMO
egg
OZMO
egg
Kinder
ÜBERRASCHUNG

GERALDINE GOAT— THE HARD WAY TO ENLIGHTENMENT

*Stephan Dillemuth's film installation, **The Hard Way to Enlightenment**, deployed a live goat in an immanent critique of privatisation and its implications for art, research and education. Geraldine has since slipped her collar to appear in this short story by KATRINA PALMER satirising the apparently limitless masochism of the contemporary artist*

OCTOBER

The management of goats has seen a rise in disbudding – the removal of horn buds shortly after birth. The buds can be cut out of a kid's head by knife, but are more commonly cauterised with hot irons. This procedure is not always conclusive. If the horn-producing cells aren't completely destroyed, the buds can grow back. Damaged bud cells can result in irregularities in any subsequent horn. As one of Geraldine's horns re-emerged, it was evidently afflicted in this manner, instead of developing with a backwards curl, it had a deviant curving forwards aspect. From its tip, the rigid crescentiform was set on a brutal trajectory, advancing as it was towards the front of Geraldine's skull, bound to make contact at a point just above her eye. The rate of the horn's growth was slow but constant, roughly equivalent to the progress of human hair, or a fingernail.

NOVEMBER

With joy and terror mingled, in these past weeks, Geraldine tried to consider the potential benefits of a wayward horn and its impending threat to her cranium. Her instinct was to see it as material for her work. As she never let her being-as-goat constrain her life options, she was an artist, and for the most part used her own body as sculptural material. Since leaving art school, she gained a reputation for live streamed performances, including *She-Goats Have Beards* – a month-long webcast that focused on Geraldine's shaven muzzle, until her natural beard grew back to its full unkempt length. So, with the perilous nature of her condition now apparent, it seemed only natural to exploit it as artwork – a duration piece in which the progress of the horn was the subject of scrutiny via a live webcast. This would be a solo performance, from an undisclosed location. Geraldine named her new work *The Hard Way to Enlightenment,* as last year she had a role in a film of the same name by Stephan Dillemuth. His film featured a goat (that is, Geraldine) and a man (the artist who talks, paints and eats) accompanied by a voiceover lecture on the dangers of corporatisation and the need for advanced art education to be self-directed and bohemian. Geraldine was sympathetic to Dillemuth's narration, seeing the increasingly streamlined and controlled characteristics of educational establishments as counteractive to the creation of good artwork. Nevertheless, she was disappointed that her role in the film was merely symbolic.

DECEMBER

By now, if Geraldine looked upwards she could just see the tip of the horn making its approach over her eyebrow, so she chose to spend time looking down. When the tip of the horn first touched the dense hair of her fur, the pressure was so slight that she hardly noticed. A few days later, as the sharp point of the horn depressed her skin, she felt it as nothing more than the irritation of an insistent finger tapping on her forehead. The pressure grew and her skin stretched, accompanied by a prickly stinging

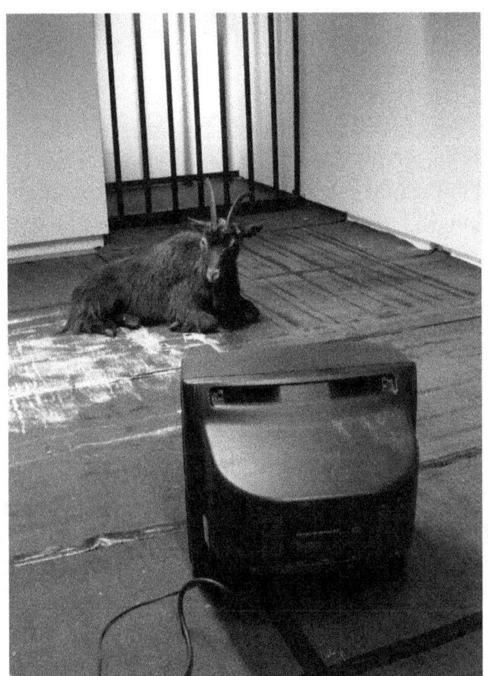
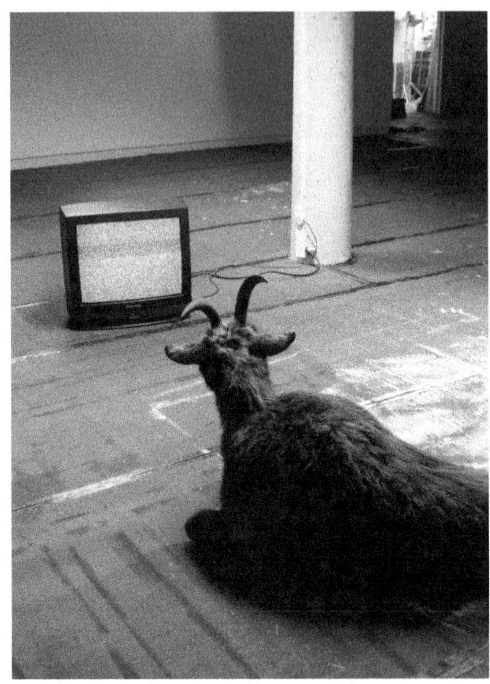

All images: Stephan Dillemuth, *The Hard Way to Enlightenment*, Transmission Gallery, Glasgow, 2010

sensation. More days passed before the feeling became truly uncomfortable and even then, when the epidermis split, there was no real pain as such, it was more of a continuous ache, and being a stalwart goat, she could tolerate it. Despite the slow pace of its progress, in the last week of December the horn made a significant and troubling move from the outside of her head, inward, casually passing through tender sebaceous glands and pulsing blood vessels. Geraldine bore the adversity well, but as the month closed her skull finally succumbed to the pressure. A crack appeared, and now the pain kicked in.

JANUARY

Geraldine found ways of managing her pain. She discovered distraction was the most effective means of counteracting trauma, and attempted to impose some methodological structure on her days, dividing her time between composition (re-positioning herself in front of the camera), dissemination (maintaining her blog) and contextualisation (researching on the net and reading emails sent in by her audience). One viewer wrote to Geraldine with a supportive message, insisting that penetrating head injuries aren't necessarily fatal, citing the case of Phineas P. Gage who survived after an explosion sent a three-foot iron through his head. By all accounts it went straight into his cheekbone, clean through his skull and landed some 25 meters away. There were reports of adverse changes to his personality, memory loss, impaired conversational skills, inappropriate sexual activity, hypomania, impulsiveness, depression, increased levels of frustration and

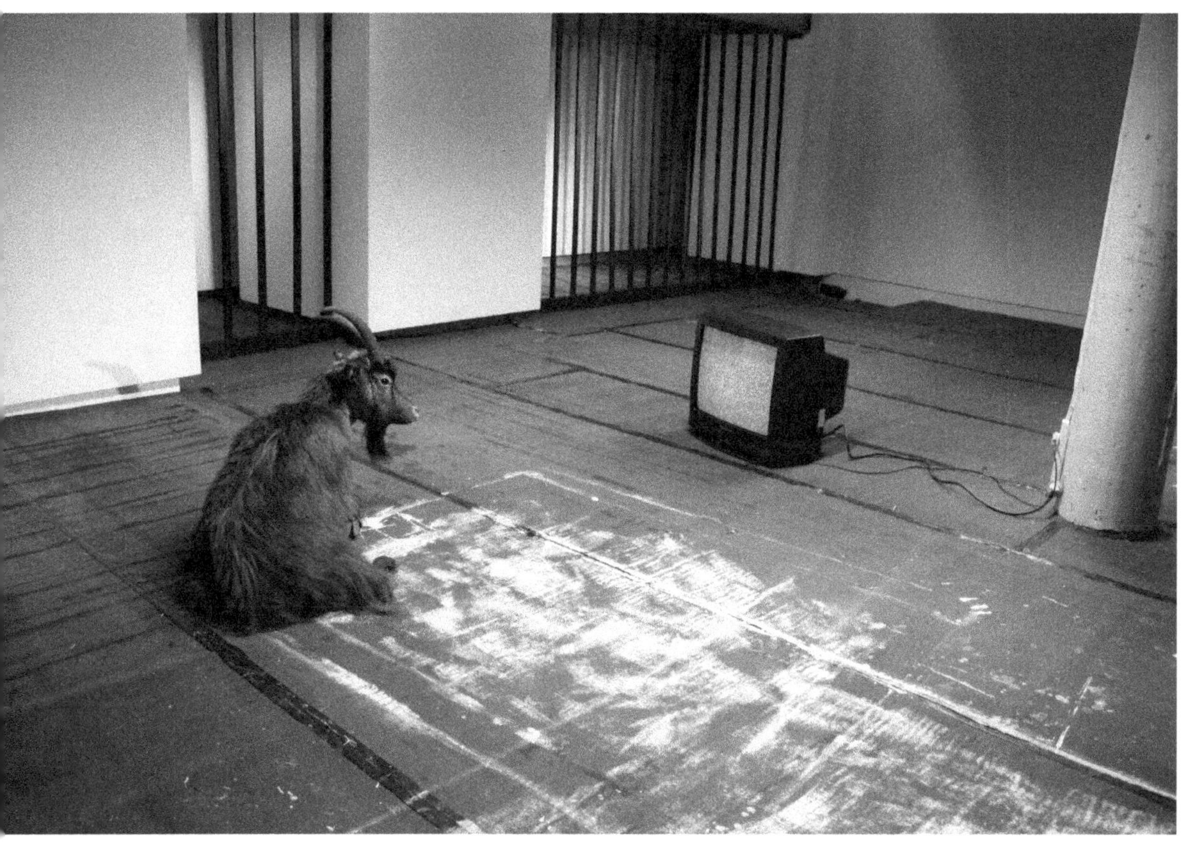

so on – but he lived. Others wrote more critically, suggesting she was bound to die for a work that was nothing more than the performance of the social and formal knowledge imposed on her at art school. She didn't reply.

FEBRUARY

The horn plunged deeper, dislodging brain matter from the frontal lobe and sending her on an hallucinatory trip. Weak from the pain and loss of vital fluids, she couldn't keep a hold of herself in her imaginings. She saw herself all coated in layers of fresh blood on top of dried, idly sucking on a juicy tomato and wondering about who she really was. Although Geraldine was never under the delusion of being human, she now began to think that she might be something other than a goat. From the arrangement of her anatomy she was fairly sure she wasn't a dog, but she thought she could easily be a rarer variety sheep or a small deer, in the same way that something at first sight might appear to be a spider, but could then turn out to be a crab; or what looks like a vegetable might really be a fruit. She became convinced that the sense of doubt about who she really was, was a direct result of her participation in Dillemuth's film. In her traumatised mind, it was Dillemuth who typecast her and undermined her potential to be anything beyond an institutionalised goat. It was his work that was explicitly and predominantly about the pseudo-libertine crude control mechanisms of art schools, and this only served to reconfirm the power of those conditions, because it allowed them to consume his creative output, and her own.

MARCH

Weeks passed in strange studio-bound isolation, interrupted only by occasional email contact. A message arrived with a link to a story about the shooting of some of her feral cousins: http://www.dailymail.co.uk/news/article-444225/Herd-goats-shot-National-Trust.html

The trust said its decision to destroy the herd of British native feral goats was based on 'animal welfare grounds' as no other suitable home was available. One local, who asked not to be named, said:

> It is absolutely disgusting, the National Trust is supposed to be a conservation group [...] They brought those poor animals on to the land and, because they didn't build adequate fencing, they shot them [...] The trust spent three weeks rounding up 15 of the goats before placing them on the grassy slopes surrounding the ruins of nearby Corfe Castle. But when they escaped again, their time was up. The hunt is now on for the last three which will also be shot if no one offers them a home.

This story disturbed Geraldine. She felt all the more determined to pursue her creative vision, unfettered. And after several viewers asked her to comment on the current state of art education, she finally gave a single and obtuse response – a statement made directly to camera:

> I, Geraldine Goat, refuse to enter the debate on the value of advanced art education, I choose instead to put my creative energy into producing work. Art education is a head-fuck, what's new? I always knew it'd be a head-fuck, that's why I went into it. I like having my head fucked.

APRIL

It was during this month that Geraldine turned away from the video camera, folded her legs underneath her barrelled torso, tucked her muzzle into her fur and made a brave attempt to sleep. In the years before the horn, when she used to close her eyes, she would gaze at the field of sludgy hues behind her eyelids. She would look into this brown, muddy terrain, and see it inflected with a multitude of tiny pale florets, budding and sprouting to form a landscape alive with efflorescence. Now, however, with the deviant horn invading her head, still growing and drawing its length and strength through her brain, when she closed her eyes and hoped to sleep, she saw the seven vertical, vibrant bands of a television test pattern: grey; yellow; turquoise; green; magenta; red; cyan. Across

---

Art education is a head-fuck, what's new?

---

these solid columns an irregular jagged white lightening flash appeared and disappeared just as suddenly. Repeated white flashes gradually became more dominant, turning the columns of warm colours to white, at which point Geraldine suffered the first of many convulsions. Her audience figures increased.

MAY

From beneath her loaded brow, Geraldine sensed her work intensifying along with the increasingly broad diameter of the horn's arc. The sharp tip had pierced through to the back of her brain and the widest part of the horn entered her frontal lobe. Then, to her surprise, a thick bubbling jet of spume discharged and as the pain reached a peak of an indescribable nature, cutting through her awareness, at this very point when she was preparing herself to lose consciousness, she discovered that she felt more awake than ever. A rapid flux of opening sensations shuddered through her, bright lights and positive exhilaration. Astonished, she wondered if the horn might be functioning as if it was a drill for self-trepanation. With results much like those associated with that peculiar procedure, she'd increased the volume of blood flowing through her brain and released the accumulation of pressure. Meanwhile messages flooded in demanding an end to the barbaric spectacle. Attempts were being made to trace her location. Geraldine began to suspect that for all her efforts to transcend her role in Dillemuth's film, she was complicit with promoting and glorifying its triumphant procession around the globe. Not only this, but she had now constructed for herself the role of victim of an art education and an association with the neurosurgical, mystical or pathological procedure of self-trepanning couldn't help. She stamped her hoof on the computer, turning off the video, shutting down the email and terminating her connection with the outside world.

JUNE

As the horn progressed through her head, Geraldine came to a private appreciation of both its presence inside her and the impressive form it created. It inched forwards and she focused not on the pain but on the sensual sensation of its slow shunting, penetrating movement inside her body. The prick took on the qualities of a fierce stabbing knife in her skull, although every now and then it would hit a nerve that sent an involuntary spasm shuddering through her stomach, down her tail and straight back up her spine, making her neck lose its control and forcing her head to jolt backwards, in a kind of ecstatic animation. With so much additional mass in her cranium, it took tremendous effort to lift the weight of her head upright, but as she did so she felt increasingly powerful. She sat back on her rump and dug her hooves in, aware of the magnificence of her presence: the conceptual and formal circularity of her horn-work; growing out of her head, as it was, and being ingested back into it. She turned the broadcast back on and positioned herself in profile to the video camera. At that moment, the tip of the horn quietly, finally, cropped up and cracked through the top of her head, feeling like the slow motion ping of an exciting idea, and looking like the protracted emergence of some stubborn and hardened seedling out of dry ground.

Katrina Palmer <katrina.palmer@network.rca.ac.uk> locates sculpture in fiction writing, recordings and live readings. Her book *The Dark Object* (published by Book Works 2010), exploits sculpture's awkward relationship with conceptualism through the paranoid pseudo-conceptual ideology of a fictional institution

INFO

Stephan Dillemuth's *The Hard Way to Enlightenment* was at the Transmission Gallery, Glasgow 28 September 2010 – 9 October 2010. The complete video, *The Hard Way to Enlightenment: a dramatisation of a lecture on the academy and the corporate public in two parts,* can be downloaded from Stephan's website here: www.societyofcontrol.com/dillemuth/2010_transmission/installtransmission.htm

EVERYONE HAS A BUSINESS INSIDE THEM

An exhibition at Gasworks singled out the thematic of 'management' as a lens through which to examine multiple artistic approaches to labour, organisation, communication and measurement. MARINA VISHMIDT *gives the show an evaluative performance review*

> No, it has to be done again, it is always to be done. Never done. As if there was no longer any movement, nor any effective gestures, nor any change, but instead an absurd simulacrum of work. Work which effaces itself as soon as it is completed as if under the effect of some curse.
>
> – Robert Linhart, *L'etabli*[1]

THAT ELUSIVE OBJECT OF MANAGEMENT

What is the object of management? And who is asking? Management is first of all exerted upon resources, be these temporal or human, rather than upon autonomous entities that can either be reasoned with or present their own reasons. Or, perhaps the autonomy of the entity is expressed through its striving to fulfil its potential as a resource, as inculcated by the homilies of human capital. As the line goes in the Stewart Marshall piece which lends the exhibition its name, 'all I can see is the management' (the context of the statement is that the protagonist cannot see 'the workers' or anything else), because management gets in our eyes. Management has set itself to measure all things, and it finds them manageable. Like its corollary 'governance', it is weakly totalising; it is the perpetual calibration of accommodation and control when all contestation over fundamentals has been eliminated from the scene. The double character of being both totalising and infinitely adjustable makes it the perfect emblem of the capital relation, whether carried out by bosses, trade unions or individuals upon themselves. At the same time, its role as the mediator of processes of valorisation brings it into ideological and actual proximity with religion and therapy, concerned as they all are with human perfectibility. But it must also be averred that the extension and elasticity of management occurs in a specific historical moment, one which is analytically punctual despite seeming experientially perpetual. And as we situate the extension of management in its historical moment, the same needs to be done for the various heuristics which we use to estrange it from us or ourselves from it, such as an art exhibition about management.

If the unthought of management is perhaps most iridescently the redundancy of thought, and the upcycling of politics as logistics, then the curt survey just set out above runs the risk of contenting itself with truism when more careful optics are solicited. And working with the premise that the exhibition itself is the occasion if not the source of this demand, the optic could initially be put in this way: what is the relationship between the art object (and its most tireless familiar, the artistic subject) and the object of management? Which amounts to saying, is it possible to build a show around the themes of management, work and the entrepreneur – particularly in the era anointed as 'communicative capitalism' – without situating art as at least a potential addressee of management's claims, not to mention their enthusiastic referee since the era of Art & Language, the Artist Placement Group or Mierle Laderman Ukeles? The poles of the aestheticisation of a study object located in a vitrine in the middle distance and a benign topos of reflexivity are equally dangerous for an aesthetic encounter with political economy. All I Can See is the Management intends to showcase

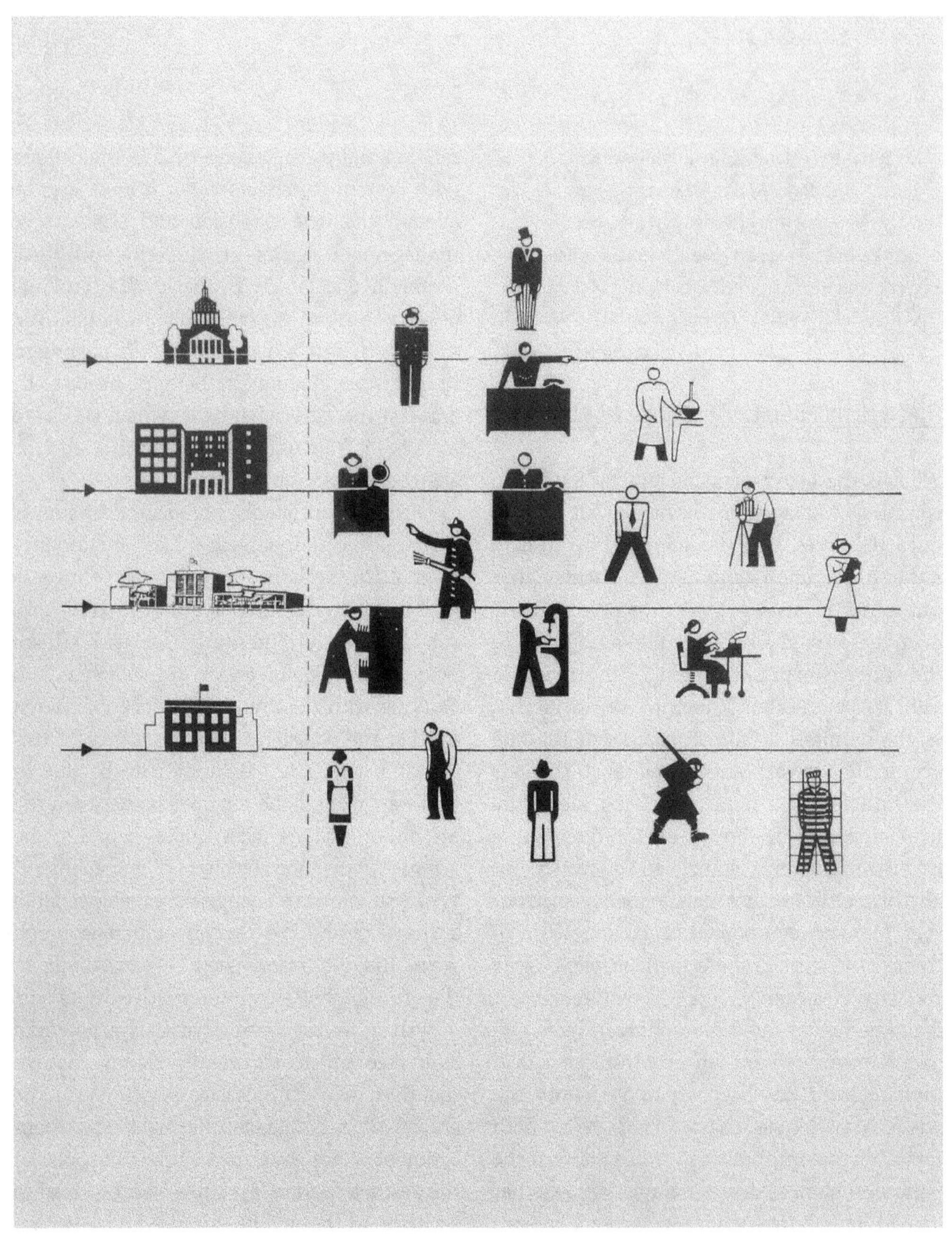

Allan Sekula, *School is a Factory*, 1978-80

'artworks that consider how late capitalist approaches to working life play out at work, in education and at home'. But the exhibition does so with a sense of excluding the immanent mimesis of the managerial role performed by culture itself from its purview (advisedly 'immanent' since management theory has for decades embraced creativity, flux, singularity and improvisation as its *passepartouts*). Does the press release's talk of a 'pervasiveness of management' include itself? Does the show take into account or see itself reflected in the culture of management within the sphere of culture or is this 'culture of management' just an eccentric ritual practised by 'workers', 'entrepreneurs' and 'managers' as the exotic others to artists? Management and art of course have a lot in common, perhaps most obviously that both of them make labour disappear, only later, if at all, to re-introduce it in the guise of a 'resource'. It could be that the exhibition sees but does not speak 'management' and the works it has assembled seem to be 'about' management. 'Management' is then an object found and summoned into a gallery space where it is expected to behave as a native informant.

But if the contention here is a certain neglect of the immanence of object to concept, then the contention must be specified a bit better. Rather than identifying a 'blind spot' in the show's thinking, it should be more interesting to see how the exhibition can or should 'perform' the logic of management, and not just see it everywhere, that is, nowhere. It might be proposed that the characteristic problem management has with locating its object – management is notoriously autotelic, that is, formalist and concerned with the control of processes, thoroughly immersed in its own logic – is paralleled in the exhibition's trouble deciding on a curatorial object.[2] It holds up and puts down management, work, and the mediating figure of the entrepreneur, but declines to put them into relation or posit a thesis that could guide the viewer in such assembling. Perhaps here sits the common misapprehension that an argument, when made by an exhibition, is bound to be didactic or illustrative and definitely semantic. Yet fostering a productive ambiguity (rather than the doxa entailed by most iterations of artistic ambiguity) itself requires a strong curatorial conceit which an exhibition put together with this degree of diffidence willingly forsakes. What may be fostered in its stead is the perception of an arbitrariness resolving into aestheticisation on the one hand, and its corollary, nostalgia, on the other. The result may be an occlusion of insights into the contemporary dynamics

Management and art, of course, have a lot in common

of management, which would have to include the communalised management of austerity, along with the management of the business 'in' us, as the Department of Trade and Industry's new slogan would have it, painting its dazzling future of mass unemployment. But if it should be said that the remit of an art exhibition that cites work, management and entrepreneurship is to be suggestive and not topical, there would still be the questions of focus and the deliberate sidestepping of the immanence of the object to the inquiry. But supposing this operation had been performed successfully, would it still fall under the rubric of reflexivity?

One dramatisation of this question was supplied by Filipa César's video, *Rapport* (2007,

15 min.), in an installation which dominated the Gasworks space both visually (it was a large projection on standing screens which diagonally bisected the space) and auditorily. The video watched a group of aspiring German managers take part in an neuro-linguistic programming (NLP) session.[3] This work evoked Harun Farocki's videogrammes of 'modern life' in its impassive scrutiny and incidental emotiveness, although César's editing preferences are more aleatory and nervous. Reflexivity here, as in most therapeutic regimes, was clearly acting as homeopathy and training for heteronomous goals ('success') which had been internalised to the point where any change to behaviour would be not just strictly personal but totally homeostatic.

DESIST, DESIST: REFLEXIVITY AS TOTAL QUALITY MANAGEMENT

Reflexivity is a highly valorised term in critical art production and mediation, signalling an awareness of tradition, contradiction, situatedness and responsibility. It may be an agonised awareness or an ironic one, an emblem of complicity or militancy, and it has numberless affective and political sources. However, against a wider backdrop of massified consumption of critical cultural practice, it is also a highly normative term and technology. One need only look at the prominence of 'criticality' in art school curricula to recognise it as the bureaucratic form of critique, and that such a training in criticality nearly always marks the spot from whence critique has been expunged.

As such, its constative is critical, while its performative is virtuous. In this respect, it functions in analogy with instruments of feedback and measure which signal management in other spheres, like consultation, evaluation, or assessment – it is the internal standard operating procedure of the field. And it is in this way that we would have to qualify the demand for reflexivity from an art exhibition about management, before we can hope to distinguish from this demand another desire, that for immanence of object to inquiry. Which is to say, the demand for reflexivity is a product of the necessity of situating the exhibition itself in the 'pervasiveness' of management seen and unseen, but this demand may issue from the same field it wants to survey.

A demonstration of 'reflexivity' here could take the form of seeing if Gasworks' or any comparable organisation's (and the whole gist would be in determining what is meant by 'comparable') own administrative structure and relationships constitute an object for a show about management? If, as is likely, this would fall fairly within the exhibition's conceptual limits, what would be the practical implications of situating its own operations within the field of management? Its own funding applications in a vitrine, its own overeducated invigilators and administrators enunciating their subjectivities in a video? Wouldn't this capture the double (-bind) prize of not only being 'about' management but also being reflexive about the role of small publicly-funded arts organisations in reproducing the managerial paradigms they query? This critique could instantaneously be generalised to represent the formation of the neoliberal subject per se through the tangled idioms of self-expression and submission. Such a configuration is of course familiar from mid-decade and pre-crisis critical art discourse centring on the cultural producer as the model subject of precarity, and one which animated practices such as Berlin's kpD (kleines postfordistisches Drama), prominently featured in the last exhibition project at Gasworks comparable to All I Can See: 2007's Lapdogs of the Bourgeoisie. The latter was a much more psychoanalytic affair, tracing an 'internal' object, and thereby worrying the symptomatic rather than taxonomic mode: its scrutiny was into how class structured the dimmed background of artistic careers. Here, the demand for reflexivity was anticipated, and, if memory serves, diverted and defused. The press release noted that '[t]he participating artists have not necessarily been chosen for a specific engagement with issues of class within their work' but hoped instead to 'ask whether the traditional analytical tools at our disposal are helpful in such an examination of the art world today.'

Now might be the time to pause and take stock of the traction of the 'hypothesis': that the logic of management is already cultural; or, how it has been sung in art's own dialect as the modernist principle of self-reflexivity. If modernism is the self-awareness of modernity (the notion of art as the research and development branch of society), what makes this reflexivity impossible now, what kind of self-awareness is required now, when the modernist temporal horizon is no longer a viable frame of reference and all we can do is manage the present? In order to show how the modernist self-reflexivity that art cannot help but perpetually engage, be it in the mode of denial or affirmation as 'criticality', is both like and unlike the closed loop of managerial auditing, a history of art's own self-definition as and against the available economic subjects of social labour is required – a history which constitutes a substantial part of the self-reflexivity or 'autonomy' of artistic production. Art, when it reflects on 'management', is not just reflecting on its outside; it is defined and traversed by its antagonism with productive relations,

what makes modernist reflexivity impossible now?

with abstract labour.[4] Artists have continually identified and misidentified their labour and their social relations with work, management and entrepreneurship. An exhibition that talks about management without alluding to the cybernetic social-engineering baroque of Stephen Willats, the Saint-Simonian consultancy schemes of the Artist Placement Group, or even – to take a current practice – the marketing training psy-ops of Pilvi Takala, might as well be talking about botany as about management, not to say handling its works as specimens. An even more prosaic way of staging the immanence of management to the field of art production would be a glance at the labour relations in its midst: the curators as managers, artists as workers and entrepreneurs. This kind of distinction itself obtains less and less. When it is the capacity to consume with distinction and sensitivity that qualifies curators and artists alike as managers of experience such profiles are tendentially subsumed into the managerial.[5] Viewers, then, are the unpaid work placements in this valorisation scheme. Another and related schema could inspect the determinations of speech and performance as emblematic of success in both management and art production: the iterability of practices, that they be original – 'visionary' – yet amenable to be reproduced and adapted in disparate contexts, which is to say, commodified, is another binding thread or shared structure.

Management, or 'the conduct of conduct', is operational, and reflexive in an instrumental way, not an immanent one; it can never 'revolutionise' its own telos – the dominance of capitalist accounting and the unchallenged legitimacy of this ontology. The structure of reflexivity in art and the structure of assessment native to management have such different genealogies, though optimised for compatibility in today's managerial dogma as it inflects and infects the 'governance' of the realm of freedom (culture) as much as it does the realm of necessity (industry). Perhaps a more generative lens to juxtapose or align them is the currently voguish curatorial rubric of 'fiction' – the fiction of management, and the fictions mobilised in contemporary art.[6] Could we call the artist/curator a manager of 'fictional' resources? This could potentially open up the whole managerial ontology to an understanding of 'purposiveness' very different to the formalism of management without end.

SPECIMENS

In some ways, the exhibition presents one with a less than straightforward task when it comes to discussing the works, since there isn't a thesis to measure them against. The diffuseness of the focus – work, management and entrepreneurship – also creates some opacity. Management is rendered as training (in works by Amy Feneck, Darcy Lange, Filipa César, and, to some extent, Allan Sekula); as an anecdote of irrationality prompted by the cultishness of much 'guru-centred' management theory and ritual (Pil and Galia Kollektiv's video), and that eternally elusive object of management, the *Seele und Gefühl eines Arbeiters* (Soul and Feelings of a Worker). This set of works by KP Brehmer was made in 1978-1980, and they disclose how the mimesis of measure produces a spooky and sublime abstraction.[7] Sublimed into human capital, the fictitious analogy between employee creativity and the boundlessness of self-valorising value is here turned into a minimal chromatic allegory, implying an absent manager to survey these charts and scry the runes of exploitation. Brought up to date, the key here may be that the secret of the value

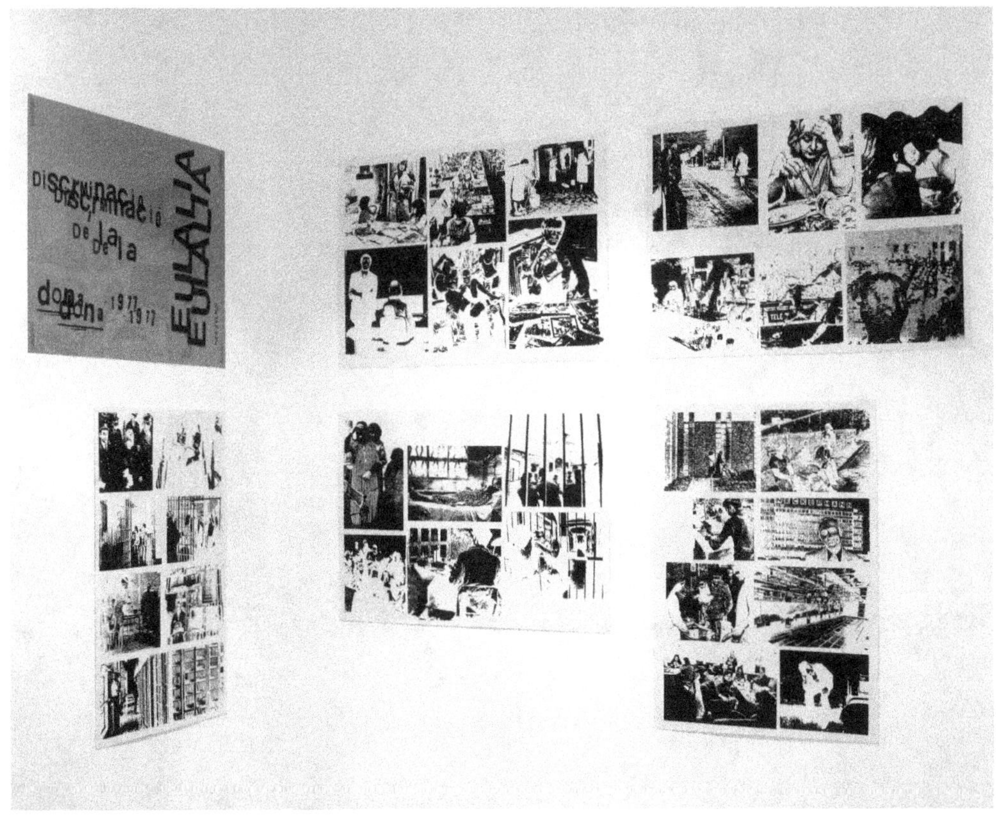

Eulàlia, *Discriminació de la dona / Discrimination Against Women*, 1977

of both fictitious capital and labour-power is not just unpaid labour (surplus-value) but the speculation on labour that has not been *done*, and will not be; not just because of propensities for 'human strike' but due to the systemically senseless nature of such labour.

Darcy Lange and Amy Feneck are interesting choices insofar as their work accentuates state (and in Lange's case, also private) education as a dimension of 'governance' in the present and recent past, while also indexing the show's signifiers to yet another domain of modular control i.e. 'management' in its broadest sense. However, Feneck only has her title, *Government Workers* (2010, 6 min.) to bear this out in what is otherwise a very rote documentation of institutional space (a Hackney primary school) that does not speak for itself. The old critique of artistic objectivity or its innocuous character mask, 'observation', such as that made by Brecht in *The Threepenny Trial* about the image of the thing as incapable of speaking for itself, targeting the rough pieties of *neue sachlichkeit*, arises here.[8] Lange's films, in the meantime, are presented very much as an object: their length and durational quality lend them vitality as documents, but are needlessly reified as the incidental qualities of an art object, and prove forbidding to the viewer's engagement, rather than leaving them open to the comparison

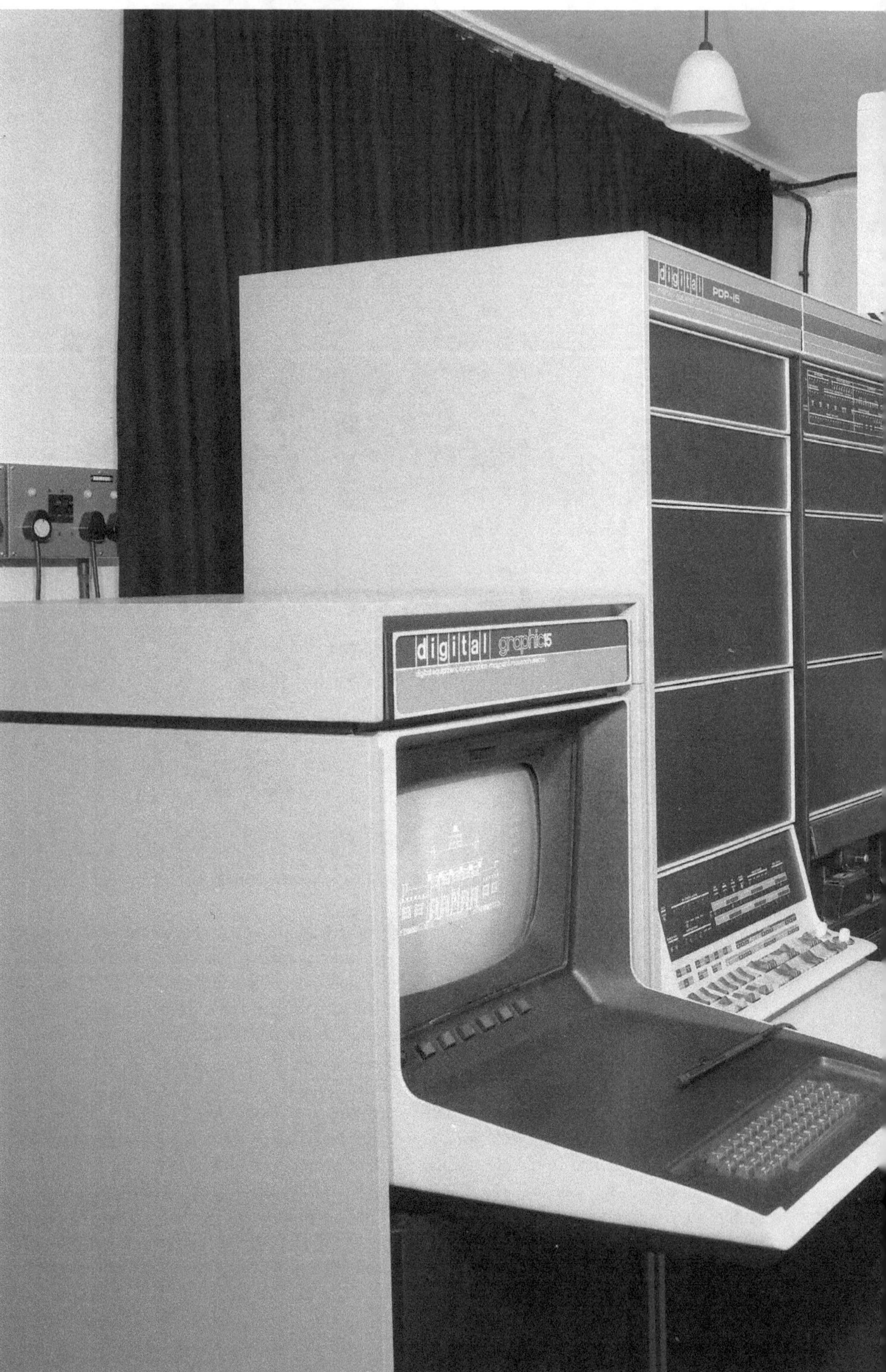
digital PDP-15
digital graphic15

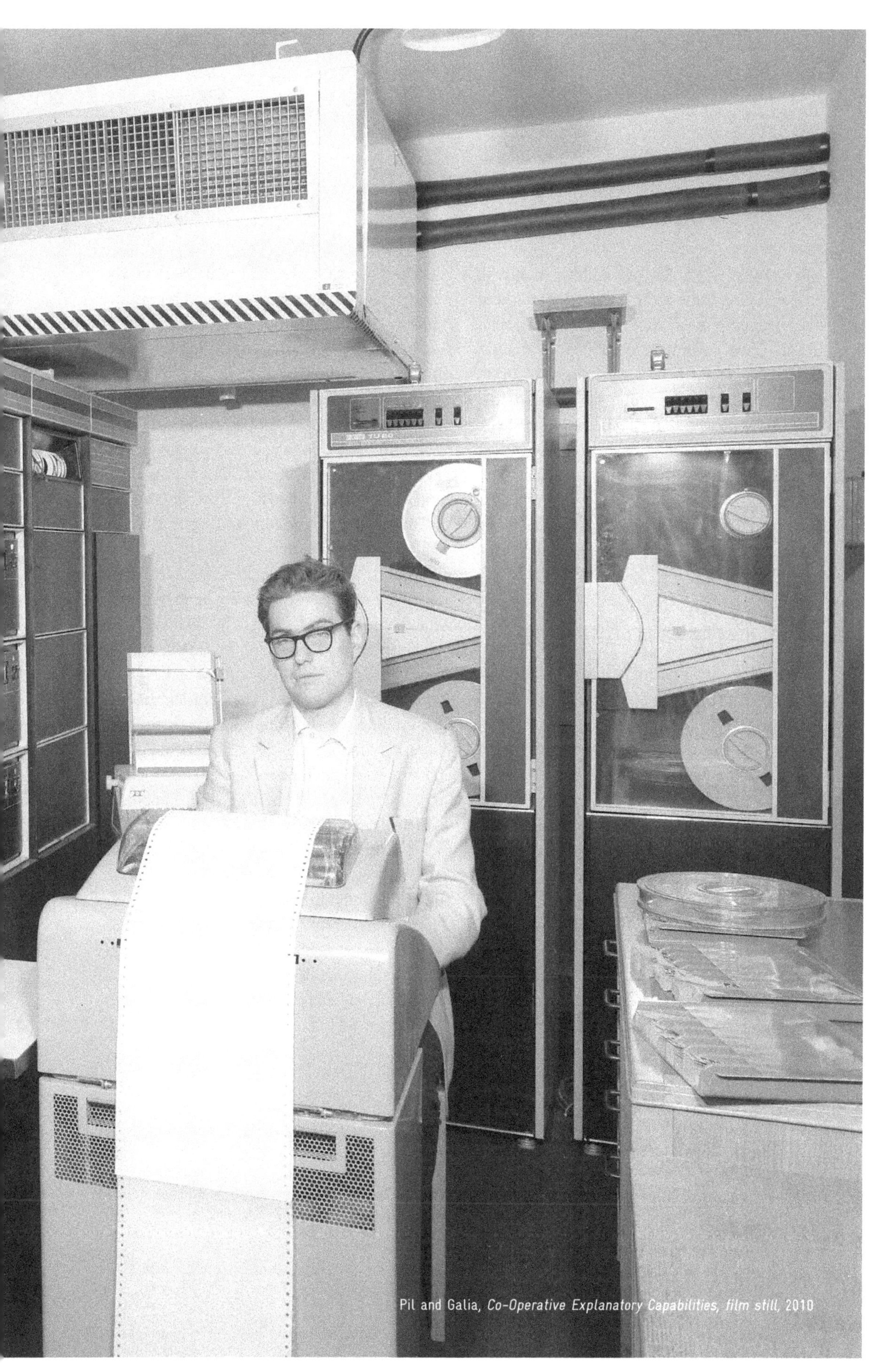

Pil and Galia, *Co-Operative Explanatory Capabilities*, film still, 2010

and analysis which Lange's archive sought to enable. Going into so many classrooms and interviewing pupils and instructors at such length, itself a component of a longer term audiovisual research into workplace relations, enacts an intriguing mimesis of industrial sociology; at least its porosity to such uses raises a question for art's relationship to management which is not taken up. Pil and Galia Kollektiv's piece *Co-Operative Explanatory Capabilities in Organisational Design and Personnel Management* (2010, 23 min.) can be seen as metonymic for the world view of the entire show – its fascinated, fabulating approach to found material echoes the show's approach to its 'object' at its best, but also exemplifies the noticeable though not overpowering 'wrong-end-of-a-telescope' impulse of nostalgia. Allan Sekula's *School is a Factory* (1978-80) is, on the other hand, perhaps the best synthesis of the show's stated concerns, with its critical realist diagramming of class, education, shifts in accumulation, and the de-skilling which management nearly always favours in its drive to submit the hard-won autonomy of labour to the automatism of the organisation. Stewart Marshall's video *Distinct* (1979, 38 min.) is a finely honed absurdist parlour drama depicting standardisation as the ineluctable drift of all human projects, from a couple's relationship to the productive relations on made-for-television film sets.

management nearly always submits the hard-won autonomy of labour to the automatism of the organisation

The diversity of All I Can See is the Management's excellent talks programme understandably could not be emulated within the exhibition.[9] As the exhibition is not a discursive medium, such a multi-layered constellation of topics and tropes was bound to suffer in the absence of a strong curatorial argument, and this was embodied by oblique or tenuous curatorial choices. One such was the *Normal Work* (2007) video and photograph suite by Pauline Boudry and Renate Lorenz. It might well be about work, but it is 'about' a number of other things as well, and none of them seem discernibly germane to 'management'. Arbitrary-seeming also was the inclusion of a buoyantly punk collage series by Eulàlia entitled *Discriminació de la dona* (Discrimination Against Women, 1977). To give an art exhibition the task of unfolding the subsumption, or redefinition, of work by management, while concomitantly charting the emergence of the entrepreneurial subjectivities dictated by this shift, is perhaps unrealistic, and the show's eschewing of didacticism underscores its appreciation that this is the case. Yet the concatenation of, at times painfully, unrelated work reflecting on different aspects of this unwieldy proposition could perhaps been avoided, or alleviated, had the telescope been turned in on itself and created an object in its own image.

Marina Vishmidt ‹maviss@gmail.com› is a London based writer and PhD candidate at the School of Business and Management at Queen Mary, University of London

All I Can See is the Management took place at Gasworks Gallery, London, 7 October 2011 - 11 December 2011

FOOTNOTES

1 Robert Linhart, *L'etabli*, (Paris: Les éditions des minuit, 1981, pp 13-14); quoted in Diane Morgan, 'Are you working enthusiastically? Fourier, Proudhon and The Serial Organisation of the Workplace', *Parallax*, 2011, vol. 17, no. 2, pp.36-48; 42.

2 The focus on 'outcomes' in the 'managerial regime' can be deceptive – 'outcomes' are the final stage in a sequence of processes, and thus cannot be analysed as normative or practical goals. 'Outcomes' can only be sought in the conditionality of management, that is, the environment which makes its processes tenable and operable.

3 The talks programme also offered an NLP session, with an explanation of its principles by a practitioner.

4 'Yet it is precisely as artifacts, as products of social labor, that [artworks] also communicate with the empirical experience that they reject and from which they draw their content.' Theodor W. Adorno, *Aesthetic Theory*, London: Continuum, 2004. p.5.

5 I owe the terms of the decidedly incipient analysis here to discussions with Stefano Harney, who proposes that the management of attention is an imperative shared by cultural workers (artists and art professionals) and 'regular' workers, a signal mode of the local subsumption of labour to the 'managerial'. In this framework, art becomes internal to labour as the suspension or diversion of attention.

6 As the significantly abridged article 'The Conduct of Management and the Management of Conduct: Contemporary Managerial Discourse and the Constitution of the "Competent" Manager' by Paul du Gay, Graeme Salaman and Bronwen Rees, included in Gasworks' 'Pipeline' reading resource for the exhibition, has it, 'It is perfectly possible and legitimate to conceive of the "manager" as a fiction, for example, because that category of person has not always existed.' http://pipeline.gasworks.org.uk/2011/08/04/constituting-the-%E2%80%98competent%E2%80%99-manager/

7 See note 5. With regard to Brehmer, he is noted as an exponent of the early 1970s West German art movement *kapitalistschen realismus*, somewhat prior to Mark Fisher's coinage. Like his contemporary Marianne Wex, Brehmer was concerned with the behavioural effects of visual communication, abstracting and staging these motifs, so that their disciplinary character might be better revealed.

8 'For the situation is complicated by the fact that less than at any time does a simple reproduction of reality tell us anything about reality. A photograph of the Krupps works or GEC yields almost nothing about these institutions. Reality proper has slipped into the functional. The reification of human relationships, signalled by the factory, can no longer be revealed by the photograph. Therefore something has actually to be constructed, something artificial, something set up. For this reason, art is indeed necessary. But the old concept of art, the one that rests on experience, is superseded. For whoever represents that which is experienceable in reality, also does not capture it. Reality is no longer experienceable in its totality.' Bertolt Brecht, *Schriften: Grosse Kommentierte Berliner und Frankfurter Ausgabe*, Werner Hecht et al (eds.), 1, vol. 21, Berlin 1988, p.469; quoted in Esther Leslie, 'Happy Knowledge', (unpublished).

9 The programme was not only illustrious but unusually considered, with the participation of critical organisation theorist Peter Fleming, Marxist anti-work and feminist political theorist Kathi Weeks, artist and trade union activist Fred Lonidier, and a screening of Joaquim Jordà's *Numax Presenta*... (1980, 105 min.), a documentary about an occupation of a textile factory in Franco-era Barcelona.

FROM THE CULT OF THE PEOPLE TO THE CULT OF RANCIÈRE

A radical social historian as well as philosopher, Jacques Rancière has spent many years rescuing vivid fragments of proletarian life and thought from the vested interests that claim to speak for them. But, in thwarting the instrumentality of intellectuals, he also risks obscuring the material he cherishes and the energies it carries – write ANTHONY ILES *and* TOM ROBERTS

Jacques Rancière is recognised today as an important aesthetic theorist and philosopher, but here we will argue that his greatest contribution is to social history. A stronger than usual emphasis will be therefore placed on Rancière's relation to the tradition of writing 'history from below', which is enjoying some degree of exposure and rediscovery at a time of renewed global revolt and struggle. In this light, it is worth considering Rancière's critical investigations of the way conceptions of the 'people' and of classes are constructed, and whose interests these constructions serve.[1]

Of the three books we discuss, *Proletarian Nights* is the best known. This book, which first brought Rancière widespread acknowledgement in the US and Europe, was published in French in 1981 and in English in 1989. Long out of print, it is republished this year alongside two collections of his work with the journal and research collective *Les Révoltes Logiques*. With the English translation of Rancière's first book, *Althusser's Lesson*, appearing last year, the constellation of these works allows English readers at last to read Rancière backwards, in the sense that the formative thoughts and arguments he subsequently refined over the course of 30 years are contained in these volumes.

FROM THE CULT OF ALTHUSSER TO THE CULT OF RANCIÈRE

In discussing these books, it's necessary to situate them in relation to Rancière's participation in the French left of the '60s and '70s. The key reference point for Rancière's work is Louis Althusser, a thinker who came to dominate French Marxist thought in the early 1960s. Rancière was a pupil of Althusser at the elite *École normale supérieure*, part of the seminar that assembled *Reading Capital*. His loyalty to Althusser was such that his contribution to this book has been cited as an example of the limits to which his master's philosophy can be taken.[2] Yet the overbearing dynamic by which he later characterised Althusser's thinking is one Rancière went on to elaborate and resist throughout the course of his work:

> The idea that the dominated are dominated because they are ignorant of the laws of domination. Eventually [for intellectuals] this exalted task dissolves into a pure thought of resentment which declares the inability of the ignorant to be cured of their illusions, and hence the inability of the masses to take charge of their own destiny.[3]

Rancière's initial split with his master was prompted by Althusser's loyalty to the Parti Communiste Francaise (PCF) during the events of 1968. Returning to Althusser's theory later, Rancière worked to widen the breach that May '68 had thrown open.[4] Henceforth, Rancière follows, in the most minute detail, the mediations which surround the subaltern subject, the proletarian or worker. The problem of theory, of Marxist science and the condescension of the intellectual to his subject, is raised to a general principle traceable back from the perspective of the present through the entire history of the left.[5]

The break of which Rancière was a part in 1968 mirrors the break of UK historians with the Communist Party of Great Britain after the invasion of Hungary by Russian troops in 1956, yet this delay is perhaps significant. During this period much of the European left distanced itself from Stalinist policy, but the primacy of the PCF in France softened this break, arguably helping to defer, and effectively trigger, what in '68 became an open revolt against the party.

AFTER '68

After 1968 and the split with Althusser, Rancière became associated with the group Gauche Proletariane (GP) - partly made up of former Althusserians and Maoists who, inspired by China's cultural revolution, rebelled against the PCF and threw themselves into the class struggle as militants during May '68, and as 'etabli' in the months that followed the cessation of the strike wave in September.[6]

The breach of '68 completely shook up the former separation of intellectuals and workers. As well as rejecting Althusser (the party intellectual), those around the GP became self-critical about not having engaged in the May revolt earlier. They had waited for the industrial workers to get involved - held back by their fetishisation of a pure working class, from which they had excluded students. As GP's pursuit of class struggle developed, they tried to overcome this division through the figure of the *etabli*. Rancière contributed to these debates within GP, criticising the placement of the *etabli* for providing a privileged situation from which to represent the working class to the activist class, thus creating a dynamic of mutually reassuring distance which retained workers as mute, romanticised others. In crisis under the pressure of this debate, state repression and the sense that workers themselves were beginning to take control of the direction of their own struggle, GP began to fall apart.[7] The situation was formative for Rancière: in activism he again met the problem of the intellectual's mediating role between the exploited, their exploitation and its overthrow. Rancière began to turn to social history to uncover the complex origins of this relationship.[8]

LA PENSÉE D'EN BAS

In 1975 Rancière joined a group of philosophers and historians, including many ex-GP militants, to research a television series on *The Meaning of Revolt in the Twentieth Century*. The series never transpired because the state-owned channel Antennae 0, withdrew backing on the advice of Prime Minister Jacques Chirac. But the group developed its research in a journal, *Les Révoltes Logiques*, based at the philosophy department of the University of Paris VIII. Inspired by a line from Arthur Rimbaud's poem 'Democratie', and addressed to both an academic and general readership, LRL was intended as a 'purposefully inconclusive problematisation of the history of the workers' and women's movements.'[9] Rather than retrieving a continuity of revolt, of invariant class antagonism, the group was more focused on the discursive content of working class articulation and the manifold means by which it has been stifled.

In a kind of manifesto, printed on the inside back cover of the first issue of the journal, the LRL group vowed to:

> listen again to [*reentendre*] the findings of social history and to re-establish thought from below [*la pensée d'en bas*] and the issues which were debated therein.[10]

French social history has, for Rancière, a specific lineage which he began to explore within the *LRL* group.[11] This is reflected in their collective work which was as interested in historiography as history itself and spent as much energy criticising other historical accounts as writing history. This is particularly evident in the extensive intra-left critiques assembled in Volume II of *Staging the People*, but the vituperative and polemical context is somewhat elided here through the extraction of Rancière's own writing from the collective output amongst which it first appeared.

The collective waged a struggle which churned up the landscape of left history. As much against history as it had been told as against how it was being made in their present; against the tradition of left militancy from which they had come. For LRL this meant opening 'a battle on several fronts' confronting dogmatisms of all kinds, including purely empirical history but also the anti-historical diminishment of empirical fact by activists.[12] It was against 'la mode retro' – a nostalgic and sycophantic relation to the past. Against the 'strict proletarian of Marxist Science' but also its post-Marxist opposite – the heroic plebs who would resist all authoritarianism; the 'noisy and colourful people' which became the 'imaginary correlate of the socialist intelligentsia [...] about to take power in 1981'.[13]

> *Les Révoltes Logiques* [questioned] the practices of identification common to the discourse of both activist vanguards and academic historians [...] It was not a history of voices from below against one of discourse from above, [...] It was a history that questioned the very functioning of these pairs of opposites, and also those that opposed realities to representations.[14]

LRL sought to complicate the framework of post-WWII left history by philosophically developing the trend of turning away from party representation and towards the complex of identification, beliefs and solidarities which made up the (pre-industrial) working class. This general trend, begun after 1956, was compounded by the events of 1968. The strategic response of many left historians in Britain, France and elsewhere, even if they remained complicit with pro-Stalinist parties, had been to steer away from 20th century history; away from battles, revolutionary events, and towards writing and thinking through the minor, and pre-capitalist histories of the proto-working class or early workers' movement.

In France, this work had been monopolised by historians working around the journal *Annales* (known as the *Annales* school), who had developed microscopic analyses of statistics, and the interactions of the material, environmental and ideological frameworks structuring action, culture and economic change over the long term.[15] However, Rancière developed strong criticisms of the Annales group, situating them in a left tradition established by pioneers such as Jules Michelet who, as Rancière saw it, founded social history on conditions which constructed and perpetuated the left historian's mediating role between people and their own history.[16] For LRL, *Annales* historians indulged a particular contemporary spirit of nostalgia and through their ultra-localist view, stressed continuity at the expense of revolutionary rupture.[17]

Yet, in some ways this drew *LRL* and Rancière closer to the studies developed by peers of the UK Communist Historians Group working on 'history from below' (who themselves had been heavily influenced by *Annales*). The groundbreaking post-WWII studies of C.L.R. James, E.P. Thompson and Christopher

Hill had flowed into and been modified by the '60s and '70s culture of the new left which no longer bracketed off questions of race, sex and class from revolutionary politics.

Rancière shares some affinities with the English historiography of 'history from below', especially in the emphasis on agency over structure. Both affirm some autonomy, in everyday life and self-perception, in the formation of popular consciousness; both perceive and animate the space for people to think differently with and against the forces determining them.

However in *LRL* there is a sharper awareness of both the authority of the historian, and of the forms of domination that are enacted within dominated groups. Equally, *LRL's* constant sniping at the self-serving nostalgia or revisionism of left intellectuals and historians was an attempt to follow and critically derail the development of left thought as it headed into the relativist impasses of postmodernism.[18]

Commonalities with the UK movement extended to participation in a debate on people's history and socialist theory organised by History Workshop, a group founded in 1967 which, sought, like *Révoltes Logiques*, to span and connect discussions between professional historians, workers' and feminist movements. However, Rancière also caused friction within the History Workshop. The editorial board of its journal is said to have refused to publish some translations of Rancière's articles in 1979 because they 'insulted the working class'.[19]

'LE SOCIAL' AND FRENCH HISTORY

In an essay published in a History Workshop anthology, *People's History and Socialist Theory*, Rancière traced the expansion of French social history in the 1880s as developed by civil servants (who were often former trade unionists) within the Labour Office of the Republican government to 'effect a conciliation between the Republic, the state and the working classes.'[20] This role for social history, according to Rancière, was further developed by anti-communist and anti-anarchist aspects of the trade union movement, and later the Socialist Party (following a split between socialist and communist parties after 1914-18). Rancière argues that as far as Marxists or the communist party were interested in history, it was not a history of the working class, but the history of revolution – the revolution of 1789 – which lent them legitimacy as the party of national democracy. Therefore, up to WWII, working class history in France continued to develop as a discussion between the workers' movement, trade unions and the State within the framework of 'industrial democracy'. This sustained the close relationship between aspects of the working class movement and the generation of its own history, but the tradition suffered a 'material loss' after WWII as its political goals had close proximity to those of the corporate state of Petain, Vichy and the Nazis. The controversial traffic of workers' ideals is discussed in Rancière's essay, 'From Pelloutier to Hitler' in *Staging the People* Volume I. It describes the relationships by which advocates of an image of the people mobilised this image in a unilateral dialogue with the State.

The power of projections and models of 'the people' is in their capacity to be appropriated by hostile interests. This is evident in the way an emphasis on working class autonomy in left history has recently been co-opted to fit the UK coalition government's austerity agenda. Phillip Blond, author of *Red Tory* and director of ResPublica, who was initially seen as an ideologist for the renewal of the Tory Party, draws directly upon an unqualified reading which credits E.P.

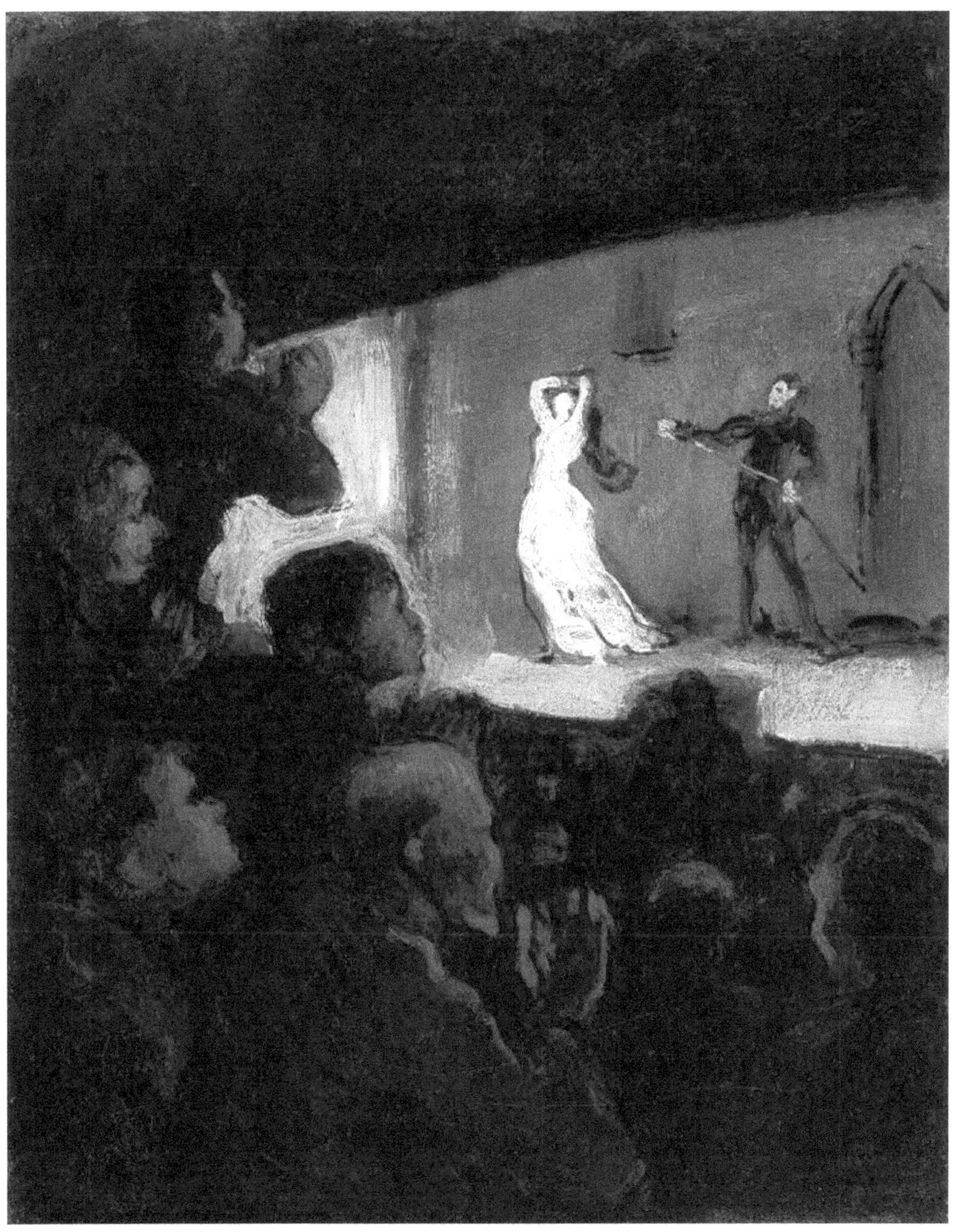

Honoré Daumier, *The Drama*, c.1860

Thompson's narrative of working class agency in *The Making of the English Working Class* to justify the dismantling of public services:

> The welfare state, I believe, began the destruction of the independent life of the British working class[...] making the populace a supplicant citizenry dependent on the state rather than themselves.[21]

Blond disingenuously characterises welfare as the invention of a 'middle-class elite' partly to 'deprive the poor of their irritating habit of autonomous organisation'. His model of social solidarity is drawn up not in the interests of working people, but of capital: if the working class can look after itself, it can act as a caretaker for the effects of neoliberalism.

As Rancière shows us, partisans of working class autonomy frequently turn out to be apologists of the worst abuses of the state and capital. In the lost tradition of 'le social' – a term which specifically emphasises the link between social history, the social question of labour and capital's reciprocal antagonism, and social movements – he recovers a marker of the false separation between the proper revolutionary destiny of the working class and an intimate self-understanding of the class in its contradictory identifications and interactions with bourgeois culture. Rancière has put tremendous efforts into tracing this division through archives to show the particular forms it takes in discrete historical moments.

STAGING THE PEOPLE

Rancière's writing for *Les Révoltes Logiques* are translated from a French collection which appeared in one volume entitled *Les scènes du peuple* in 2003. The English version is split into two volumes and titled respectively, *Staging the People: The Proletarian and His Double*, 2011 and *The Intellectual and His People: Staging the People Volume 2*, 2012.[22] Three longer essays collected in Volume I of these writings for LRL particularly stand out as original and concrete contributions to the contentious historical vicissitudes of working-class thought and culture. These build a dynamic bridging analysis between the 19th and 20th centuries which is revisited and enriched across Rancière's oeuvre. An exemplary essay in the deployment of this technique is 'Off to the Exhibition' which assesses reports made by trade delegations to the Exposition Universelle of 1867; a spectacle, Rancière insists, 'the workers perceive [...] as a product of their dispossession'. Rancière presents the reports as an example of the very juncture of politics, economics and ideology which bourgeois thought would rather keep separate. It is a key example of Rancière's delicate juxtaposition of fragments of proletarian self-articulation and historical hindsight. Through them he examines a meeting point of 'class and domestic power' which is both significant and somewhat self-defeating.

The workers' reports remonstrate against employers' deployment of machines as a tool against their class which is accompanied by an attack on the employers' efforts to introduce women into the workplace. Machines are attacked because they deskill the worker rather than freeing him from work time, therefore removing from the worker his power over his own production – his craft and intelligence 'in order to produce a bit more, to produce regardless.'[23] The introduction of women into the workplace is attacked by male workers for threatening to remove the worker from his power over his domestic situation. This is not only a matter of scandal judged by contemporary attitudes to gender equality in the workplace, but could already at the time be understood as an outmoded attitude: only a few years later the Women's Union for the Defence of Paris and Aid to the Wounded recognised attempts to discriminate against female workers as the defence of privilege and sought to abolish all competition between male and female workers.[24]

Rancière's presentation of these reports is sympathetic. Here, workers (albeit elite ones) pass judgement on their own conditions, in terms which correspond closely to Karl Marx's analysis of the introduction of machines, thus challenging the emerging power of employers to reorganise work, catalyse competition and force downward pressure on the wage across all industries.[25] The reports grasp the machine not as a 'cold-blooded monster to be destroyed' but rather, as Rancière's presentation goes to lengths to show, imagine a moral and social 'collective appropriation of the machines'.[26] Nonetheless, Rancière also gives due attention to a contradiction: here the retort to one particular division of labour production marks a second division in the social reproduction of the class itself.

While Rancière identifies this moment as a transition from 'corporative thinking' or 'Bonapartiste "socialism"' to a 'new revolutionary working-class ideal', a contradiction in the class is not resolved, but rather carried over. In Rancière's somewhat reductive formulation, the foundation of this split is 'the power of the working man over his wife'. If the way forward is for the working class movement to retract from the compact with bosses and move to open struggle over the means of production, towards either a revolutionary state or workers' control, this trajectory of productivism leaves these two powers – at work and at home – separated and unexamined parts of a never-to-be-whole.

Here, workers pass judgement on their own conditions, challenging the emerging power of employers

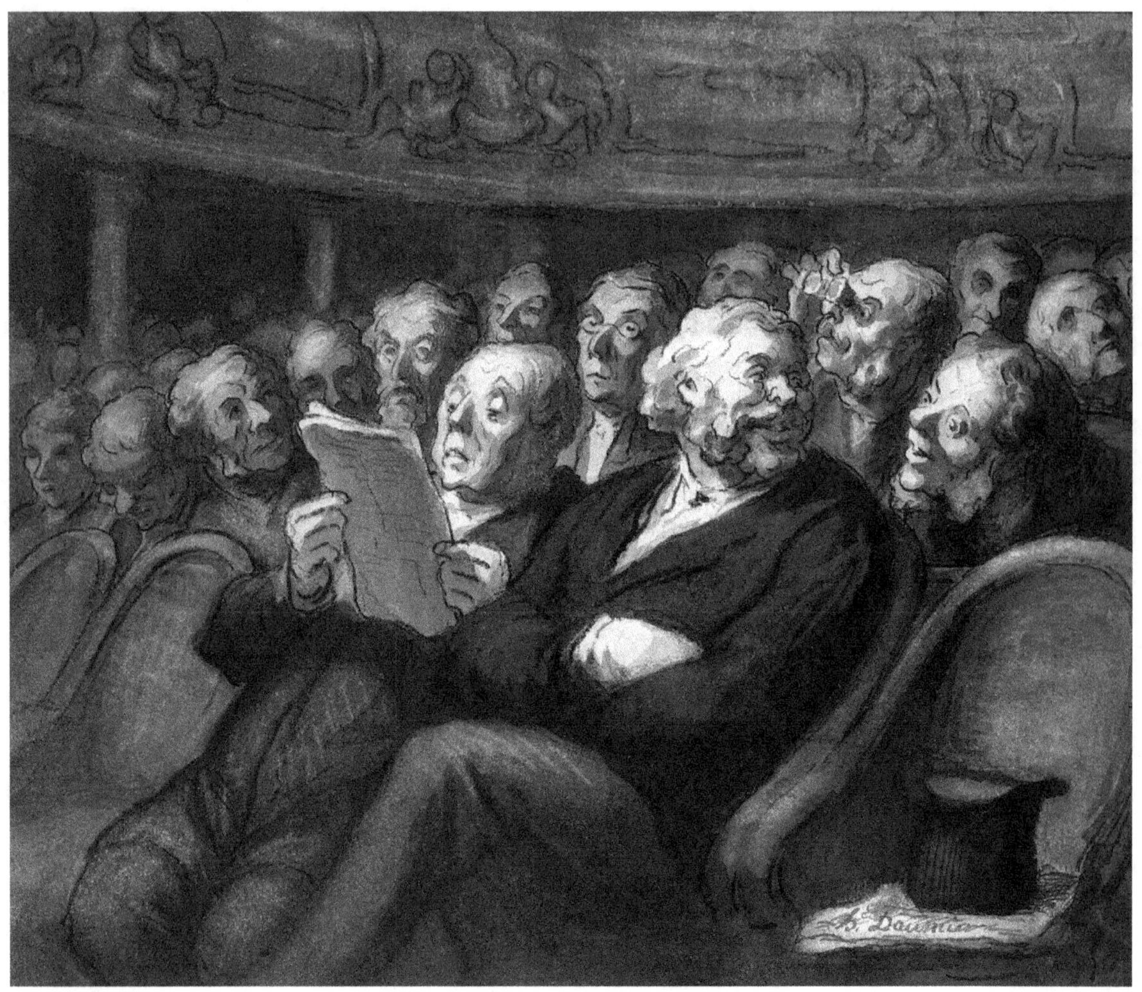

Honoré Daumier, *Intermission at the Comédie Française*, 1858

The 1975 essay marks a crucial development in Rancière's thinking. Initially sympathetic to the threats to working class autonomy, he latterly recognised this as a problematic example by which proletarian resistance and power can be formed at the expense of other denigrated subjects, i.e. women.[27] Henceforth, it will become impossible for the workers to affirm themselves as workers – for their gains will also be their losses, unless the workers' movement becomes only the movement of those who identify and wield power over other parties as men. The anti-work ethos which Rancière situates elsewhere on more individualistic terms finds, here, a structural rapport.

'From Pelloutier to Hitler' for which the shorter essay, 'Links in the Chain' provides a theoretical prelude and ally, examines the way certain forms of workerism and productivism were absorbed by Petain's collaborationist State leading to collusion between pro-Nazis and trade unionist elements in France. It is a powerful reminder to social historians that the Nazi movement drew its origins from the Left and closer examination might find painful proximities in the history of any territory. Even more controversially, it is a powerful rebuke to those in France who would like to imagine, without complication, a glorious continuum of socialist history cemented by the victory over Nazism.

The opportunity is not missed to hammer home the reactionary character of idealist forms of anticapitalism: alternative currencies, reformism (e.g. workplace hygiene), democratic negotiation between bosses and workers, even workers' autonomy. During this brief period all these measures were recommended by trade unions or militants in favour of collaboration and found some approval from the Vichy powers. These workers' advocates greatest treason lay in the way they sought to organise workers' needs in order to better direct them via the State. Rancière conveys well the complex context through which such arguments unfolded, found material motivation, were contorted and contested. Moreover, the attempt to mobilise heroic socialist traditions of hard work, loyalty and dignity in the service of collaboration lends great power to his thorough questioning of whether these ideals were native to the working class at all. In the context of the PCF's debates over the relationship between workers and intellectuals this research had the function of authorising GP's ultra-leftism and discrediting the more distanced and economistic approach of the party. However, the celebration of 'workers against work' could equally end up on the opposite pole of the political spectrum by affirming tendencies to work less for more outside of any revolutionary perspective.[28]

'Good Times, or, Pleasure at the Barrière' details the interactions between state censors, the organised left and theatre managers, singers, actors and revellers who took their pleasures beyond the limits set by censorious authorities. It is the companion piece to the essay collected in volume II, 'The People's Theatre: A Long Drawn-Out Affair'. This essay lends its theme of *Staging the People* to both volumes. In it, Rancière revisits the 150-year long persistence of an idea: the people's theatre, and its moralising role. It is here that Rancière first posited a socialist tradition which understood 'theatocracy' as coeval with democracy and thus a defining framework of 'self-representation' through which the people 'could view their own actions.'[29] However, in each case the course advised by the people's champions is none too distant from the use of theatre the State's advisors recommended to itself, albeit for different reasons. In 'Good Times' the problematic is situated in the ideal of a worker's culture untainted by bourgeois mediation:

> [...] the definition of a workers' morality of labour and devotion reflects the desire to free workers' initiative from bourgeois tutelage. But at the same time, the image of the worker is asserted as a cornerstone of the system of dependence to which the proletarians are reduced [...] it is in this way [...] that the demands of the working-class elite take up a position parallel to those of the discourse of the state.[30]

In Rancière's hands these parallels unravel - between the left and its 'image of the worker' and the workers themselves; between the left and the state; and between the subversions of underground culture and the state censors. Whilst the puritanism of the left and the state mirror each other in the grapple for limitation or control over working class bodies and minds, it is a fun-loving anti-politics which escapes to entertain:

> A plague on politics!
> To make a song
> my simple muse
> takes up a Bacchic chorus.
> Long live the gurgle of bottles
> And the sweet kisses of lovely girls[31]

It is by such heresies that left guardians of the period felt most threatened, but Rancière does not celebrate these occasions as simply unmediated. Rather, he is compelled to develop the problematic mediations of such retorts and their echoes in the present.[32] However impure, it is the tenacious escapes from the controlling discourses from above, be it left condescension or state paternalism, which interest Rancière and it is to them that he entrusts working class agency.

Yet Rancière, having turned over this question of the relationship of the intellectual to 'his people' from the break with Althusser and realisation that the class won't do the intellectual's bidding, to his own forays into rewriting history from below, still finds himself in need of an image of the people. He deposes a classical proletariat as negation in favour of the figure of the declassé, sometimes artisan, sometimes refusenik wage-slave who abandons the divisions forced upon body and mind.

> The genuinely dangerous classes were perhaps less those savages supposedly undermining the basement of society than the migrants who moved on the boundaries between classes[33]

It is this *declassé* subject - or subtraction from an ideal subject - foreshadowed in this earlier work for *LRL* which Rancière put at the forefront of his ambitious study, *Proletarian Nights*.

PROLETARIAN NIGHTS

Proletarian Nights, developed from Rancière's research for his doctoral thesis and first published in English under the more suggestive title *Nights of Labour*, is a hefty study of a relatively small group of Paris artisans who were active in writing poetry, prose, polemics, letters and diaries outside of working hours, under the July Monarchy (approximately 1830-1848).[34] The book has a three-part structure. The first follows the writings of joiner Gabriel Gauny, and through them, his attitudes to his work, his nocturnal explorations and those of his friends. The second explores the relationships between the Saint Simonians (a group of utopian socialists), and those workers whom they recruited. The third section analyses the way moral conceptions of the working class were constructed in contemporary workers' journals such as *L'Atelier* and through the Icarians, followers of Etienne Cabet's communitarian movement much influenced by Owenism.[35]

he stops his arms and glides in imagination toward the spacious view to enjoy it better than the possessors of the neighbouring residences

Taken together, Rancière's project in *Proletarian Nights* is to bring into tension the ambitions of the worker intellectuals and their construction as political subjects. He seeks to problematise conceptions of both the ideological separation between workers and intellectuals, and perceived unities of class identities, experiences and demands.

While seeking to avoid ventriloquism, the book might partly function as a veiled allegory of the dynamics of the post-'68 French left, particularly in Volume II wherein Rancière hints at echoes between the Saint Simonians and the *etabli* of the 1970s, only in reverse. Those workers disposed to join the Saint Simonians were more or less ambivalent about their ideology, finding instead the 'possibility of another world' which led them to begin to occupy the symbolic spaces of the intellectuals.

In making use of their night hours to pursue this 'other world', Rancière argues that the worker-poets' activities were 'entirely material and entirely intellectual at the same time.' The artisans not only appropriated languages and discourses, but also the material conditions which facilitate intellectual activity:

> Emancipation for those workers [...] was the attempt to conquer the useless, to conquer the language of the poet [...] the leisure of the loiterer. It is the attempt to take the time that they have not. To go to the places where they are not supposed to have anything to do.[36]

This entails a triple mastery: of time; of the effects of work on the body and mind; and also of the symbolic space of literature itself.

The logic of appropriation is central to Rancière's concept of emancipation. He suggests that 'the power of a mode of thinking has to do above all with its capacity to be displaced'. Rancière draws upon a text by Gauny about a fictional floorlayer who temporarily makes himself at home working alone and unwatched in unfinished bourgeois houses:

> Believing himself at home [...] he loves the arrangement of a room, so long as he has not yet finished laying the floor. If the window opens out onto a garden or commands a view of a picturesque horizon, he stops his arms and glides in imagination toward the spacious view to enjoy it better than the possessors of the neighbouring residences.[37]

Making oneself at home where one supposedly 'does not belong', might be a precondition for radical change. Rancière certainly floats this possibility throughout *Proletarian Nights*. Elsewhere he has suggested of the floorlayer's tale that 'what is at stake in emancipation [is] getting out of the ordinary ways of sensory experience. This thought has been important for my idea of politics, not being about the relations of power but being about the framing of the sensory world itself.'[38]

Rancière foregrounds the individual aspirations of the artisans in a complex, dialectical way as producing a form of agency which is not incompatible, indeed feeds into collective action and structural change. However the development between the worker's encounter with the symbolic space of poetry and philosophy, and concrete practices of emancipation, is often only hinted at in *Proletarian Nights*. Rancière suggests that the 'night-time socialisation of vanities' contributed towards opening up a much broader space of possibilities for the working class, a 'general movement of people getting out of their condition' and 'prepared for' the July revolution of 1830. They may well have had a motivating effect, but the specific ways in which they did are sadly not adequately explored in the text.

Rancière shifts between analysis of the relative status and dispositions of the artisans, and empathetic passages in which he chooses to write *with* their accounts. Emphasising a literary trajectory against tendencies in French historiography to treat history as science, Rancière refuses separation from his sources, except as an arguing consciousness alongside them. His work on them coincides with proliferation and amplifications of the questions within them. Irritatingly obfuscating perhaps, but this is joined to Rancière's own refusal to separate philosophy from history or literary creation from both.

Rancière's choice of worker intellectuals as his subjects attests to a common investment in literature as a means of transformation and agency by philosopher and artisans. He initially presented a smaller selection of the material revisited in *Proletarian Nights* in a book, written with Alain Faure, collecting the writings (including brochures, letters, poems, articles and posters) of workers of the 19th century across two key revolutionary periods 1830-34 and 1848-51.[39] However while *The Voice of the People* presented the worker poets as an exceptional contribution broadening the range of 'voices of the people', they assume an exemplary position in *Proletarian Nights*. It goes without saying, but it's important to add given the reception of Rancière in the culture industry, that literature offers significant forms of political agency and enriches broader movements, but culture is not the only terrain of struggles.

It is clear that Rancière himself harbours

a strong identification with the worker intellectuals. The 2012 edition of *Proletarian Nights* receives a new preface in which he suggests that the experiences of the precarious workers of the present day may come to resemble those of the artisans of his 19th century. However, it is not clear how Rancière's celebration of the subversion of the separation of work and play by the 19th century artisan translates into contemporary terms, given that capital has by now 'subverted' and enclosed both domains. The relative ease with which today's proletarianised academic or student reading *Proletarian Nights* may identify themselves with its heroes risks flattening not just the past, but the present too.

THE VOICE OF TRUTH

Rancière's truths emerge through writing and thinking alongside workers' thought and speech. Shifts in what it is possible to say or to imagine under a particular set of historical relations take precedence, and surface with the contradictions which allow us to experience the distance from our own present and from a future we might hope for. Rancière is able to move from the image of class as unitary to the continuous intervention into debates in order to complexify the situation and destabilise its certainties, thereby exposing the polysemy, intelligence and fragmentation through which the working classes found ways to act, and express their condition.[40] There is a determined self-criticism of the historian's traditional authorial power in this ongoing non-distinction between subject and historian – a refusal to become or pretend the 'voice of truth'. Rancière appears uninterested in acquiring the stable mastery of historians who engage in haughty professionalised combat with each other at a safe remove from the situation from which they draw their historical source material. But whilst Rancière gestures towards another form of history writing, one inseparable from the activity of its subjects, he has not, other than rhetorically, attempted to close this gap.

Rancière's prose undermines its own authority by being deliberately inconclusive, but this can often amount to a certain vagueness. Although *Proletarian Nights* is more rigorous, in the other volumes under review Rancière almost never gives away complete sources or references for the material he works on. We cannot easily squabble over footnotes, re-read and re-present the same material in a different and contradictory light.

it is Rancière's contrarian circumbendibus voice which determines the route

Though the books under review are peppered with insightful and poetic fragments of speech emanating from working class voices, it is Rancière's contrarian circumbendibus voice which determines the route. A route which, whilst it holds open the prospect for violent rupture and the overturning of routine perspectives – the very potentiality of revolt – mostly meanders off and then back onto the familiar road of the intellectual and his subject. He worries, pauses and reflects upon this relationship over and over, but never overcomes it.

Rancière neither wishes to ignore the formation of class in its complexity, nor totally abandon the revolutionary trajectory of 'the class' as the agent of its own abolition. But his grip upon this second axiom loosens over time. On the one hand a singular idea of the worker restricted, in the discourse of the employer, to his *métier* and on the other hand restricted, in Marxist discourse, to the task of revolution is opened up to a plurality of possibilities and as yet unknown capacities. But does writing history in a way which is both provisional and densely resistant to misappropriation preclude appropriation by 'a people who are missing', those who might transform it through struggle?

Rancière argues that a book inherently travels wherever it can; at the point of availability, anyone might pick it up and make use of the ideas contained in it, regardless of its intended audience. But Ranciere's evasiveness, his latter-day lack of real critical friction and tendency to waffle inconclusively might be said to limit his audience and thus the potential uses of his ideas.

Perhaps because he foregrounds the traction of symbolic transformation on material change, Rancière's work has been most readily absorbed into contemporary art discourse. The problem lies in allowing symbolic transformation to take precedence over the material change to which it should be intimately joined. The power of Rancière's contribution is in his assumption of equal capacity and his celebration of the imaginative transgressions against ideologies that might wittingly or unwittingly contribute towards 'keeping each to his or her place'. But to advocate the potential universality of ideas whilst at the same time leaving structural and material inequality intact, is simply another way of keeping everybody in their place.

Anthony Iles <anthony@metamute.org> is Assistant Editor of *Mute*. Tom Roberts <to_mroberts@hotmail.com> is a writer and artist. They are co-authors of the pamphlet *All Knees and Elbows of Susceptibility and Refusal*, due to be revised and reissued by Strickland Distribution in Autumn 2012

INFO

Books Reviewed: Jacques Rancière, *Proletarian Nights*, London: Verso, 2012; Jacques Rancière, *Staging the People: The Proletarian and His Double*, London: Verso, 2011 (Staging the People, Vol.I); and Jacques Rancière, *The Intellectual and His People: Staging the People*, London: Verso, 2012 (Staging the People, Vol II).

FOOTNOTES

1 For more on the development of 'history from below' see Anthony Iles and Tom Roberts, *All Knees and Elbows of Susceptibility and Refusal*, published as part of the alt.SPACE festival, July 2007. http://caughtlearning.org/files/all_knees_and_elbows_v2.pdf

2 Donald Reid, Introduction to *Proletarian Nights*, London: Verso, 2012, p.xiv.

3 Jacques Rancière, *Althusser's Lesson*, London: Continuum, 2011, p.xvi.

4 *Althusser's Lesson* was first published in 1974.

5 Anglophone commentators frequently invoke Rancière as a critic of Marxist economic determinism, yet he is less a critic of Marx than the critic of Althusser who leaves the latter's interpretation of Marx's largely intact.

6 *Etabli* or 'establishment' was a tactic by which activists, often students or intellectuals, were clandestinely placed in factories to promote worker agitation with the support of militant left groups. Rancière discusses the phenomenon in the article, 'Factory Nostalgia' in *The Intellectual and His People: Staging the People* Volume 2, London: Verso, 2012. In which, among other books, he reviews Robert Linhart's novel, *L'etabli*.

7 In 1973 an occupation at the LIP factory in *Besançon* led to worker self-management. See: Jacques Rancière, *Althusser's Lesson*, pp.119-120 and for a more critical account; 'Lip and the Self-Managed Counter-Revolution' in *Negation*, No. 3, 1973, http://libcom.org/library/lip-and-the-self-managed-counter-revolution-negation

8 Introduction to *Proletarian Nights*, 2012, p.xix

9 Oliver Davis, *Jacques Rancière*, London: Polity, p.40.

10 *Les Révoltes Logiques* 1 (Winter 1975), quoted in Oliver Davis, op.cit., p.40.

11 This is explored in Jacques Rancière, '"Le Social": The Lost Tradition in French Labour History', in Raphael Samuel (Ed.), *People's History and Socialist Theory*, London: Routledge, 1981; and later

in further detail in Jacques Rancière, *The Names of History*, Minneapolis: University of Minnesota, 1994.

12 Jacques Rancière, *Staging the People: The Proletarian and His Double*, (*Staging the People*, Vol.I), London: Verso, 2011, p.9 and p.11.

13 Ibid., p.8.

14 Ibid., p.13.

15 During its appropriately long history, the journal has used four titles: *Annales d'histoire économique et sociale* (1929-39); *Annales d'histoire sociale* (1939-42, 1945); *Mélanges d'histoire sociale* (1942-4); *Annales: économies, sociétiés, civilisations* (1946-1994); and presently: *Annales: Histoire, Sciences sociales* (1994-). See: Peter Burke, *The French Historical Revolution: The Annales School 1929-89*, Malden MA / Cambridge: Polity Press, 1990 and Lynn Hunt and Jacques Revel (eds), *Histories: French Constructions of the Past*, New York: The New Press. 1994.

16 See footnote 11.

17 See Oliver Davis, op.cit., p.42.

18 This is explored in greatest detail in the second volume of Rancière's collected writings for *Les Révoltes Logiques*. Attacks are directed at Rancière's former comrades from the GP, particularly André Glucksmann and the 'New Philosophers'. The revisionism of which Rancière accuses ex-GP militants is easily mapped onto Anglophone cultural theory of the 1980s which let go of the certainty of the mass worker in order to pursue the non-worker as identity, and all the better to justify the continuation of the intellectual's metier. Rancière's response to this love of labour lost is best summed up thus: '[...] the disappointed love of the political activist cannot be satisfied with the sociological positivity of this proletariat fallen from its pedestal.' Jacques Rancière, 'The Factory of Nostalgia', in *The Intellectual and His People*, Verso, London, 2012, p.136.

19 Adrian Rifkin, then a member of History Workshop's editorial collective, speculates that Rancière's exploration of hybridity was incompatible with what he saw as History Workshop's cast-iron conception of class consciousness. Adrian Rifkin, 'JR Cinéphile, or the Philosopher Who Loved Things', *Parallax* vol. 15 Issue 3, 2009.

20 Jacques Rancière, '"Le Social": The Lost Tradition in French Labour History', op.cit., p.269.

21 Philip Blond, *Red Tory*, London: Faber & Faber, 2010, p.15.

22 For the sake of simplicity and in reference to the order of publication, we will refer to *Staging the People*, Vol.I and *Staging the People*, Vol.II.

23 Shoemakers' report cited in 'Off to the Exhibition: The Worker, His Wife and the Machines', in *Staging the People*, Vol.I, p.68.

24 See: Adrian Rifkin and Roger Thomas (eds.), *Voices of the People*, New York: Routledge, 1988, p.14.

25 Karl Marx, *Capital* Vol.I Chapter 15.

26 *Staging the People*, Vol.I, p.73.

27 Introduction to *Proletarian Nights*, op.cit., pp.xxv-xxvi.

28 See footnote 18 and Michael Seidman, *Workers Against Work: Labor in Paris and Barcelona during the Popular Fronts*, Berkeley: California University Press, 1991.

29 Jacques Rancière, 'The People's Theatre: A Long Drawn-Out Affair', in *Staging the People*, Vol.II, p.10.

30 Jacques Rancière, *Staging the People*, Vol.I, p.201.

31 Unknown street singer quoted in the workers' newspaper, *L'Atelier*, in *Staging the People*, Vol.I, p.43.

32 The essay, 'The Cultural Historic Compromise', in *Staging the People*, Vol.II, documents misunderstandings between a group of gauchist painters who tried to take their paintings to the workers, the activists who encouraged them and the local communist party officials who censored them.

33 *Staging the People*, Vol.I, pp.181-182. The full quote continues: '- individuals and groups who developed within themselves abilities that were useless for the improvement of their material life, but suited to make them despise this.'

34 Although most of the subjects in Rancière's book live in this period the latter half of the book follows their legacy into the 1890s.

35 The Icarians, who generally attracted skilled and literate artisans, went on to found communes in Texas and Illinois.

36 Jaques Rancière, 'Revisiting Nights of Labour', lecture at Sarai 6th February 2009 http://www.youtube.com/watch?v=Lr6ZfzbumVo

37 Jacques Rancière, *Proletarian Nights*, p.81.

38 Jacques Rancière 'Art is Going Elsewhere and Politics has to Catch it', *Krisis*, 2008, Issue 1, (English), and available at http://www.egs.edu/faculty/jacques-Rancière/articles/art-is-going-elsewhere-and-politics-has-to-catch-it/ 2010, p.40

39 Alain Faure & Jacques Rancière, *La Parole Ouvriere 1830-1851*, 1976. See: Adrian Rifkin and Roger Thomas (eds.), *Voices of the People*, op. cit., p.8.

40 '[...] there is no single 'voice of the people'. There are broken, polemical voices, each time dividing the identity they present.' *Staging The People*, Vol.I, p.12.

THE GENDER RIFT IN COMMUNISATION

In a contested 'swerve' in debates around communisation, issues of gender, class and race are coming to the fore. Reviewing key texts in this debate, P. VALENTINE *discusses the material basis of the gender distinction in capitalism, and its centrality to class exploitation*

A Communisation theory is primed to do what only a minority of Marxist-feminists have attempted to do over the last 50 years of inquiry: re-articulate the capitalist mode of production as being constituted no less by the man/woman relation than by the class relation.[1] What would ideally emerge from such a project is a 'single system' in which the gender relation and the class relation are equally necessary elements within a totality, rather than the subsumption of one to the other, or the erection of a 'dual system' of two different and autonomous systems of patriarchy and capitalism. We say communisation is 'primed' for this project because one of the major interventions of communisation theory has been to theorise communism as the abolition not only of capitalists, but also of workers; of work itself and thus of value; of *the wage labour relation itself* and thus of the distinction between 'work' and 'life'. This distinction is cast in a variety of terms including the conceptual dyads public/private; social/non-social; public/domestic, and is almost unequivocally understood by gender theorists as a grounding element in the production of gender.

Communisation's very starting point is a demand for the abolition of fundamental material elements of the reproduction of gender – the division of social life into two 'spheres'. This implies an analysis of the system of gender and class as a unity, and because it focuses on the gender binary as a material relation of exploitation or oppression in which the two sides are produced rather than given, it also articulates the patriarchy in a way which, opens avenues of new and more rigorous theories of gender oppression that are able to link the exploitation and oppression of women with violence and oppression based on hetero-normatvity and cis-normativity. However, until the work of Théorie Communiste (TC) and recently Maya Andrea Gonzalez, conversations around communisation had completely ignored gender, or had merely added gender to the list of things to be abolished through communisation, amounting to little more than buttering the toast of communisation with radical cultural gender theory.[2] A critique of the gender binary, of the essentialist identities of 'woman' and 'man', which could lead equally to their destruction or proliferation, is attached to a theory of communisation without affecting the concept of what constitutes the capitalist totality. The mere shift from women's liberation to gender abolition cast in these basic terms represents little advance in theory over the well-trodden 'postmodern' shift to de-essentialise identity (an important move, but not particularly new or rare). As TC have written,

> If the abolition of the gender distinction is necessary from the point of view of the 'success' of communization, it is not in the name of the abolition of all the mediations of society. It is in its concrete and immediate character that the contradiction between men and women imposes itself on the 'success' of communization, against what that relation implies in terms of violence, invisibilisation, the ascription to a subordinate position.[3]

Only a substantive theory of the production and reproduction of gender in capitalism can give real non-idealist content to the abolition of gender. The important questions are: *what is 'woman' and 'man', what is the gender relation,* and *what is its relation to class?* The nascent forays into gender theory from the communising tendency have tended towards two major elisions: avoiding the problematic of race and its relation to class and gender, and displacing an analysis of sexual violence to the sidelines of the production of the gender distinction. We will here attempt a brief overview and assessment of existing communisationist gender theory and point towards some obvious gaps.

THE COMMUNISING CURRENT ON GENDER

TC's initial texts on gender claimed: 'it's immediately apparent that all societies hinge on a twofold distinction: between genders and between classes' and '[t]he evidence of the abolition of genders will be a revolution in the revolution'. The initial texts – 'Gender distinction, programmatism and communisation' and the two supplements, 'Gender – Class – Dynamic' and 'Comrades, but Women', published in *Théorie Communiste* issue 23, were still filled with inner conflict and tension around how exactly to describe *the material basis of the gender distinction and the way in which it is related to the class relation.*[4] Their stronger, and more provocative analysis (which are not often referenced by other male-dominated theory collectives) addressed women's role and experience in working class struggle. TC understands that women experience an entirely different realm of oppression and exploitation than men, so that whenever they rise up, this rising up calls into question the differential positions of men and women – namely, that men do the appropriating of women and women are those who are appropriated by men (even and especially the men who are supposed to be their 'comrades'). When women call this relation of appropriation into question, men will fight back, fight against the women, in an attempt to put the women 'back in their place'. As Lyon, a member of TC, says in the recently published *SIC* journal: 'The defence of the male condition is the defence of male domination. It is the defence of the existence of two separated spheres of activity.'[6]

However, the real material ground of the gender distinction is not fully formed in these early texts. The concept of separate 'spheres' or 'realms' was concretely raised, but the material genesis and reproduction of the distinction between these spheres, as well as the consistent description of 'women' as loosely but not systematically associated with 'biological' traits such as childbearing, XX chromosomes, breasts, vaginas and so forth, was not explained. In particular, they attributed the production of 'women' (which they generally equate with the production of the gender distinction) with the fact that the increase in the population is the primary productive force in classed societies.

When queried further TC wrote 'Response to the American Comrades on Gender', a dense and lengthy text that left many important questions unresolved.[7] They do argue that class societies are defined by surplus being expropriated by some portion of society, and that 'up until capital [...] the principal source of surplus labor is the work of increasing the population.' We might cast this in more concrete terms by saying: the way to increase surplus labour in classed society is to produce more people, and this is made difficult by high infant death rates and/or vulnerability to death from the environment, war and attack. In many places the way to ensure the continued production of surplus *at all* was to ensure that women produce as many babies as possible, to avoid a decrease of the population.[9] TC write,

> Population can be called the principal productive force only insofar as it becomes the *productive force of labor* (rather than science or the means of production, etc). It becomes this [...] insofar as a specific social arrangement has population as its *object*.[10]

This begins to answer the question of 'what is woman', and the inchoate answer is *woman is she who is appropriated by society for the purpose of increasing the population*. It is easy to see also that severe gender distinctions will necessarily arise in places where there are intense pressures on population stability, and thus intense conscription of women to constant childbearing.

Both Gonzalez and TC correctly articulate the way this ontologically negligible feature (child-bearing) comes to ground a hierarchised social relation:

> The possession of a uterus is an anatomical *feature*, and not immediately a *distinction*, but 'baby maker' is a social distinction which makes the anatomical *feature* a *natural distinction*. Within the nature of this social construction, of this system of constraint, that which is socially constructed -women - are always sent back to biology.[11]

> [...] sexual difference is given a particular social relevance that it would not otherwise possess. Sexual difference is given this fixed significance within class societies, when the category woman comes to be defined by the function that most (but not all) human females perform, for a period of their lives, in the sexual reproduction of the species. Class society thus gives a social purpose to bodies:

theorising gender amounted to little more than buttering the toast of communisation

> because some women 'have' babies, all bodies that could conceivably 'produce' babies are subject to social regulation.[12]

But the questions remain: why and how? While countless activities slip easily between the boundaries dividing the two gendered 'spheres', why is baby-bearing not only confined to the female/domestic/private/non-social/non-waged sphere, but *constitutive of* it? Why, then, is baby-bearing so pernicious a domestic activity, if others (cleaning, laundry, emotional labour) traverse the spheres more easily? Why haven't we started making babies in test tubes? Why hasn't surrogate motherhood become more popular (though its popularity is dramatically rising)? Why aren't women paid to bear children? These questions must be answered in order to explain why and how baby-making can be understood as the essential activity which *constitutes* the female, non-waged sphere.

Further, and more fundamentally, how does this appropriation of women, on whatever basis (baby-making or no) begin? In other words, what is the origin of the gender distinction and how is it reproduced?[13] These questions are outside the scope of this article, but we do believe that the answers both involve gendered physical violence and sexual violence, which we will address cursorily below. These questions are displaced and de-emphasised within communisation theory, currently.

GENDER IN CAPITAL

TC and Gonzalez both agree that, once capital comes on the scene, there is a shift in the material basis for the appropriation of women, because 'In the capitalist mode of production, the principal 'productive force' is the working class itself.'[14] If the production of woman emerges from a situation in which the increase in the population is the principal productive force, this means that the production of woman fundamentally changes in capitalism. They argue that 'the determination of a public sphere' is actually the 'source' of the sex difference, and we may infer that this is because the public sphere formalises the appropriation of women in/as the private sphere. Due to capitalism's absolute distinction of labour as separate from 'reproductive activities in the private sphere', we find that 'The cleavage between production and reproduction, of home and workplace, is perfect, structural, definitive of the mode of production.'[15] TC write:

> The sexed character of all categories of capital signifies a general distinction in society between men and women. This general distinction 'acquires as its social content' that which is the synthesis of all the sexuations of the categories: the creation of the division between public and private [...] the capitalist mode of production, because it rests on the sale of the labor power and a social production that does not exist as such on the market, rejects as 'non-social' the moments of its own reproduction which escape direct submission to the market or to the immediate process of production: the private. The private is the private of the public, always in a hierarchical relation of definition and submission to the public. As general division and given its content [...] it is naturalized and it actually exists in the framework of this society as natural division: all women, all men. It is not enough to say that all the categories of the capitalist mode of production are intrinsically sexed. It is necessary also that this general sexuation is given a particular form: the distinction between public and private where the categories men and women appear as general, more general even than the differences of class which are produced as 'social' and 'natural.' The distinction

> between men and women acquires its own content at its level, specific to the level produced, which is to say, specific to the distinction between public and private: nature (that which the social has produced at the interior of itself as non-social and which actually comes to appear as obvious, natural, because of the anatomical distinction).[16]

We agree that the categories of the capitalist totality are sexed; that this sexuation arises from a distinction between the realm of wage labour and that of something else. But is the distinction that grounds the hierarchical gender binary that between 'public' and 'private', or between 'production' and 'reproduction', or between the 'social' and the 'non-social'? This ambiguity of the real, material and historical nature of the separate spheres betrays a further ambiguity concerning the real material construction and reproduction of the gender distinction, before and during capitalism. How are women produced and kept in such a relation of hyper exploitation and appropriation? What are the material mechanisms that enable men to reproduce themselves as men, the appropriators?

Why haven't we started making babies in test tubes? Why aren't women paid to bear children?

Because capital does not consistently face dwindling populations (and in fact, the opposite is often true) both TC and Gonzalez agree that gender comes to mean something different when capital comes on the scene. Child-bearing can no longer be the functional reason for appropriating women in their totality, because it is no longer the principal productive force. Here there is some ambivalence about how to theorize women as a 'problem' for capitalism: Gonzalez continues to posit childbearing as the ground for the gender distinction in capital and women's experience in both spheres, while TC defer primarily to the ever more materially distinct separation of spheres necessitated by the wage-relation as the material ground for gender in capital.[17]

WHITHER SEXUAL VIOLENCE

It is important to note also that sexual violence and rape are consistently displaced or left out of a schematic account of the gender relation within TC and Gonzalez's accounts. Gonzalez effectively draws the notion of separate 'spheres' of activity into more concrete terms, where we are able to talk about the real patterns of employment women experience, and the real, concrete ramifications of pregnancy and childrearing on the appropriation of women inside and outside the wage relation. However she ends up treating the relation between actual men and actual women of similar classes in an abstract space where violence does not occur. It is impossible to accurately theorise the feminised 'sphere' without referring to sexual violence, and so this represents a serious oversight in the existing theory. Women's subordination in the home; women's experience in waged labour; baby-bearing – all these things are produced *directly* through sexual violence as a mechanism of control over women's bodies. Sexual violence is not an unfortunate side effect in the appropriation of women – it is a necessary element of that appropriation, Sexual and domestic violence ('private' violence within intimate family or friend relations) are the types of violence that *are constitutive of* the gender relation.

Gonzalez's mention of violence against women in general is confined to two footnotes, and only one mentions sexual violence. The first reads

> [...] violence against women, sometimes carried out by women themselves, has always been necessary to keep them firmly tied to their role in the sexual reproduction of the species.[18]

Here, 'violence against women' refers to the amount of women who die in childbirth and the taxing experience of bearing upwards of eight children in a lifetime. This violence has no immediate perpetrator. The only thing to blame is the whole system. Even though violence against women is *almost always at the hands of men, Gonzalez immediately reminds* us that it may be carried out even 'by women themselves.' Here, she distances violence on women's bodies from the structural relation between men and women, effectively *sanitising* the relation between men and women by shifting violence to the abstract social totality. Globally, including in the US, women are more likely to be raped *by a man* than to have high levels of literacy. Women in the military are more likely to be raped *by a man* than to die in combat. Women are raped at home and at the workplace by men. Rape and sexual assault functions, among other things, to keep women confined to their duties which either benefit men of their own class or a higher one (through their unpaid work – be it sex, emotional labour, cleaning, etc.) or capitalists who employ them (under threat of rape and assault, women are coerced into working longer, harder and not to complain or organise in the workplace). For Gonzalez, sexual violence is more or less dismissed as an 'ahistorical' ground for a theory of gender.[19]

In the 'Response...' TC make several references to violence and to sexual violence, and even to rape, as mechanisms of the gender relation,[20] but in their formally published texts on gender, in *Théorie Communiste* Issue 24 and *SIC*, TC do not mention rape or sexual violence. They do put a strong emphasis on the direct physical violence that proletarian men inflict upon proletarian women, *when those women attempt to struggle in a way that problematises the separation of the spheres*. They draw from accounts of Argentina's piquetero movement:

> There are female comrades who declare in the assembly: 'I couldn't come to the "piquete" (road blockade) because my husband beat me, because he locked me down.' For that, the women-question helped us quite a bit[...] because you've seen that it was us, the women, who were the first to go out for food, job positions, and health[...] And it brought very difficult situations – even death. There were husbands who did not tolerate their wives attending a meeting, a 'piquete'.[21]

It is meaningful that rape and systematic sexual violence make no appearance in the formally published texts of TC on gender, nor in the entirety of *SIC*, nor *Communisation and its Discontents*. The neglect of rape and sexual violence as structural elements of the gender distinction, and thus of the capitalist totality, leads to an account of gender that cannot make sense of an enormous amount of gendered social relations. Some have argued correctly that certain strains of feminist emphasis on rape have served a racist or classist function within struggles and analysis, but it is also true that the neglect of rape and sexual violence is just as easily used in racist or classist attacks.[22] If it is not a systematic structural relation, rape and sexual violence are 'bad things' that some 'bad people' do, and on these accounts, those bad people blamed by law, media and white supremacist popular opinion, are more often than not poor and of an ethnic or racial minority. We observe some beginnings of structural theories of rape and sexual violence in Kathy Miriam's elaboration of Adrienne Rich's concept of 'sex right', which she articulates as 'the assumption that men have a right of sexual access to women and girls [which] allows for specific acts of coercion and aggression to take place.'[23] This theory also grounds Miriam's expanded theory of *compulsory heterosexuality.* Although too philosophical and non-material/historical to immediately cohere with a structural communist theory of capitalist social relations, Miriam describes processes which *must* be included in our accounts. To ignore sexual violence and compulsory heterosexuality in an account of structurally gendered capitalist social relations is equivalent to ignoring the way in which the threat of unemployment and the growth of unemployed populations structures the relation between labour and capital.

Understanding sexual violence as a structuring element of gender also helps us to understand how patriarchy reproduces itself upon and through gay and queer men, trans people, gender nonconforming people and bodies, and children of any gender. Gendered divisions of labour within the waged sphere, in conjunction with baby-bearing, do not account for the particular patterns in which, e.g., trans people are economically exploited within capitalist economies, which differs dramatically from cis-women, as well as the endemic murder of trans women of colour which amounts to a sort of geographically diffused genocide.[24] It cannot account for the widespread rape of children by male family members. But if we consider sexual violence as an essential material

'the determination of a public sphere' is actually the 'source' of the sex difference

> *there is truth in these theories of sex-right and black death*

ground in the production of hierarchised gender relations, then we can begin to see how such patterns relate to the production of the categories women and men and the distinction between the spheres of waged/unwaged; social/non-social; public/private.

ABOLITION OF RACE?

Many have argued that the category 'women' is not required for the social functions currently performed by women to 'get done' – that is to say, capitalism could rid itself of gender, and still maintain the necessary distinction between 'spheres' of social/non-social or waged/unwaged. The emerging communisationist gender theory, on the other hand, argues generally that the categories 'women' and 'men' *are nothing other than* the distinction between the spheres of activity. Abolishing gender while retaining the waged/unwaged division is like abolishing class while retaining the split between the owners of the means of production and those who are forced to work for a wage in order to survive.

The very same manoeuvres are used to make similarly deflationary arguments about what is usually called 'race' or 'ethnicity'. Even the more militant theorists of race often claim that, at base, race and ethnicity are historical leftovers of past violences that capital has picked up, found useful, and mobilised to its advantage. Even some of the theorists most intent on elevating and integrating a theory of racial and ethnic oppression into the analysis of capitalism – from autonomists like Harry Cleaver and Selma James to canonical theorists of white supremacist, capitalist society like Stuart Hall – continue to insist that race is in some sense subordinate to or an inflection of (or in Hall's terms, an articulation of) class.

The race question has yet to be put on the table for communisation theory. Theorists who analyse race and racialisation as a fundamental social relation that grounds and reproduces capitalist society, (from Cedric Robinson's epic *Black Marxisms* to the recent 'afro-pessimists' like Frank Wilderson and Jared Sexton) have not been addressed within communisation. This is a testament to the persistent Eurocentrism of current communisation theory, even as it is drawn into the American context.[25]

Frank Wilderson claims that white supremacy: 'kills the Black subject that the concept, civil society, may live' and later,

> We live in this world, but exist outside of civil society. This structurally impossible position is a paradox because the Black subject, the slave, is vital to civil society's political economy: s/he kick-starts capital at its genesis and rescues it from its over-accumulation crisis at its end. Black death is its condition of possibility. Civil society's subaltern, the worker, is coded as waged, and wages are White. But Marxism has no account of this phenomenal birth and life-saving role played by the Black subject.[26]

Similar to Miram's phenomenological and hermeneutic account of the sex-right, this language is not yet legible to existing communist or Marxist conversations. The limits of such conversations are threatening to their strength, for there is truth in these theories of sex-right and black death that, if ignored, leaves an account of the totality not only incomplete but a potential tool of capitalist violence.

We believe that capital is a totality which is 'classed', 'gendered' and 'raced' by virtue of its own internal logic. These are not three contradictions which sit on three thrones in the centre of the capitalist totality, homologous with one another, dictating its logic. We must reveal exactly how race and gender are necessary social relations based on particular material processes within the capitalist mode of production.[27] Through the recent work of communisationist gender theory, we have come to understand 'women' as the category describing those whose activity, unwaged and waged, is appropriated in their totality by society ('men'). This relation inscribes two distinct 'spheres' that ground the gender binary. The fact that the boundaries around these spheres are violently policed does not mean they are static - in fact their policing also involves a constant manipulation of the boundaries. We understand 'proletariat' as the category describing those who do not own the means of production, and are forced to either sell their labour to those who do (the 'capitalists') or are cast out to waste away. How are we to understand the category of 'racialised', or perhaps of 'black,' or perhaps 'ethnicised'? It seems possible that these categories are necessarily related to capital's necessary overproduction of humans within the movement of capitalist development, and its consequent need to kill, obliterate, remove and dispossess such bodies.[28] But how do we structure this theory, and how does it relate to waged exploitation and to the two 'spheres'?

For now, despite our revulsion at relegating the race question to so brief a moment within this conversation, we merely note, especially for our European comrades (who continue to be more resistant to these questions than any other comrades we've encountered around the world, in our experience), the obvious fact that the reproduction of racial and ethnic hierarchies affect, form and constitute every moment and place of capital's reproduction. A range of feminists, from African-American feminists like Patricia Hill Collins to eco-feminists like Maria Mies, have noted and argued that gender is *produced through racialisation*, and that racialisation is *produced through gender*. Communisation has now been able to say, *there is never a* proletarian *who is not gendered*, so we must also be able to say there *is never a proletarian or a 'woman' who is not raced*. There is never a 'woman' who is not also a woman *who is raced*. Communisation has now been able to say, there is never a proletarian who is not gendered, so we must also be able to say there is never a proletarian or a 'woman' or 'man' who is not raced. There is never a 'woman' or a 'man' who is not also a *woman who is raced*. Communisationists can't afford to turn a blind eye to these necessary processes of the capitalist totality.

P. Valentine lives and spanges in Vancouver, BC, and is currently en route to Montreal, QC to join in festivities. They dedicate everything forever to the American Metropolis. Probably the coolest thing they've got going on right now is liesjournal.info. They can be reached at <unruhe.unruhe.unruhe.unruhe@gmail.com>

FOOTNOTES

1 Examples are: I. M. Young; Silvia Federici; Katherine Mackinnon; Fulvia Carnevale and others. Others, e.g. Gloria Joseph, Evelyn Nakano Glenn, Maria Mies and Angela Davis, demand a theory which also articulates race as a necessary structural element.

2 Maya Andrea Gonzalez, 'Communisation and the Abolition of Gender' in Benjamin Noys (Ed.), *Communisation and its Discontents: Contestation, Critique, and Contemporary Struggles*, New York: Minor Compositions/Autonomedia, 2011.

3 Théorie Communiste, 'Response to the American Comrades on Gender', http://libcom.org/library/response-americans-gender-theorie-communiste

4 These two supplements are translated into English and made available at http://petroleusepress.com

5 'When women fight, whether in the private or public sphere, when they attack the very existence of those spheres which is constituted by their separation into public and private, they must confront their male comrades, insofar as they are men *and* insofar as they are their comrades. And they (the women) are the men's comrades, but women.' (Théorie Communiste, 'Comrades, But Women', originally published in *Théorie Communiste*, Issue 23, English pamphlet (2011) available here: http://petroleusepress.com/

6 Bernard Lyon, 'The Suspended Step of Communisation' in *Sic: International Journal for Communisation*, Issue 1, 2012, p.163.

7 TC were posed the following questions: '1. Why do all class societies depend on the increase in population as principal productive force? 2. What does it mean for the increase in population to be the main productive force? 3. TC often write that 'labour is a problem for capital'. Does this mean the falling rate of profit? Or does it mean the increasing surplus populations pose a problem of revolt? Or both? 4. TC say that women/the family are a problem for capital. Is this merely because labor is a problem for capital, and women/the family reproduces labor?'

8 Théorie Communiste, 'Comrades, but Women', op. cit.

9 Gonzalez mentions this also, Maya Gonzalez, op. cit., p.226.

10 Théorie Communiste, 'Response to the Americans on Gender', op. cit.

11 Ibid.

12 Maya Gonzalez, op. cit., p.224.

13 TC disavow a serious discussion of the origins of the gender distinction, which seems disingenuous considering the important role that the theory of the origin of capitalism (in primitive accumulation) plays for the theory of class exploitation.

14 Théorie Communiste, op. cit.

15 Ibid.

16 Ibid.

17 Though TC also sometimes lean towards Gonzalez' point: Lyon writes that gendered domination 'would always have had the allocation of women to childbirth as its content, that by which women exist as such.' and 'The public/private distinction shows that, in the capitalist mode of production, the definition of women is globally constrained to their role as childbearers.' Bernard Lyon, 'The Suspended Step of Communisation', p.164.

18 Maya Gonzalez, op. cit., footnote 192.

19 'Radical feminism followed a curious trajectory in the second half of the 20th century, taking first childbearing, then domestic work, and finally sexual violence (or the male orgasm) as the ground of women's oppression. The problem

was that in each case, these feminists sought an ahistorical ground for what had become an historical phenomenon.' Maya Gonzalez, op. cit., footnote 203.

20 'Domestic labor, positioned within the division of labor, forms of integration/interpellation in the immediate process of production, 'atypical' forms of the wage system, everyday violence of marriage, family, negation and appropriation of female sexuality, rape and/or the threat of rape, all these are the frontlines where the contradiction between men and women plays out, a contradiction whose content is the definition of men and women and the ascription and confinement of individuals to these definitions (none of these elements is accidental). These frontlines are the loci of a permanent struggle between two categories of society constructed as natural and deconstructed by women in their struggle. The frontlines are never stable. The public-private distinction is constantly redefined: the present "parity" is a redefinition of its boundaries but also a redefinition of what is private.' Théorie Communiste, 'Comrades, but Women'.

21 Théorie Communiste, op. cit.

22 For a critique of Susan Brownmiller see: Alison Edwards, 'Rape, Racism, and the White Woman's Movement: An Answer to Susan Brownmiller', http://www.sojournertruth.net/rrwwm.html

23 Kathy Miriam, 'Towards a phenomenology of Sex-Right', *Hypatia,* Vol.22, Issue 1, February 2007, p.225.

24 The visibility of this genocide, as with most, is almost totally nil. Its invisibility is only emphasised when social movements recognise some isolated incidents, which makes it only more important to mention; for example, in the United States the recent, somewhat more publicly recognised, murder of Brandy Martell in Oakland, as well as the severe sentencing of CeCe Macdonald, who merely defended herself from a violent transphobic attack. These types of transphobic murders and victim-blaming punishment happen every day worldwide unnoticed.

25 Communists have certainly not dealt with race *well* elsewhere, but European ultra-left and communisationist theory remains somewhat uniquely unconcerned with race – as does its American counterparts.

26 Frank Wilderson, 'Gramsci's Black Marx: Whither the Slave in Civil Society?', *We Write,* Vol.2, Number 1, January, 2005, p.9. and p.15.

27 There are some inchoate formations that we know of in the US which are beginning to take on this task. See http://escalatingidentity.wordpress.com and http://liesjournal.info. We are sure there are many more we do not know of.

28 See *Endnotes* #2, 2011.

SELF-COMPRESSION: AN INTERVIEW WITH JESSE DARLING

Involving a conceptual engagement with technical environments, self-risking and cathartic performances, and a profound thinking around gender and subjectivity, Jesse Darling's art illuminates deep links between technology, power and experience

A Jesse Darling is an artist and writer whose practice, while dispersed beyond that of conventional critical art, centres around a critique of the prosuming performative self produced by late capitalism. Her work steers away from a formalist appropriation of this discourse and instead explores, sometimes in a celebratory way, the mediative forms of this post-Fordist, IKEA-furnished, playbouring phase of user-generated capitalism. After her solo exhibition Stockholm Syndrome and Other System Failures (March 2012) at Arcadia_Missa, co-directors Tom Clark and Rózsa Farkas spoke to Darling to explore some unresolved questions raised by the show.

TOM CLARK: How did you arrive at making art? Your practice, including your blog, and conversations around your practice, feel quite natural in a way that doesn't suggest the strictures of a conventional A-levels-to-foundation-to-art-school route.

JESSE DARLING: I did do art at A-level: it was the only subject I came into school for, I suppose because it helped me survive. It legitimised the articulation of my otherness somehow, which is what art is good for in general. This was before the internet was a ubiquitous fact of life. I give thanks on bended knee that there wasn't anything like Tumblr or MySpace in my early teens, but I sometimes wonder how things might have been different if I'd been able to access the internet communities of self-identified weirdoes, autistics, queers and 'otherkin,' who contain and support one another through recognition of a shared sense of marginality, like the street communities I hung around in later on. I did have a virtual existence of some kind, or a secret life in which I could express my 'true existence', but this just meant cruising around the streets all night by myself looking for trouble. I had big issues with institutional learning, since I felt like the *real* education was all out there in the streets and in bodies – mine and other people's; plus, state school careers advice doesn't really understand 'artist' as a viable profession, and neither did my parents, so it just didn't count as something I could end up doing. This is as much a question of class values as anything else (one of the many elephants in the big white room of the art world). Later I (accidentally) ended up in Amsterdam's Rietveld Academie, this prestigious, cerebral institution, but they threw me out for failing to conform to any of the basic tenets of studentship. I was doing a lot of drugs by that time, living in squats, working in the sex industry. 'Making art' – as recognised by the academy – just felt impossibly removed, rarefied and arbitrary, a million miles away from all the stuff happening on the streets and in the world, which came at me with a kind of urgency and immediacy that I couldn't find in the classroom or the studio. I was like, where's the *real* work at? I went back to art school eventually (Central Saint Martins College of Art and Design) and it was quite productive, although I did notice that the academy has a peculiar relationship with lived experience. In other words, some people do it, then some people write about it, and some only ever read about it. I don't want to posit any kind of hierarchy of learning here, but when those people end up in a position to decide what is and isn't valuable or worthwhile, that can sometimes be problematic.

TC: You were involved with earlier permutations of what is described as 'net art', can you say a bit about this and what you feel characterises this particular moment of that history?

JD: I've always been into virtualism, but I'm not really into the term 'net art'. It's a bit cheesy and specific, and implies a false commonality in what I see as a diversity of practices. Having said that, I do think there are art communities, on and offline, who do share a common aesthetic, and whose practice inevitably ends up echoing some of the same themes. I will also say that what's now being described as net art seems to be (self-)defined by the employment and deployment of a common space and/or reference point for a generation: online platforms like Facebook and Google, Twitter and Tumblr, and to a lesser extent (often in combination with) the imaging software we use and live in. Hannah Black, who's an artist and theorist friend of mine, coined the term 'techno-povera', derived from 'arte povera', which I think defines it perfectly. If Arduino consoles and robots are the new marble and oil paint, then YouTube and Google are the new 'materials of the everyday'.

TC: Would you describe your practice as coming under this net art rubric?

JD: I think pretty much every artist who is practicing today is working in negotiation with the conditions of a changing time: virtualism, globalism, hypercapitalism, precarity. Artists in Africa and China are addressing different kinds of questions, for example, and it's good to remember that our experience (of the internet, etc.) is not universal; there's probably someone living next door to me who doesn't know what Photoshop does or what Tumblr is. For me personally, virtual spaces are a big part of what I'm thinking about, in as much as they provide a very live metaphor for the kinds of marginal and interior spaces I've known IRL. I'm not interested in making art about the internet, per se; but the internet is part of a matrix of conditions that shape my experience as a human in the world.

TC: You've said that you were mentored by early net artists but chose not to engage in coding or the network architecture, which was part of their practice, how come?

JD: I speak a little 'MySpace pidgin' html and I can read it pretty good. I don't code mostly because it feels very difficult, and I'm an immediatist. My practice has been shaped by what was available: the time, space and money I had to work with. It's for the same reason that I don't work with bronze or clay; I don't have a foundry, you know? It's also why my own body shows up so much in the work – it's a powerful technology I have at my disposal, for 'free'. I don't have to ask permission or rent out a space. If I started coding I'm sure I'd get into it – there's a great poetry in it – but I don't want the complexity of the process to become the product (of my art). Art about technology often ends up making both art and technology look really dated and capricious within a year or two. Great big wow, great big innovation award at Arts Electronica or somewhere, and next year it's an app on everyone's smartphone and nobody gives a shit. Plus, this nerdist or generational elitism – we're-the-only-ones-who-know-how-to-use-this-stuff-ism – isn't interesting to me. I'm interested in the human condition, as it changes with the times, and/or abides despite everything.

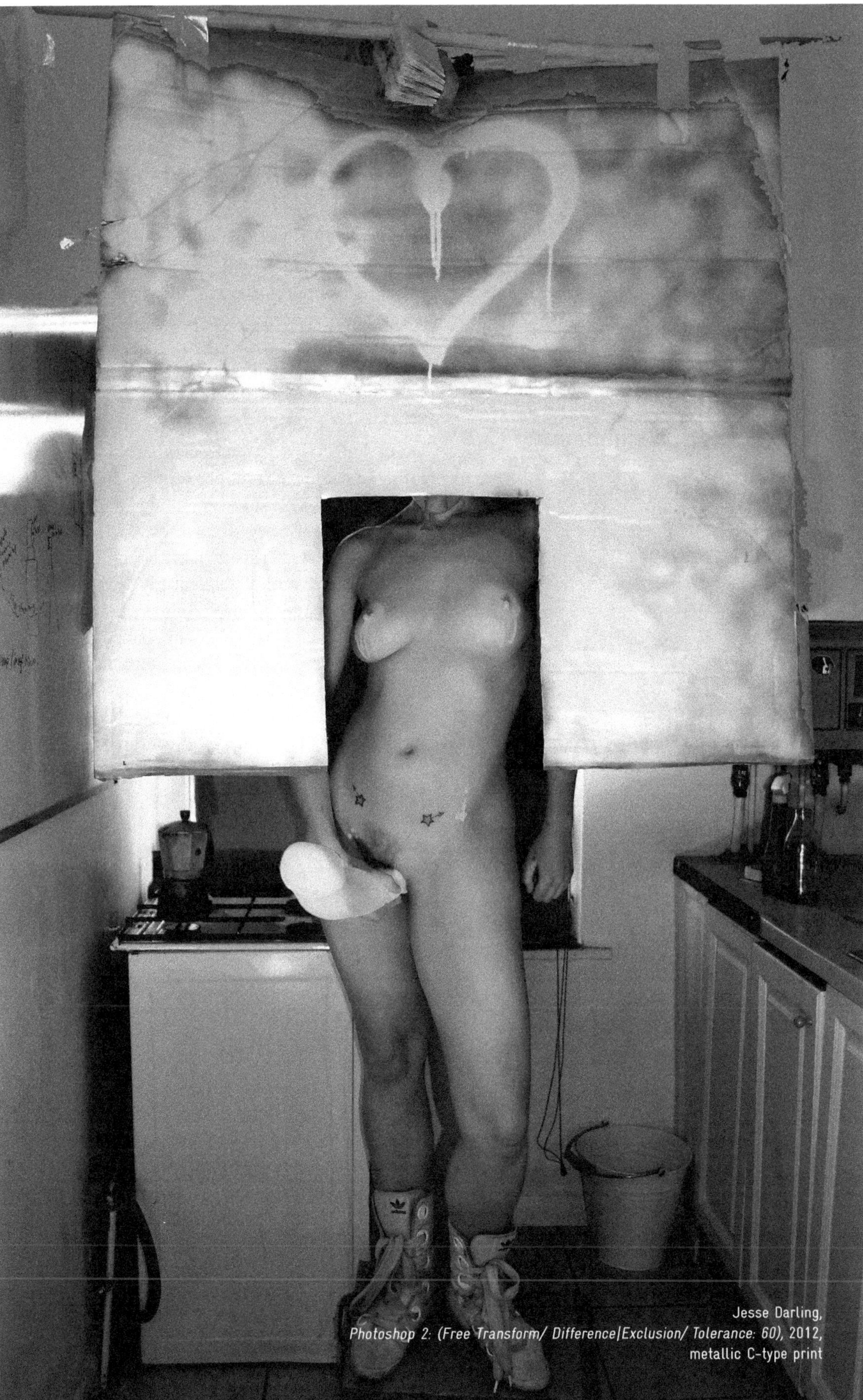

Jesse Darling,
Photoshop 2: (Free Transform/ Difference|Exclusion/ Tolerance: 60), 2012,
metallic C-type print

I'm afraid of all the high-definition images in advertising and increasingly in art; the world appears decayed and muddied beside its representation

TC: Do you think that this move in focus, to your articulation of a user's rather than just the author's experience, also has anything to do with parallel shifts from web 1.0, to the more user-centric web 2.0 environments?

JD: Coding culture is pretty authorial. Even open source stuff has strict protocols that reinforce authorial culture. The author was supposed to have died in 1967, but keeps coming back, like a zombie, in variously striated forms, despite all the discourse; I suspect that this has to do with a deep historical relationship to goods and property, and it's gonna take more than the creative commons movement to change that. Web 2.0, meanwhile, *can't* be too authorial: as users, we're just making hay on someone else's land, the use of which is strictly prescribed and often policed. But as far as I'm concerned I've never known any other condition. I grew up in a city: there was no wilderness or free space anywhere. I wrote an essay for the *New Inquiry* in which I likened Web 2.0 to the suburban sprawl of strip malls and shopping centres that many of us spent time in growing up and often still inhabit. The fact that all public space was essentially privatised space, the fact that there wasn't anything to *do* or anywhere to *go*, didn't stop us from being curious, bored, rebellious teenagers, finding ways to express our nascent subjectivity and finding ways to subvert the use of that space much as the NEET kids do today, just by virtue of existing.

I used to hang around with a bunch of hackers in Amsterdam who ran a semi-squatted troglodyte computer club in the basement of the anarchist bookstore. They had really strong filter coffee and free internet, with a bunch of old boxes running Linux and Ubuntu. You wouldn't get far in that place if you didn't know how to navigate the bash shell. As far as they were concerned, the world was divided into Morlocks who could code, and Eloi, who couldn't. I had plenty of caffeine-fuelled arguments about the elitism of that. And although I loved the interiority of the shell and the intimacy of the command line, I liked the daylight better, and having sex, and arguing with cops on the street. The two concerns seemed incompatible so I picked my battles. Later, I did a residency with with art-prankster hacktivists monochrom in Vienna. There's a lot of serious coding and data-activism in that scene. Jacob Appelbaum was hanging around; I was doing stuff with the local cell of the Graffiti Research Lab. But since monochrom are basically absurdist situational performance artists, there was a lot of good stuff about hacking narrative, or hacking life – expanding, subverting what's encoded in culture – and I took a lot from that.

RÓZSA FARKAS: OK, so after your exhibition at Arcadia_Missa I wanted to think again about your IKEA work and, in light of what you've said so far about your practice, ask why you transformed the IKEA performance into a gif?

JD: During a residency at 319 Scholes in New York I started doing a lot of thinking about the body, about how it can be a weapon to hurl against the membrane of hermetic reality and consensual oppression. It's a kind of shamanic objective, cathartic embodiment for the greater good, channelling the sickness of society. I like this idea very much – that I should suffer for my art – and I'm committed to it, though probably not cut out for it. Anyway, I planned to go to IKEA and just start screaming until they came and took me away. We had all these contingency plans: What if they taze you? What if they put you in an ambulance? I spent two days preparing myself for a breakdown in the best way I know how – I didn't sleep, didn't eat, drank too much coffee, went into a really hideous drunk-sober-drunk cycle, took weird pills. But when the time came, I just couldn't do it. It felt too theatrical, and anyway, I didn't want to pull focus like that, and risk upsetting all those people shopping. My own failure, compounded by a genuine distress which many of us always feel in IKEA, just made me want to cry. But all my preparations made sure I was deep inside it, kneeling on the floor sobbing while people went past with their trolleys. That was the only authentic response. And in retrospect, I think, the right one: anger is so performative, and there are plenty of ways to codify violent behaviour in public places, but tears in the shopping centre are for children and crazies. It's very uncomfortable to see adults experiencing extreme distress in public. Ann Hirsch's *Just Some Girl Crying in a Corner*, in which she sat on the gallery floor and cried for an hour at an opening, works in a similar way. I should add that I dressed neatly and conservatively for the occasion: I wore a skirt and sandals, very gendered-bourgeois. In this sense, it was a performance: there was a costume, there was a stage. But in fact it was a kind of anti-performance. I wanted it to be real and it was.

But when I watched the footage, in beautiful, slick HD - it just looked like the worst, hammiest acting ever. Straight-up video is a really bad way to document performance, I think – or anything, really; and it got me thinking about other ways to show what had happened there. So I started thinking about animated gifs because they are embedded media; they cannot extricate themselves from their context, i.e. they belong in the ether, it's their natural habitat; just as me-the-body cannot extricate itself from late-capitalist conglomerates who aestheticise an ideology of the disposable and precarious. The form (of the animated gif)

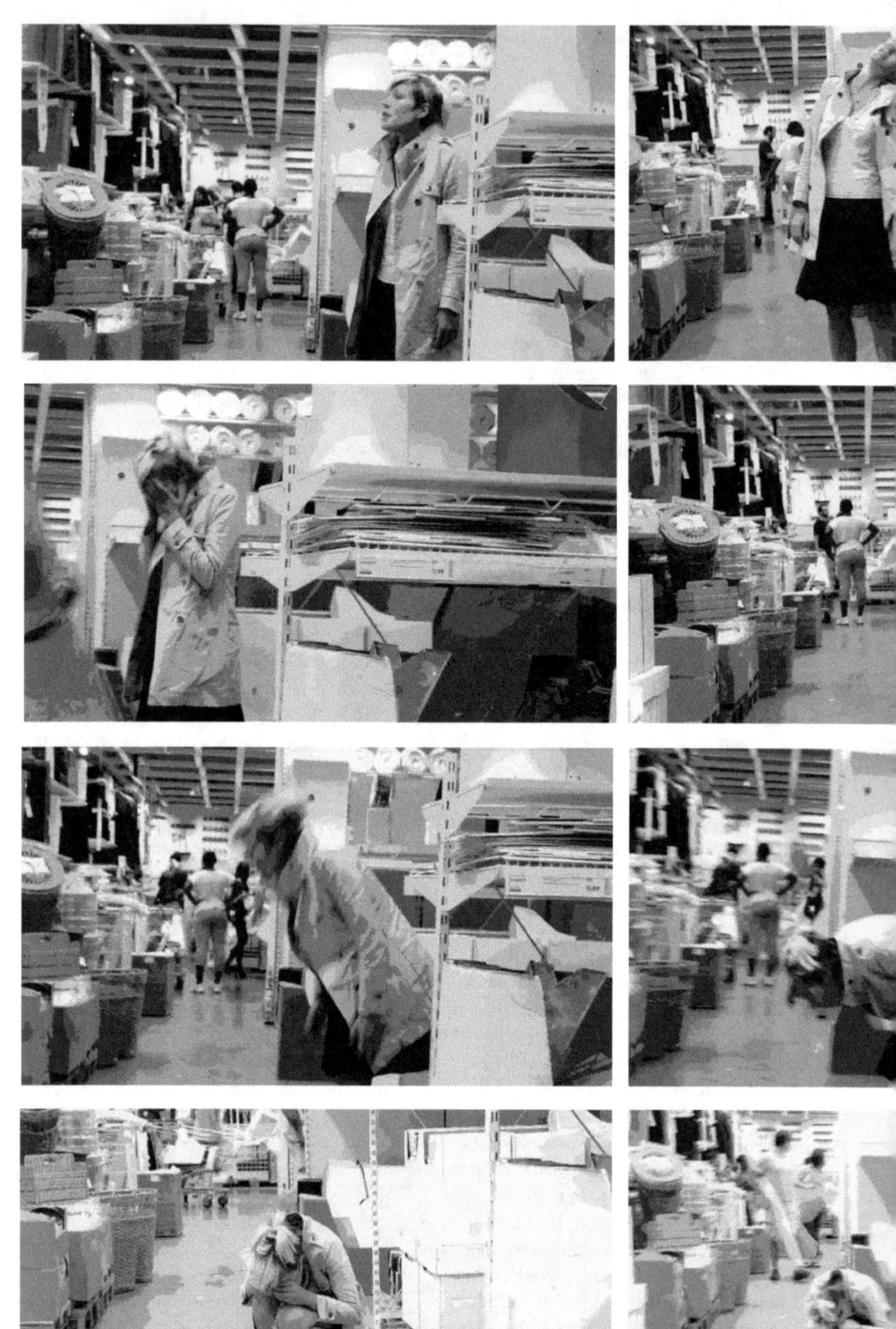

Jesse Darling, *iKea*, 2012, single-channel video, LCD TV screen

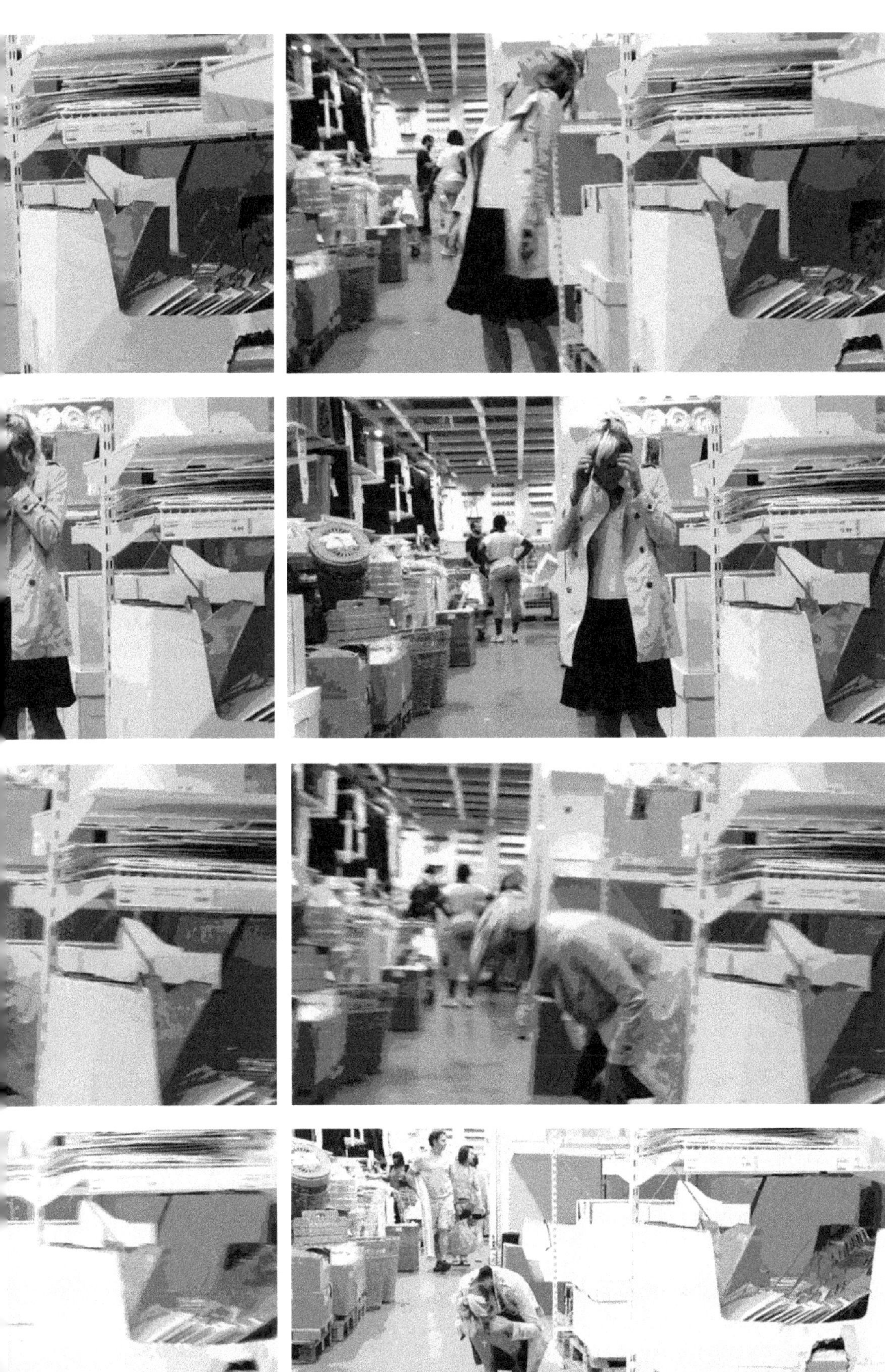

reflects the futility of action, since it's like this endless cycle of oops! LOL, oops! LOL etc., a really purgatorial immortal coil. Animated gif culture is down there at the bottom of the barrel, so you have to deal with that context, too: the form also ends up being a comment on the *absurdity* of the act in the face of certain failure. I started thinking about Brecht's idea of *gestus*,

The animated gif reflects the futility of action

the moment of truth, as it were: a single gesture that encapsulates a whole paradigm. I started thinking about animated gifs as a parallel to *gestus*, and you don't think about Brecht without thinking of populist political theatre. Maybe it's a stretch to say that animated gifs are populist political theatre for the micro-modular age; and maybe it's not.

TC: Is the use of the gif's jumpy techno-povera sensibility a decision to use the technology to destabilise our easy relationship to the image of performance?

JD: I think I'm engaged in a struggle with mediation; the compulsion and futility of trying to capture the moment. I want to reflect this in the image. The process of encoding an image into gif format is a process of systematic decay and degradation, reflected in the end product; this makes transparent the difference between 'real life' and mediated life. This to me is also the closest thing I've found to something like 'the aura' in digital imaging; the transmissible sense of a temporal process, by which we understand that a gesture has been performed; something like 'the painter's hand'. That there was once, at some point, a true moment, now gone forever and succeeded or replaced by this (decayed and muddied) representation, like a painting: it isn't *supposed* to look like life. I'm afraid of all the high-definition high-DPI images on and offline, in advertising, in commerce, increasingly in art; they point to an inverted faith-reality in which the world appears decayed and muddied beside its representation, which – through relentless ubiquity and repetition in every area of our physical, virtual and psychological space – then starts to assume a hegemonic function. The animated gif, by virtue of its vileness and its limitations, stands in defiance of all that stuff. And yes, it also declares a contextual and historical alliance with the low-brow, the low-budget, the low-concept and low-culture aspects of internet culture, in a way that is comparable to street art IRL. My (aesthetic) values were incorrigibly influenced by street and squatter culture as a kid, so I also feel an affinity to all that is cheap and disgusting and immediate.

RF: Why then did the gif have to be displayed on a high-quality advertising monitor in the show?

JD: In the end, the piece became a video that went through several cycles of compression. This came about because I was trying to make the file small enough to parse it into a gif, and it wasn't happening, so I ended up with something else. I started with the raw HD and made it into a basic movie file using Final Cut, but it was still too smooth – it looked more real than real life, which wasn't representative – so I put the file through Quicktime and exported it as an .avi, which is a 'lossy', chunky codec; then Photoshop, etc. The whole process was like putting something through several rounds of

Xerox. It just got noisier and messier with every compression. So I was getting into the idea of compression, in a poetic-anthropomorphic sense, to communicate what was happening to me in IKEA after two days of systematic self-abuse. I'd become a 'lossy' codec myself, 'I was losing it', glitched-out and full of interference. The advertising monitor I used to screen the video was partially as an analogue to the hermetic space of IKEA itself. Those things have no stereo out (for sound), because in advertising nobody can hear you scream; and then the monitor became the medium, because in trying to read my dirty little file it came up with all kinds of horizontal interference which completed the work, as though we were collaborating, my bad compression versus the machine.

I planned to go to IKEA and just start screaming until they came and took me away

RF: Can you talk a bit more about why you honed in on IKEA and, in your eyes, the correlation between something like this and Facebook.

JD: IKEA and Facebook both propose a kind of space, an aesthetic which is also an ideology. The space of the IKEA catalogue is a virtual one, of course; like Facebook, a hygiene of form that would do away with inconsistency, spillover and decay. One thing I've been thinking about lately in my own work is how and why IKEA and Facebook have become such world-dominating psychospatial paradigms. And I think it's because they offer a very seductive paradigm of place-ness and order, which appeals to the psychological homelessness of a generation. We love this shit because it makes us feel like the contingency and terror of growing up in such precarious times can be controlled, or at least temporarily eluded; but of course the aesthetic imposes its own conditions, boxes us in, our very selves compartmentalised into

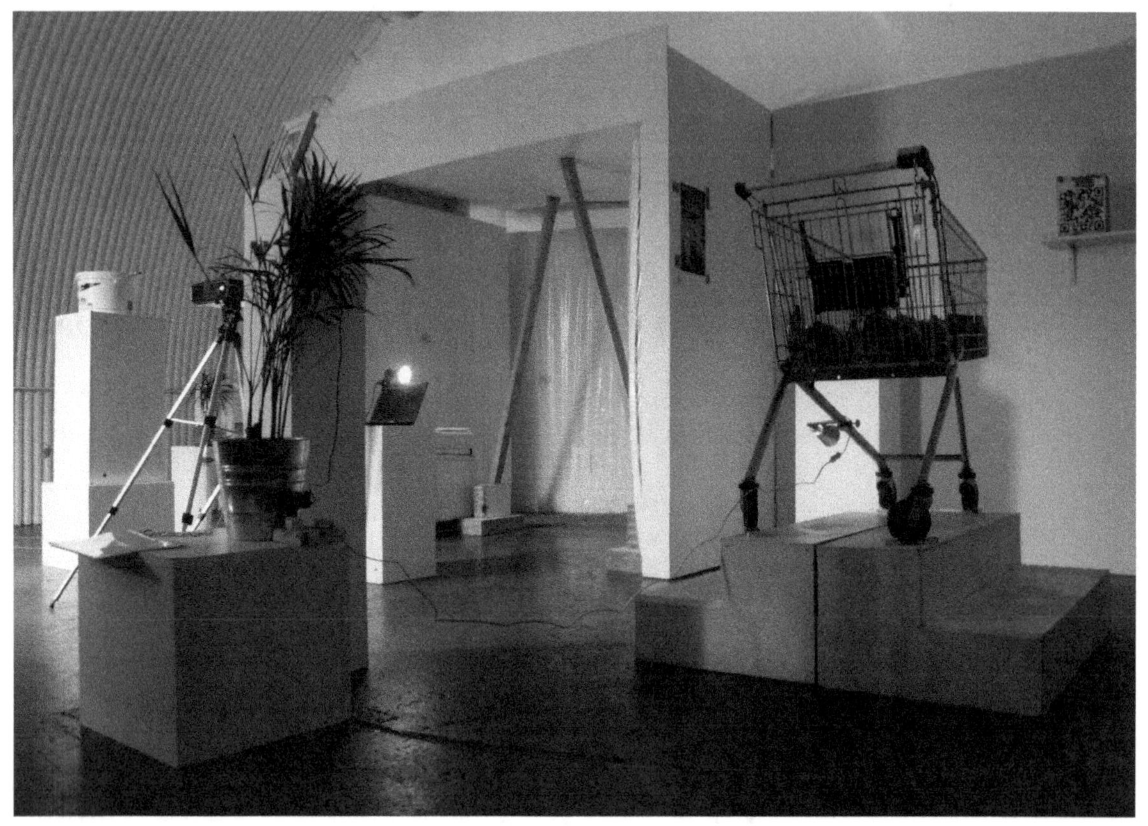

Jesse Darling, Stockholm Syndrome & Other System Failures, Installation view, Arcadia_Missa, London, 2012

fill-in forms and space-saving storage solutions like shiny little horcruxes.[2] I think about it as a form of Stockholm Syndrome: when the captive learns to love the captor as a mechanism of survival.

TC: To follow on from this conflation of identity and the interface, and looking specifically at your work, *Image Macro* (2012), in which a fairly urgent element is the statement 'please let this be real', is this a critique, personal cry or what?

JD: It's both of those things: it's an incantation, a sort of secular prayer. A lot of our discourse and behaviour surrounding technology is starting to look like magical thinking or faith – which is more an affective notion than a religious notion at this point; having no choice but to believe in it, longing to trust it. The installation (*Image Macro*, 2012) is a feedback loop in which a camera gazes at a screen, which is fed back into a projector. The forms and patterns that appear projected are the result of the camera trying to figure out the right depth of focus, shuttling back and forth between the image on the screen and the dust on the screen's surface and coming up with this beautiful organic decay. It's a kind of animism, forcing the camera into negotiating the Gaze. 'Please let this be real' is a kind of post-ironic statement, in that by the time the subject(ivity) shows up it's nothing but a shadow on a projection. But it's there nonetheless (that's why it's a prayer; there's no proof of God's existence but we construe the smallest signs as something to work with). This is compounded by the embodied subjectivity of the viewer, the implied – and imparted – subjectivity of the camera, and the 'bodies' of the tripods holding the camera and projector, triffids engaged in doggy-style coitus. 'We are no longer a part of the drama of alienation; we live in the ecstasy of communication. And this ecstasy is obscene.' (Baudrillard)

TC: The idea of cyborg is being mentioned again recently, particularly within the discussion around the potential for using the web to transcend ordinarily fixed identity markers such as gender, is this something you could talk about?

JD: If this is so, I think it comes from a general shift in focus: from the machine and its processes to the user/subject and her processes, since we don't believe in sentient technology any more, only corporate apparatus and intuitive interfaces, and the power of the panopticon. There is something of the cyborg about the camwhore, reply girl, Tumblr femme – as Haraway puts it 'a creature of social reality as well as a creature of fiction [...] The cyborg is a matter of fiction and lived experience that changes what counts as women's experience in the late twentieth century.' It comes back to negotiating the Gaze, and forcing the body back into the frame as a statement of feminist subjectivity: if we could really negate our bodies and live in the cool matrix of post-gendered networketopia, then abortion rights wouldn't be an issue; transgender kids wouldn't be murdered in small towns. As women and queers we are not allowed to forget what it means to be a body in the world, and I think this is where the internet archetype of the contemporary cyborg comes from: the gazed-at, gazing back. Finally,

I'd become a 'lossy' codec myself, I was losing it

we recognise that we don't only make the machines, as in modernity, but that they make us, too; and some of us are necessarily more aware of how we are being constructed in that. 'The machine is us, our processes, an aspect of our embodiment.' (Donna Haraway)

RF: So is your use of social media celebratory or critical of it as a platform? Is it a medium in itself for you?

JD: It's both celebratory and critical, and it's neither. It's what's at hand. Certainly it is a platform, although it's one among many; and it's also a medium, because it has quite specific formal possibilities and limitations that we can all agree on, like paint or photography or anything. And like any other medium, there are artists who try to subvert it, and artists who just want to excel at it. In this case there's an argument to suggest that to excel it at it – deliberately and with a certain cynicism, matched only by the data overlords themselves – is an act of subversion *an sich*.

RF: Within your practice is this performance art? If so, then is everyone becoming a performance artist through their online avatars?

JD: It is a form of performance, of course. But everything's a form of performance, both on and offline. I wouldn't go so far as to describe social intercourse as performance art, but I do think that social media has set up this space in which the Gaze (and by that I mean the curiously neutral gaze of the voyeur, but also the heterosexist normative capitalist-hegemonic gaze of *He-Who-Bestows-Or-Denies-Value*) has become ubiquitous and omnipresent, perpetuated by one's own friends and colleagues and compounded by the *pollice verso* of the Facebook 'Like'. The Gaze is something that women have always engaged in intimate struggle with; we work with it, or against it, or we work through it, but never are we free of it. Now we're effectively all gazing at each other, and the Big Other gazes through us. So in a sense we're all part of that negotiation now, which points to a condition in which a thing can't exist until it's captured and transmitted – pix or you didn't happen. And habitual users of social media are all fully aware of this as a basic condition, either knowingly or not; so we're all out there performing like crazy, either overtly and knowingly, or being performatively non-performative, playing ourselves, 'being the best we can be.' This evokes a different kind of performance, like 'high-performing dividends' and 'improved sexual performance', the stuff of spam mails and corporate webinars. Etymologically very similar; 100 percent Web 2.0.

TC: So lastly, contingency was a key factor in how you wanted to construct your exhibition at Arcadia_Missa, as well as making new works for it in this process. Why does this play such a large role in your working process?

JD: I think because I'm ambivalent about the notion of authorship (and what it means in a gendered historical context) and also because I'm uncomfortable with the rarefied space that art occupies, which is somehow removed from life. The white cube functions as a container, like the padded cell; within that space anything is permitted, which implies that immediately outside that space all permissions are withdrawn. This is not only vaguely paternalistic but it's a false dichotomy as well; the white cube isn't this big free-for-all, it's also an oppressive paradigm. So using contingency as a medium is almost political for me. But it's personal too, in that I get bored and sad when I feel like I'm fully in control of something; it's too little like life, or living (which is an experience of problem-solving, rolling with solutions, falling in and out of love with things and ideas and people). If I'm genuinely afraid of what might happen next, then I know I'm onto something, and if I'm proud of a finished work, the pride is about having overcome that fear. Our lives are very precarious at the best of times, and especially at this moment in history; this precarity is our basic condition, like swimming in a choppy sea. If you keep trying to fight it, you'll drown. So you need to learn to surf, which means learning to watch for and ride the contingent factors. Be afraid - but stay afloat.

Arcadia_Missa <info@arcadiamissa.com> is an art group and publisher running Arcadia_Missa Gallery. It focuses on digital, experiential, collaborative and performative practices. Arcadia_Missa was born out of a want, and need, to continue a collective and self-initiated means of learning post-university. Via self-education as public gallery programme, Arcadia_Missa hopes to counteract (micro)institutional teaching and by deliberately positioning itself as apprentice, attempting to stay in a liminal, exploratory space that can continually develop with all its participants

Print and digital *How to Sleep Faster* publications are available from arcadiamissa.com as well as information about Arcadia_Missa's upcoming Open Office 0-0 project

FOOTNOTES

1 Jesse Darling, 'Arcades, Mall Rats, and Tumblr Thugs', *The New Inquiry*, February 2012, http://thenewinquiry.com/essays/arcades-mallrats-tumblr-thugs/

2 '"Horcrux" is a term from JK Rowling's *Harry Potter* meaning powerful object in which a Dark wizard or witch has hidden a fragment of his or her soul for the purpose of attaining immortality. Creating one Horcrux gives one the ability to resurrect oneself if the body is destroyed; the more horcruxes one creates, the closer one is to true immortality.' From http://harrypotter.wikia.com/wiki/Horcrux

BITCOIN – FINALLY, FAIR MONEY?

Bitcoin is a decentralised digital currency deploying peer-to-peer networking to enable secure and anonymous transactions without a central bank. Unlike many economic commentators, THE WINE AND CHEESE APPRECIATION SOCIETY *and* SCOTT LENNEY *take the currency seriously but ask, how exactly does it differ from 'real' money?*

In 2009, Satoshi Nakamoto designed a new electronic or virtual currency called Bitcoin, the goal of which was to provide the equivalent of cash on the internet.[1] Rather than using bank or credit cards to buy stuff online, a Bitcoin user will install a piece of software, the Bitcoin client, on his computer and send Bitcoin to other users directly under a pseudonym. One simply enters into the software the pseudonym of the person one wishes to send Bitcoin, the amount to send, and the transaction will be transmitted through a peer-to-peer network.[2] What one can specifically obtain with Bitcoin is somewhat limited to the few hundred websites which accept them, but includes other currencies, web hosting, server hosting, web design, DVDs, coffee in some coffee shops and classified adverts, as well as the ability to donate to WikiLeaks and to use online gambling sites despite being a US citizen.[3] However, what allowed Bitcoin to break into the mainstream – if only for a short period of time – is the Craigslist-style website 'Silk Road' which allows anyone to trade Bitcoin for prohibited drugs.[4] On 11 February, 1 BTC (Bitcoin) exchanged for $5.85, 8.31 million BTC were issued so far, 0.3 million BTC were used in 8,600 transactions in the last 24 hours and about 800 Bitcoin clients were connected to the network. Thus, it is not only some idea or proposal of a new payment system but an idea put into practice, although its volume is still somewhat short of the New York Stock Exchange.

The three features of cash which Bitcoin tries to emulate are anonymity, directness and lack of transaction costs, all of which are wanting in the dominant way of going about e-commerce using credit or debit cards or bank transfers. It's purely peer-to-peer just like cash is peer-to-peer. So far, so general. What makes the project so ambitious is its attempt to provide a new *currency*. Bitcoin is not a way to move Euros, Pounds or Dollars around, it is meant as a new money in itself – it is denominated as BTC not £s. In fact, Bitcoin is even meant as a money based on different principles to modern credit monies. Most prominently, there is no 'trusted third party', no central bank in the Bitcoin economy and there is a ceiling limiting supply to the final figure of 21 million.[5] As a result, Bitcoin appeals to libertarians who appreciate the free market but are sceptical of the state and, in particular, state intervention in the market.

Because Bitcoin attempts to accomplish something well known – money – using a different approach, it allows for a fresh perspective of this ordinary thing, money. Since the Bitcoin project chose to avoid a trusted third party in its construction, it needs to solve several 'technical' problems or issues in order to make it viable as money. Hence, it points to the social requirements and properties which money must have in order to function as such.

In the first part of this text we want to explain how Bitcoin works using as little technical jargon as possible and also what Bitcoin teaches us about a society where free and equal exchange is the dominant form of economic interaction. From this follows a critique of the libertarian ideology behind it.

The first thing one can learn from

Bitcoin is that the characterisation of the free market economy by some (libertarian) Bitcoin adherents (and most other people) is incorrect; namely, that exchange implies mutual benefit, cooperation and harmony.

Indeed, at first sight, an economy based on free and equal exchange might seem like a rather harmonious endeavour. People produce stuff in a division of labour such that both the coffee producer and the shoemaker get both shoes and coffee; and that coffee and those shoes reach their consumers via money. The activity of producers is to their mutual benefit or even to the benefit of all members of society. In the words of one Bitcoin partisan:

> If we're both self-interested rational creatures and if I offer you my X for your Y and you accept the trade then, necessarily, I value your Y more than my X and you value my X more than your Y. By voluntarily trading we each come away with something we find more valuable, at that time, than what we originally had. We are both better off. That's not exploitative. That's cooperative.[6]

In fact, it is consensus in the economic mainstream that cooperation requires money and the Bitcoin community does not deviate from this position: 'A community is defined by the cooperation of its participants, and efficient cooperation requires a medium of exchange (money)'.[7] Hence, in their perspective on markets, the Bitcoin community agrees with the consensus among modern economists: free and equal exchange is cooperation and money is a means to facilitate mutual accommodation. They paint an idyllic picture of a 'free market' whose ills are attributed to misguided state intervention and sometimes the misguided interventions of banks and their monopolies.[8]

CASH

One such state intervention is the provision of money and here lies one of Bitcoin's main features: its function does not rely on a trusted third party or even a state to issue and maintain it. Instead, Bitcoin is directly peer-to-peer not only in its handling of money – like cash – but also in the maintenance and creation of money; as if there were no Bank of England but instead in its place, a protocol by which all people engaged in the British economy collectively printed sterling and watched over its distribution. For such a system to accomplish this, some 'technical' challenges have to be resolved. Some of which are trivial, some of which are not. For example, money needs to be divisible, two £5 notes must be the same as one £10 note, and each token of money must be as good as another – it can't make a difference which £10 note one holds. These features are trivial to accomplish when dealing with a bunch of numbers on computers, but two qualities of money present themselves as non-trivial.

DIGITAL SIGNATURES: GUARANTORS OF MUTUAL HARM

Transfer of ownership of money is so obvious when dealing with cash that it's almost not worth mentioning or thinking about. If Alice hands a tenner to Bob, then Bob has the tenner and not Alice. After an exchange (or robbery, for that matter) it is evident who holds the money and who does not. After payment there is no way for Alice to claim she did not pay Bob, because she did. Nor can Bob transfer the tenner to his wallet without Alice's consent except by force. When dealing with bank transfers etc., it is the banks who enforce this relationship, and in the last instance it is the police.

One cannot take this for granted online. A banknote is now represented by nothing but a number or a string of bits. For example, let's say 0xABCD represents 1 BTC.[9] One can copy it easily and it's impossible to prove that one does not have this string stored anywhere, i.e., that one does not have it anymore. Furthermore, once Bob has seen Alice's note he can simply copy it. Transfer is tricky: how do I make sure you really give your Bitcoin to me?[10] This is the first issue virtual currencies have to address and indeed it is addressed in the Bitcoin network.

To prove that Alice really gave 0xABCD to Bob, she digitally signs a contract stating that this string now belongs to Bob and not herself. A digital signature is also nothing more than a string or large number. However, this string/number has special cryptographic/mathematical properties which make it – as far as we can ascertain – impossible to forge. Hence, just as people normally transfer ownership, say a title to a piece of land, money in the Bitcoin network has its ownership transferred by digitally signing contracts. It's not the note that counts but a contract stating who owns the note. This problem and its solution – digital signatures – is by now so well established that it hardly receives any attention, even in the Bitcoin design document.[11]

Yet, the question of who owns which Bitcoin in itself already problematises the idea of harmonic cooperation held by people about economy and Bitcoin. It indicates that in a Bitcoin transaction, or any act of exchange for that matter, it is not enough that Alice, who makes coffee, wants shoes made by Bob and vice versa. If things were as simple as that, they would discuss how many shoes and much coffee was needed, produce it and hand it over. Everybody happy.

Instead, what Alice does is to exchange her stuff for Bob's stuff. She uses her coffee as a lever to get access to Bob's stuff. Bob, on the other hand, uses his shoes as a leverage against Alice. Their respective products are their means to get access to the products they actually want to consume. That is, they produce their products not to fulfill their own or somebody else's need, but to sell their products such that they can buy what they need. When Alice buys shoes off Bob, she uses her money as leverage to make Bob give her his shoes; in other words, she uses his dependency on money to get his shoes. And vice versa, Bob uses Alice's dependency on shoes to make her give him money.[12] Hence, it only makes sense for each to want more of

Alice uses Bob's dependency on money to get his shoes

the other's for less of their own, which means depriving the other of her means: what I do not need immediately is still good for future trades. At the same time, one wants to keep as much of one's own means as possible: buy cheap, sell dear. In other words, they are not expressing this harmonious division of labour for the mutual benefit at all, but seeking to gain an advantage in exchange, because they have to. It isn't only that one seeks an advantage for oneself, but that one party's advantage is the other party's disadvantage: a low price for shoes means less money for Bob and more product for her money for Alice. This conflict of interest is not suspended in exchange but only mediated: they come to an agreement because they must, but that does not mean it would not be preferable to just take what they need.[13] This relation they

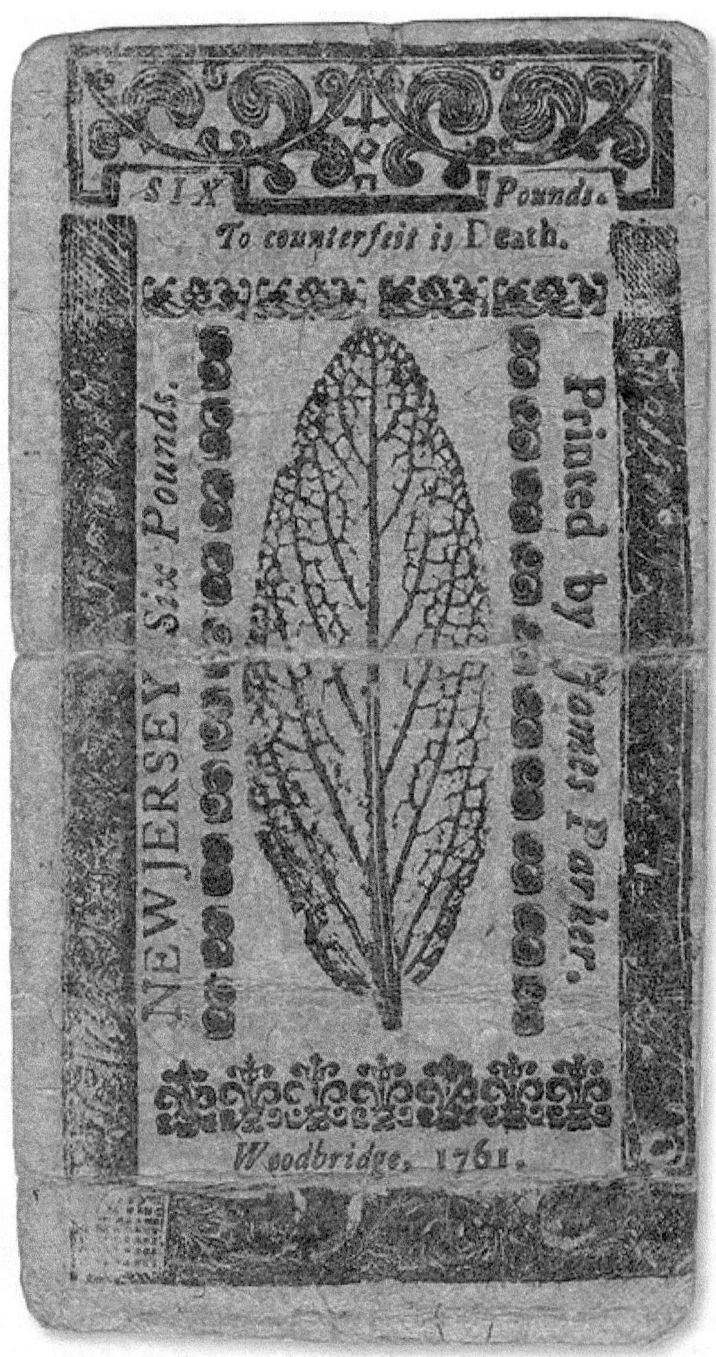

Bill of credit issued by James Parker, 1761

have with each other produces an incentive to cheat, rob and steal.[14] Under these conditions – a systematic incentive to cross each other – answering the question who holds the tenner is very important: it's a matter of getting what one needs or not.

This systemic production of circumstances where one party's advantage is the other party's disadvantage, also produces the need for the state's monopoly on violence. Exchange as the dominant medium of economic interaction, and on a mass scale, is only possible if parties in general are limited to the realm of exchange and cannot simply take what they need and what they want. The libertarians behind Bitcoin might detest state intervention, but a market economy presupposes it. Wei Dai describes the online community as:

> a community where the threat of violence is impotent because violence is impossible, and violence is impossible because its participants cannot be linked to their true names or physical locations.[15]

In this way he not only acknowledges that people in the virtual economy have good reasons to harm each other but also that this economy only works because people do not actually engage with each other. Protected by state violence in the physical world, they can engage in the limited realm of the internet without the fear of violence.

The fact that 'unbreakable' digital signatures – or law enforced by the police – are needed to secure such simple transactions as goods being transferred from the producer to the consumer implies a fundamental enmity of interest of the parties involved. If the libertarian picture of the free market as harmonious cooperation for the mutual benefit of all was true, they would not need these signatures to secure it. The Bitcoin construction – their own construction – shows their theory to be wrong.

Against this, one could object that while by and large trade is a harmonious endeavour, there will always be some black sheep in the flock. In that case, however, one would still have to enquire into the relationship between effort (the police, digital signatures, etc.) and the outcome. The amount of work spent on putting those black sheep in their place demonstrates rather vividly how the expectation is that there would be many more without these countermeasures. Some people go still further and object on the principle that it's all down to human nature, that it's just how humans are. However, by proposing such a view, one first of all agrees that this society cannot be characterised as harmonious. Secondly, the statement 'that's just how it is' is no explanation, even though it claims to be one. At any rate, we have tried above to make some arguments as to why people have good reason to engage with each other the way they do.

PURCHASING POWER

With digital signatures, only those qualities of Bitcoin which affect the relation between Alice and Bob are treated, but in terms of money the relation of Alice to the rest of society is of equal importance. The question needs to be answered – how much purchasing power does Alice have? When dealing with physical money, Alice cannot use the same banknote to pay two different people. There is no double spending, her spending power is limited to what she owns.

When using virtual currencies with digital signatures, on the other hand, nothing prevents Alice from digitally signing many contracts transferring ownership to different people: it is an operation she does by herself.[16] She would sign contracts stating that oxABCD is now owned by Bob, Charley, Eve etc.

The key technical innovation of the Bitcoin protocol is that it solves this double spending problem without relying on a central authority. All previous attempts at digital money relied on some sort of central clearing house which would ensure that Alice cannot spend her money more than once. In the Bitcoin network this problem is addressed by making all transactions public.[17] Thus, instead of handing the signed contract to Bob, it is published on the network by Alice's software. Then, the software of some other participant on the network signs that they have seen this contract certifying the transfer of Bitcoin from Alice to Bob. That is, someone acts as notary and signs Alice's signature and thereby witnesses Alice's signature. Honest witnesses will only sign the first spending of one Bitcoin and will refuse to sign later attempts to spend the same coin by the same person (unless the coin has arrived in that person's wallet again through the normal means). They verify that Alice owns the coin she spends. The witness' signature again is published (all this is handled automatically in the background by the client software).

Yet, Alice could simply collude with Charley and ask Charley to sign all her double spending contracts. She could get a false testimony from a crooked witness. In the Bitcoin network, this is prevented by selecting one witness at random for all transactions at a given moment. Instead of Alice picking a witness, it is randomly assigned. This random choice is organised as a kind of lottery where participants attempt to win the ability to be witness for the current time interval. One can increase one's chances of being selected by investing more computer resources, but to have a decent chance one would need computer resources as great as the rest of the network combined.[18] As a side effect, many nodes on the network waste computational resources solving some mathematical puzzle by trying random solutions to win this witness lottery. In any case, for Alice and Charley to cheat they would have to win the lottery by investing considerable computational resources, too much to be worthwhile – at least that's the hope. Thus, cheating is considered improbable since honest random witnesses will reject forgeries.

But what is a forgery and why is it so bad that so much effort is spent – computational resources wasted – in order to prevent it? On an immediate, individual level a forged bank note behaves no differently from a real one: it can be used to buy stuff and pay bills. In fact, the problem with a forgery is precisely that it is indistinguishable from real money, that it does not make a difference to its users - otherwise people would not accept it. Since it is indistinguishable from real money it functions just as normal money and more money confronts the same amount of commodities and as a result the value of money *might* diminish.

So what is this value of money, then? What does it mean? Purchasing *power*. Recall, that Alice and Bob both insist on their right to their own stuff when they engage in exchange and refuse to give up their goods just because somebody needs them. They insist on their exclusive right to dispose of their stuff, their private property. Under these conditions, money is the only way to get access to each other people's stuff, because it convinces the other party to consent to the transaction. On the basis of private property, the only way to get access to somebody else's private property is to offer one's own in exchange. Hence, money indicates how much wealth in society one can get access to. Money measures

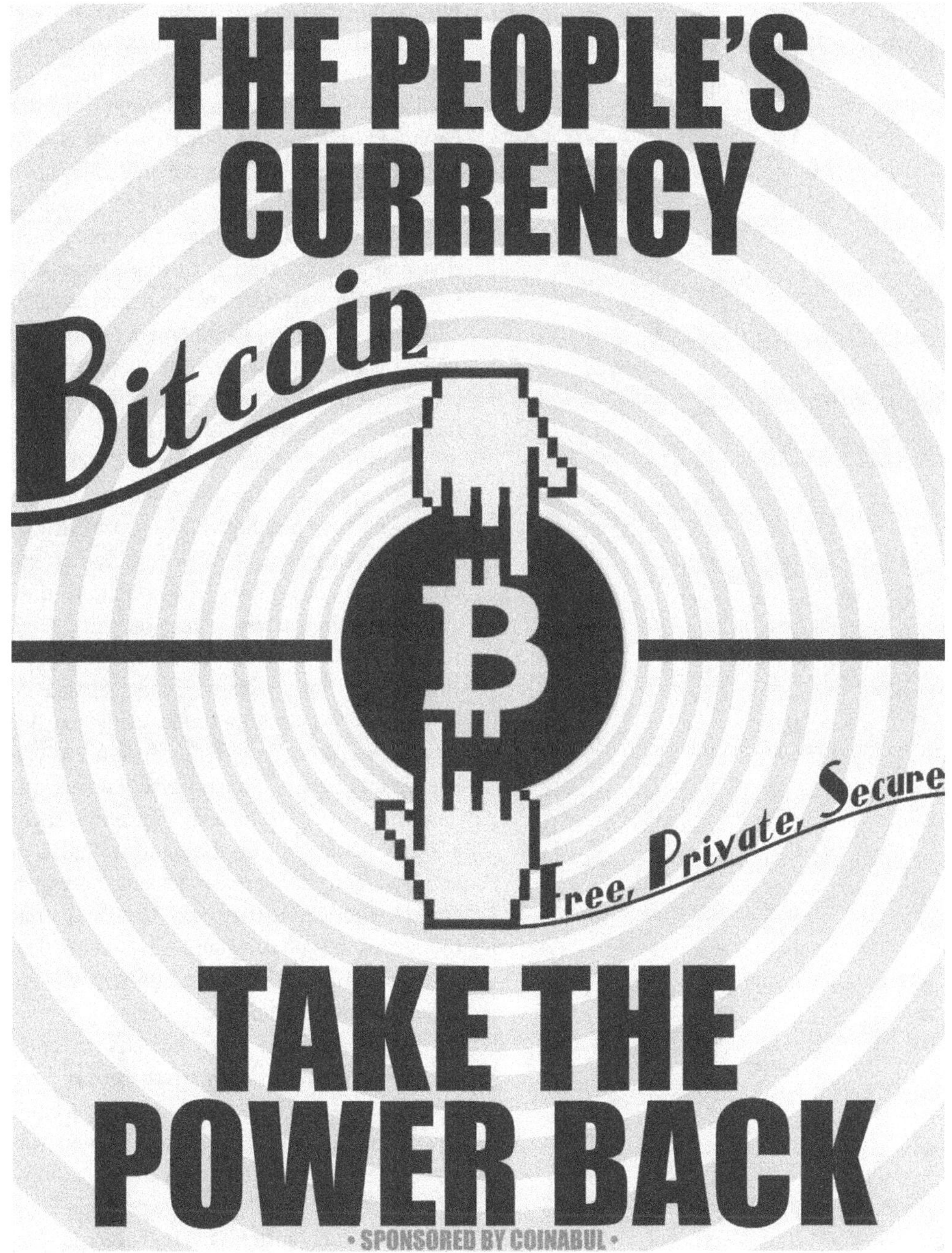

Bitcoin flyer

Money is power one can carry in one's pockets

private property *as such*. Money expresses how much wealth as such one can make use of: not only coffee or shoes but coffee, shoes, buildings, services, labour power, anything. On the other hand, money counts how much wealth as such my coffee is worth: coffee is not only coffee but a means to get access to all the other commodities on the market. It is exchanged for money such that one can buy stuff with this money. The price of coffee signifies how much thereof. All in all, numbers on my bank statement tell me how much I can afford, the limit of my purchasing power and hence – reversing the perspective – from how much wealth I am excluded.

From this it is also clear that under these social conditions – free and equal exchange – those who have nothing will not get anything, that the poor stay poor. Of course, free agents in a free market never have anything, they always own themselves and can sell themselves – their labour power – to others. Yet, their situation is not adequately characterised by pointing out that nature condemns us to work for the products we wish to consume, as the libertarians have it. Unemployed workers can only find work if somebody else offers them a job, if somebody else deems it profitable to employ them. Workers cannot change which product they offer, they only have one. That this situation is no pony farm can be verified by taking a look at the living conditions of workers and people out of work worldwide.

Money is *power* one can carry in one's pockets; it expresses how much control over land, people, machines and products I have. Thus, a forgery defeats the purpose of money: it turns this limit, this magnitude into an infinity of possibilities, anything is – in principle – up for grabs just because I want it. If everyone has infinity power, it loses all meaning. It would not be effective demand that counts, but simply the fact that there is demand, which is not to say that would be a bad thing, necessarily.

In summary, money is an expression of social conditions where private property separates means and needs. For money to have this quality it is imperative that I can only spend that which is mine. This quality and hence this separation of need and means, with all its ignorance and brutality towards need, must be violently enforced by the police and on the Bitcoin network - where what people can do to each other is limited - by an elaborate protocol of witnesses, randomness and hard mathematical problems.

THE VALUE OF MONEY

Now, two problems remain: how is new currency introduced into the system (so far we have only handled the transfer of money) and how are participants persuaded to do all this hard computational work, i.e., to volunteer to be a witness. In Bitcoin the latter problem is solved using the former.

In order to motivate participants to spend computational resources on verifying transactions they are rewarded with a certain amount of Bitcoin if they are chosen as a witness. Currently, each win earns 50 BTC plus a small transaction fee for each transaction they witness. This also answers the question of how new coins are created: they are 'mined' when verifying transactions. In the Bitcoin network money is created 'out of thin air', by solving a pretty pointless problem. That is, the puzzle whose solution allows one to be a witness. The only point of this puzzle is that it is hard, that's all.[19] What counts is that other commodities/ merchants relate to money as money and use it as such, not how it comes into the world.

BITCOIN, CREDIT MONEY AND CAPITALISM

However, the amount of Bitcoin one earns for being a witness will decrease in the future - the amount is cut in half every four years. From 2012 a witness will only earn 25 BTC and so forth. Eventually there will be 21 million BTCs in total and no more.

There is no *a priori* technical reason for the hard limit of Bitcoin; neither for a limit in general nor the particular magnitude of 21 million. One could simply keep generating Bitcoins at the same rate, a rate that is based on recent economic activity in the Bitcoin network or the age of the lead developer or whatever. It is an arbitrary choice from a technical perspective. However, it is fair to assume that the choice made for Bitcoin is based on the assumption that a limited supply of money would allow for a better economy; where 'better' means 'fairer', more stable and devoid of state intervention. Libertarian Bitcoin adherents and developers claim that by 'printing money' states - via

No matter what the substance of money, credit is guaranteed by success

their central banks - devalue currencies and hence deprive their subjects of their assets.[20] They claim that the state's (and sometimes the banks') ability to create money 'out of thin air' would violate the principles of the free market because they are based on monopoly instead of competition. Inspired by natural resources such as gold, Satoshi Nakamoto chose to fix a ceiling for the total amount of Bitcoin to some fixed value.[21] From this fact most pundits are quick to speculate over the likelihood of a 'deflationary spiral'; i.e., whether this choice spells doom for the currency due to exponentially fast deflation – the value of the currency rising compared to all commodities – or not. Indeed, for these pundits the question of why modern currencies are credit money hardly deserves attention. Consequently, they miss what would likely happen if Bitcoin were to become successful: a new credit system would develop.

CREDIT

Capitalist enterprises invest money to make more money, to make a profit. They buy stuff such as goods and labour power, put these 'to work' and sell the result for more money than they have initially spent. For a capitalist enterprise, money is a means and more wealth – counted in money – is the end: growth.

If money is a means of growth, a lack of money is not a sufficient reason for the augmentation of money to fail to happen. With the availability of credit money, banks and fractional reserve banking, it is evident that this is the case. However, assume, for the sake of argument, that these things did not exist. Even then, at any given moment, some companies have money which they cannot spend yet while other companies need money to spend now (to buy new machines, say). Hence, both the need and means for credit appear. If growth is demanded, having money sitting idly in one's vaults while someone else could invest and augment it is a poor business decision. This simple form of credit hence develops spontaneously under free market conditions.

Furthermore, under the dictates of the free market, success itself is a question of how much money one can mobilise. The more money a company can invest the better its chances of success and the higher the yield on the market. Better technologies, production methods, distribution deals and training of workers, all these things are available – at a price. Now, with the possibility of credit the necessity for credit arises as well. If money is all that is needed for success and if the right to dispose over money is available for interest then any company has to anticipate its competitors borrowing money for the next round of investments, rolling up the market. The right choice under these conditions is to apply for credit and to start the next round of investment oneself; which – again – pushes the competition towards doing the same. This way, the availability of money not only provides the possibility for credit but also the basis for a large scale credit business, since the demand for credit motivates further demand.

Even without fractional reserve banking or credit money, e.g., within the Bitcoin economy, two observations can be made about the relation of capital to money and the money supply.

If some company A lends company B money, the supply of means of payment increases. Money that would otherwise be petrified into a hoard, kept away from the market, used for nothing, is activated and used in circulation. More money confronts the same amount of commodities, without printing a single new banknote or mining a single BTC. That means: the amount of money active in a given society is not fixed, even if Bitcoin was the standard form of money.

Instead, capital itself regulates the money supply in accordance with its business needs. Businesses 'activate' more purchasing power if they expect a particular investment to be advantageous. For them, the right amount of money is that amount of money which is worth investing. This is capital's demand for money.

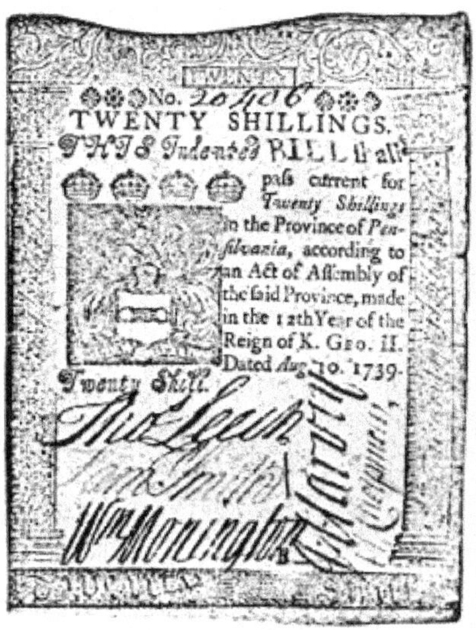

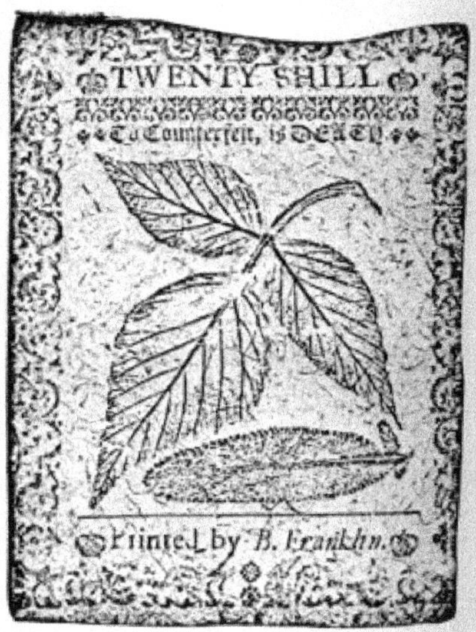

Bill of credit issued by Benjamin Franklin, 1739

GROWTH GUARANTEES MONEY

When one puts money in a bank account or simply lends it to some other business, to earn interest, the value of that money is guaranteed by the success of the debtor to turn it into growth. If the debtor goes bankrupt that money is gone. No matter what the substance of money, credit is guaranteed by success.

In order to secure against such defaults creditors may demand securities, some sort of asset which has to be handed over in case of a default. On the other hand, if on average a credit relation means successful business, an IOU itself is such an asset. If Alice owes Bob and Bob is short on cash but wants to buy from Charley he can use the IOU issued by Alice as a means of payment: Charley gets whatever Alice owes Bob. If credit fulfils its purpose and stimulates growth then debt itself becomes an asset, almost as good as already earned money. After all, it should be earned in the future. Promises of payment can assume – and have assumed in the past – the quality of means of payment.

Charley can then spend Alice's IOU when buying from Eve, and so forth. Thus, the amount of means of payment in society may grow much larger than the official money, simply by exchanging promises of payment of this money. And this happens without fractional reserve banks or credit money issued by a central bank. Instead, this credit system develops spontaneously under free market conditions and the only way to prevent it from happening is to ban this practice: to regulate the market, which is what the libertarians do not want to do.

Systematic enmity of interests, exclusion from social wealth, subjection of everything to capitalist growth – that is what an economy looks like where exchange, money and private property determine production and consumption. This does not change if the substance of money is gold or Bitcoin. This society produces poverty not because there is credit money but because it is based on exchange, money and economic growth. The libertarians might not mind this poverty, but those who have discovered Bitcoin as a new alternative to the status quo perhaps should.

The Wine and Cheese Appreciation Society of Greater London <wineandcheese@hush.com> is part of the Junge Linke gegen Kapital und Nation network. Its writings can be found at http://www.junge-linke.org/en

Scott Lenney <delasbas@hotmail.co.uk> writes about culture and politics

FOOTNOTES

1 The key white paper on Bitcoin is *Bitcoin: A Peer-to-Peer Electronic Cash System* by Satoshi Nakomoto, http://bitcoin.org/bitcoin.pdf
2 A peer-to-peer network is a network where nodes connect directly, without the need of central servers (although some functions might be reserved for servers). Famous examples include Napster, BitTorrent and Skype.
3 Probably due to pressure from the US government, all major online payment services stopped processing donations to the WikiLeaks project, see: http://www.bbc.co.uk/news/business-11938320 Also, most US credit card provides prohibit the use of their cards for online gambling.
4 After Gawker media published an article about Silk Road - http://gawker.com/5805928/the-underground-website-where-you-can-buy-any-drug-imaginable two US senators became aware of it and asked congress to shut it down. So far, law enforcement operations against Silk Road seem to have been unsuccessful.
5 'Bitcoins are created each time a user discovers a new block. The rate of block creation is approximately constant over time: six per hour. The number of Bitcoins generated per block is set to decrease geometrically, with a 50 percent reduction every four years. The result is that the number of Bitcoins in existence will never exceed 21 million.' http://www.bitcointalk.org/index.php?topic=3366.msg47522#msg47522
6 https://forum.bitcoin.org/index.php?topic=5643.0;all
7 Wei Dai, 'bmoney.txt', http://weidai.com/bmoney.txt. This text outlines the general idea on which Satoshi Nakamoto based his Bitcoin protocol.
8 'The real problem with Bitcoin is not that it will enable people to avoid taxes or launder money, but that it threatens the elites' stranglehold on the creation and distribution of money. If people start using Bitcoin, it will become obvious to them how much their wage is going down every year and how much of their savings is being stolen from them to line the pockets of banksters and politicians and keep them in power by fobbing them off with bread and circuses those who would otherwise take to the streets.' http://undergroundeconomist.com/post/6112579823
9 For those who know a few technical details of Bitcoin: we are aware that Bitcoin are not represented by anything but a history of transactions. However, for ease of presentation we assume there is some unique representation – like the serial number on a five pound note.
10 'Commerce on the Internet has come to rely almost exclusively on financial institutions serving as trusted third parties to process electronic payments. [...] Completely non-reversible transactions are not really possible, since financial institutions cannot avoid mediating disputes. [...] With the possibility of reversal, the need for trust spreads. Merchants must be wary of their customers, hassling them for more information than they would otherwise need. A certain percentage of fraud is accepted as unavoidable. These costs and payment uncertainties can be avoided in person by using physical currency, but no mechanism exists to make payments over a communications channel without a trusted party.' – Satoshi Nakomoto, op. cit.
11 For an overview of the academic state-of-the-art on digital cash see Burton Rosenberg (ed.), *Handbook of Financial Cryptography and Security*, CRC Press, 2011.
12 To avoid a possible misunderstanding,that money mediates this exchange is not the point here. What causes this relationship is that Alice and Bob engage in exchange. Money is simply an expression of this particular social relation.
13 Of course, people do shy away from stealing from each other. Yet, this does not mean that it would not be advantageous to do so.
14 'Transactions that are computationally impractical to reverse would protect sellers from fraud,

and routine escrow mechanisms could easily be implemented to protect buyers.' Satoshi Nakomoto, op. cit.

15 Wei Dai, op. cit.

16 'The problem of course is the payee can't verify that one of the owners did not double-spend the coin.' – Satoshi Nakomoto, op. cit.

17 'We need a way for the payee to know that the previous owners did not sign any earlier transactions. For our purposes, the earliest transaction is the one that counts, so we don't care about later attempts to double-spend. The only way to confirm the absence of a transaction is to be aware of all transactions' – ibid. Note that this also means that Bitcoin is far from anonymous. Anyone can see all transactions happening in the network. However, Bitcoin transactions are between pseudonyms which provides some weaker form of anonymity.

18 On the Bitcoin network anyone can pretend to be many people by creating many pseudonyms. Hence, this lottery is organised in such a way that one has to solve a mathematical puzzle by trying random solutions which requires considerable computational resources (big computers). This way, being 'more people' on the network requires more financial investment in computer hardware and electricity. It is similar to an ordinary lottery: those who buy many tickets have a higher chance of winning.

19 'The only conditions are that it must be easy to determine how much computing effort it took to solve the problem and the solution must otherwise have no value, either practical or intellectual' – Wei Dai, op. cit.

20 'The root problem with conventional currency is all the trust that's required to make it work. The central bank must be trusted not to debase the currency, but the history of fiat currencies is full of breaches of that trust. Banks must be trusted to hold our money and transfer it electronically, but they lend it out in waves of credit bubbles with barely a fraction in reserve. We have to trust them with our privacy, trust them not to let identity thieves drain our accounts. Their massive overhead costs make micropayments impossible.'– Satoshi Nakamoto, Bitcoin creator, quoted in Jashua Davis, 'The Crypto-Currency: Bitcoin and Its Mysterious Inventor', *The New Yorker*, 10 October, 2011.p. 62.

21 'The steady addition of a constant amount of new coins is analogous to gold miners expending resources to add gold to circulation. In our case, it is CPU time and electricity that is expended.' Satoshi Nakomoto, op. cit. Furthermore, the distributed generation of Bitcoin is inspired by gold. In the beginning it is easy to 'mine' but it becomes harder and harder over time. Bitcoin's mining concept is an attempt to translate the return to gold money to the internet.

BLOOMSBURY OLYMPIC

As the 2012 London Olympics looms, construction and education – two poles of an economy of despair – are destined to meet in East London. RICHARD B draws out the unlikely connections between Bloomsbury and Stratford

It is Spring 2012. The party socialists in the Bloomsbury student movement walk out of their classrooms to protest against the reforms to Higher Education, parading through the streets as if each thump on a paving stone will bring the world a little closer to political ignition. A year and a half ago, this was indeed the motion that articulated so successfully the collective, national rage against the current administration's policies towards land, labour and capital. Since then, today's student movement, in Bloomsbury and beyond, has drifted up and down. It still remains more organised and vibrant than its generational precursors have been for perhaps a decade in the UK and the active forms of co-operation between student and trade union activists are equally novel. Yet, in the face of continued, unrelenting government legislation, the movement pauses. The march is directed at the Minister for Universities, David Willets, but it seems impossible to imagine how it could move beyond accusation and into real antagonism.

The move beyond current coordinates is often deemed, in pseudo-management talk, as the key strategic aims of a campaign: with *solidarity*, with a 'linking up' how could we ever be stopped? Resistance, aggregating under the working title of convenience ('anti-cuts') comprised itself of students, proletarians and other fiscal underdogs, and proclaimed in all its self-congratulatory stellar immensity the necessity of *solidarity*. Surely if we had joined-up better, like rats biting each-others' tails, we would have mobbed into a mass with no diminishment of momentum? Thus far, ironically, it is the lofty institutions themselves which have been far more feverish and clandestine in expanding outwards into the working class communities from which the student movement was restricted, dominated as it was, in 2010 at least, by cadres from the Russell Group universities.

For while the student movement may have understandably stalled in the face of the onslaught of the fastest transfer of economic governance from nation state to private corporation in the history of our beleaguered welfare state, the *university* movement has far from subsided. Perhaps, however, we can ride its waves.

Over the past two years in the UK, two sectors of capital production have been central to the political arguments for particular strategies of economic reorganisation: education and construction. Education in the banalised, bastardised vehicle of the Higher Education sector, one which became the centrifuge of both policy and resistance; construction in the bizarre world of the Olympics. The site in Stratford is now the largest construction site in Europe, at a time when new construction projects across the UK as a whole are at the lowest rate of commission since 1980. These two sectors are about to collide with University College London's (UCL) declared intention to construct a new campus in Stratford, on the site currently occupied by a 1960s housing estate.[1] In the boulevards of Bloomsbury, the potentialities of post-Olympic capital dribble from the colonnades; in Stratford, the soft filtrations of UCL's nanotechnologies trickle into the already toxic marshland.

CARPENTERS ESTATE

Carpenters Estate is known for being the largest housing estate standing adjacent to the

Olympic Park. At one end, the High Road, broad and empty, strung with dim colour-changing lights, heralds the mix of inflated glass phalloi, surviving workers' cafés and stocky private housing with fragmented coloured surfaces which presently characterise Stratford. At the other end of the estate, a strange road blockade formed out of Olympic signs and wire mesh barriers announces the concealed entrance to the sacred Olympic Park itself: 'Demolish. Dig. Design' proclaims the multi-coloured plastic hoarding. Reflected in the luminescent cyan are the words of a discarded sign, spelling out in reverse 'We Buy Gold'. On the other side of the gate loom the Olympic stadia.

There are three large tower blocks on Carpenters Estate, designed by Thomas North and Kenneth Lund, the West Ham Borough architects through the 1960s. Each 22 storey block stands watch over rows of two and three-storey low rises, which exemplify a range of '60s to '80s council architecture. The towers themselves are built around a central core of pokey corridors, while the outer skin is dominated by windows and black cladding reminiscent of the pioneering Ravenscroft Estate in Canning Town. Each tower rests on large, pastel-coloured concrete trapezoid feet, though at James Riley point, instead of a Le Corbusier-style flow of air beneath the block, the spaces below have been gated up to fence in a myriad of large vacant waste bins.

All three blocks are nearing the end of a 'decanting' process. It's a familiar story which has already played itself out countless times, notably at the Heygate Estate in Southwark. The lack of proper maintenance suffered by the buildings from the moment construction ended is used by the council as a reason for development, promising riches for the council and impoverishment for the residents.

It's worthwhile understanding how the destruction of these blocks is built into the history of their fabric. The old Worshipful Company of Carpenters purchased land in Stratford and West Ham, and in the 19th century turned it from fields for pasture into those for industrial production, leasing it out for the manufacture of bricks, matches and linen. As the railways criss-crossing the marshes needed land from the Carpenters' Company, transformed through South-Sea bubble and colonial necessity into a financially secure apparatchik club, was awarded handsome compensation by the state in lieu of market prices.[2] Gifted these cash sums, the Company invested in supporting technical education at Imperial University, King's College London and UCL, as well as the founding of a building crafts college on the site itself. Factories and houses rose up side by side along the River Lea. Both thus suffered the mass bombing of WWII which scattered its way up the valley.[3]

Surely if we had joined-up better, like rats biting each others' tails, we would have mobbed into a mass

In the 1950s, the Carpenters Estate lay as part-ruin, part-rubble, with houses interspersed amongst the detritus. West Ham Council had 8,000 people on its waiting list for housing every year. Faced with this seemingly impossibly task of provision, the council began a program of erecting not only modernist housing estates, but cheap high rises fashioned from pre-fabricated concrete slabs. West Ham bought the Carpenters' land through compulsory purchase order in 1965

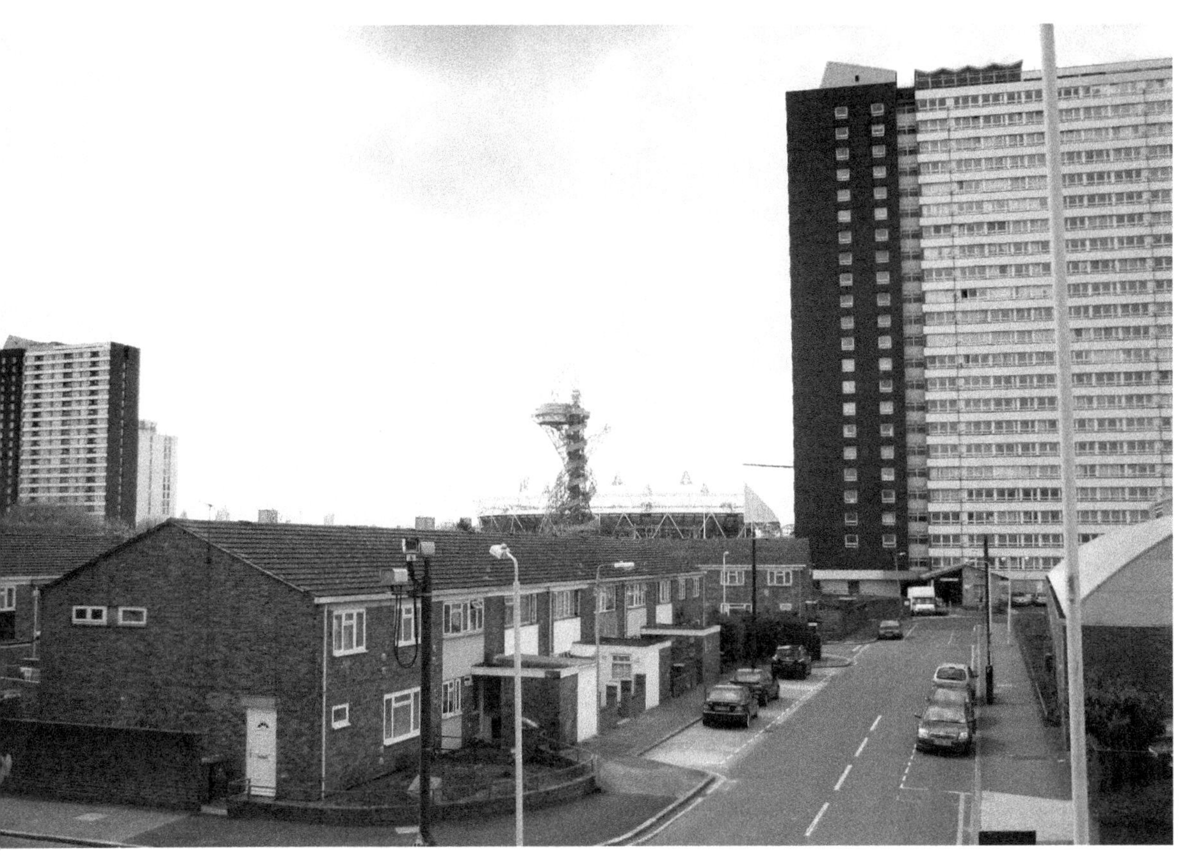

All photographs by Rose-Anne Gush

and the three towers – Dennison, James Riley and Lund points – were finished by 1968.[4]

Across East London, similar towers rose from the dust of history. From '68 onwards, it is a history of decay. In that year, as the Carpenters buildings were finished, the latest of West Ham's housing solutions revealed catastrophic cost-cutting. Ronan Point, a 200ft tower in Canning Town also designed by Thomas North, partially collapsed when a ground floor flat exploded from a gas leak. Every living room on the corner of the building, from base to top, cascaded downwards.

While damp and subsidence have caused cracks and peeling in the Carpenters towers, they remain structurally sound. Lacking such a material justification that could be leveled by council authorities in response to residents' enquiries, the estate has of course become host to bourgeois conspiracies that the buildings must be infected with the social disease named anti-social behaviour, or simply 'decline'. At the Royal Institute of British Architect's current exhibition, 'A Place to Call Home', the buildings purported to have contributed to the 'aspirational' shift in the 1970s were Ronan Point and the Broadwater Farm Estate. While the former represents a physical disaster, the latter is a social disaster. Given that the Broadwater Farm riots, stoked by a racist police force more than inadequate architectural design, did not happen until 1985, the implication can only be that this was a disaster inscribed into the mortar of the dwellings, waiting to burst out.

This attitude is no doubt helped by the desultory data provided from the national census, which records the Stratford Estate as one of the economically poorest areas in the country. Such statistics themselves, however, are unnecessary for any bureaucrat wanting to draw the useful conclusion that the estate is beyond repair, his mind dominated by the threat society perceives in itself, never mind that the real threat is quite clearly in the deleterious balance sheets of local government. And never mind, too, that residents who have lived on other estates speak highly of the lack of fear and violence at Carpenters.

Typically, despite the protestations of the Carpenters community, now in its third generation, James Riley Point was deemed unable to be repaired at reasonable cost in 2004, and has been slowly emptied out since. The other two blocks were marked for termination soon after, each announcement accompanied by the term 'regeneration', and carrying with it the appropriate subtext of class spite. Two thirds of the estate now lies empty.

What makes the Carpenters community cohere, in all its Bengali-Turkish-Polish-aging-Cockney splendour, and in spite of their dwindling numbers, are the shared amenities. There is a primary school on the site, comprising a large set of low and squat pre-fab buildings, stretching out between the blocks. The school will be closed during the Olympics themselves, but the staff still believe their future is assured. The school supported the Newham and West Ham bid for the Olympic site, seeing the games, at least in its official output, as no threat at all. At the estate pub (the Carpenters Arms) the workers are far less certain. The pub managers are hopeful that Olympics will bring more business along the new lane bisecting the estate, leading from the A road to the Olympic Park.

Indeed, despite the busy roads nearby and the roaring Westfield shopping centre just on the other side of the station, I seem to see less people on the estate each time I walk round it. Quietness holds it, cranes watch over it. On one occasion, I caught up with some students on a spliff break in the park. They were attending a ten-week course in basic construction and maintenance at the Building Crafts College next to the estate. The courses are usually funded by local housing associations, institutions which form a central part of the post-Olympic unaffordable homes bonanza. One of the students said he was hoping to get a job at the red tower on the horizon, Anish Kapoor's corporate sponsored sculpture-building, the helter-skelter 'something else' which looms through the mist. He told me how he had a friend who used to live in the Dennison Point behind us, but he and his family had been moved to another council house in Abbey Lane. Other friends had been moved as far as Barking.

This is the next step of the managed decline: breaking up communities and peppering residents through the environs. The London Plan for the Olympics set a target of one half of all new development used for affordable housing.[5] Of the 11 new blocks currently curtaining off the Carpenters Estate from the rest of the world, about one third are 'affordable'. In an interview with the BBC, the comedically villainous Mayor of Newham, Sir Robin Wales, can be heard assuring his constituents that this managed decline is not so bad; that the former residents of the estate will be rehoused *or offered loans* with which to buy new homes. Faced, effectively, with the accusation of actively impoverishing his electors, the Mayor retorts that there is no impoverishment, there's just huge bundles of good, wholesome debt waiting for them whenever they ask. So much for the lessons of sub-prime. Already, most of the houses on the Carpenters Estate are privately owned by indebted beneficiaries of the 1980s Right-to-Buy scheme. Those being decanted from the three tower blocks are being encouraged to move into the brand new Genesis Housing Association development opposite the estate, a move with which they also rescind their right to secure tenancies.

As if the throes of privatisation were not enough, the fraction of the newly built Olympic village which Newham will be offered

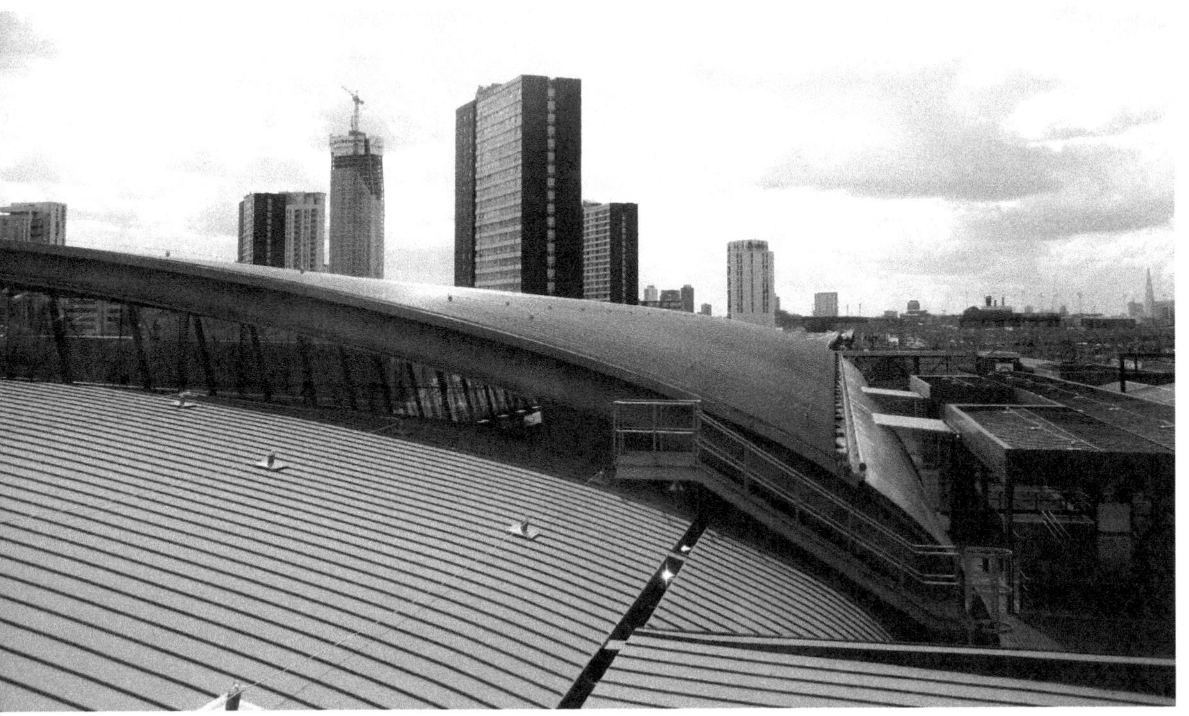

as council-owned housing stock is to be well used in the *Realpolitik* of class war. Earlier this month, the sickly Mayor revealed proposals for prioritising the allocation of the 348 new houses to 'hard-working' families and soldiers, in a patent continuation of forced labour: work or die, the administration sharply drones. Those who have had the good fortune to retire before they die are being hurried out of their too-costly state provided flats and into the private market.

But we can go further than lamenting the *unfair* infringement on the rights of proletarians to continue a specific form of life. Instead, we can see in the processes of the Olympics the effect of a high-capital growth project on a section of the working class already mutating through another, parallel process of class decomposition. Capital and class move together. Newham proletarians out, Bloomsbury capital in.

OLYMPIC-BLOOMSBURY

University College London announced last year that, as part of its beautified Masterplan, it intends to construct a bright new campus in Stratford. The 20 hectare site it proclaims ripe for this illustrious moment is of course the Carpenters Estate. A quick walk around the site makes clear that the only option for such a project, given the specific geography, would be the total destruction of the housing estate and its amenities. The Mayor of Newham, again with the perfect, honest prowess which only his class of quangocrats can deliver, laudates:

> With leading educational institutions already firmly established in the area, another university would inspire Newham youngsters to *look* at the wider opportunities available to them. As well as

> presenting *employment* opportunities, a new campus will provide a significant boost to the local economy and provide a lasting legacy for the community.

Read: 'The young people of East London may *look* upon the heights of UCL with pleasure, and dream that they too, one far off day, could achieve its greatness. But until then they can have the even greater pleasure of *employment* in the university.'

The Mayor deftly replaces opportunity to aspire with opportunity to survive – ambition for subsistence. Stratford is actually already well covered, if not saturated, with educational institutions. Queen Mary's university is only a quick bus ride away, the Building Crafts College maintains specialist as well as foundation courses, and just on the other side of the depleting old shopping centre is the original branch of the University of East London (UEL). Birkbeck University, also based in Bloomsbury, shares resources with UEL in this first Stratford building, and the two institutions are engaged in a new campus (blandly branded 'University Square') to piggy-back on the Newham building mania. But the hopes for a lasting legacy in the *economy* (and not just its whimpering cousin, the job market) will be the in-and-out flow of students from UCL, while East Londoners can make do with the service provision of the *other* institutions on their doorstep. Anywhere except the precious Russell Group spires.

Indeed, where UCL is granted laurels and stooping, the class basis of UEL students earns the full wrath of the Olympic storm. UEL housed many students at the Clays Lane housing estate, once the largest purpose-built housing co-operative in the UK, erected proudly by the National Building Agency. Clays Lane was bought and demolished in 2007 to make way for the presentation of the Olympic site to prospective developers as a symbol of the area as a whole. In other words, students and families were forced out of their homes in order to show off a pristine lot begging for ballparks and tennis courts. It was left as this manufactured wasteland for two years.

The provost of UCL, Malcolm Grant has insisted with the usual excess of management soft talk that Carpenters residents have been consulted (i.e. patronised) and their views listened to (i.e. safely contained). Carpenters Against Regeneration Plans (CARP) have witnessed the council and UCL conspiring to push ahead with development of the site despite their protestations in the sham public meetings, for which security guards were hired to discourage dissenting voices.

More recently, the residents have hit out against the capitalising efforts of the local council, who have signed a deal with the BBC allowing the top five floors of one of the *supposedly* crumbling tower blocks to be used for broadcasting during the Olympics itself. In this, the council is far from double-speak: it is in fact remarkably consistent. The tenants cannot be bled for the kind of capital which the Olympics provide, so they must be jettisoned. The Olympics must be welcomed in, first from the top of the tower blocks, their height providing the one last function in the new towering behemoths of Stratford Corp, until the dynamite can be placed at their base and the swaggering shapes of UCL can rise from the debris. Even the BBC understand this logic perfectly: they have indicated that while in residence in the top five floors of the block, they will be subletting some of the rooms to international media pundits.

There is another way in which the deterioration of the blocks, and the parallels with the Heygate Estate in this manner, has not gone unnoticed by the culture industry.

Both blocks, in their advantageously abandoned states, were used as filming locations for the horror-comedy *Attack the Block*. The film brings together gang theory and alien invasion, narrating the real and slapstick violence of a group of residents on a London housing estate as they battle against a ferocious alien invasion which seems attacking only their housing block. In the film, the police are eaten by the invading beasts quite early on; this is a world without state protection or intervention (not that any tears are shed for the local enforcement). Nonetheless, this demarcates quite clearly the lines of aggression which ground the film: it isn't a state actor which is being satirised as the invading force, but a class one. The heroic defenders of the block are mainly black: the aliens represent the gentrifying terror of white bourgeois London, tearing at the fabric of their environment, threatening their lives.

The culture industry, of course, sees the impoverishment they themselves are causing through the banality of bourgeois *neutrality*, and respond with what is – despite its comedic violence – really a nostalgic sob story about friendship and homeliness. And then, the film's profits rolling in, the same class smells the last few drops of capital which can be eked out from the top five floors of a block ready for termination – its *friendly, homely* community included – and springs on the kill.

Tenants can't be bled for the kind of capital the Olympics provide, so are jettisoned

BLOOMSBURY, OLYMPIC

The culture industry, thriving on the output of the emptied estates, is well integrated into the capital, as well as social, mesh of Bloomsbury, Olympic. Russell Square, this Summer, is media hub. Specially provided buses will ferry journos to and fro from tube stations; a special tube line will move them in their thousands

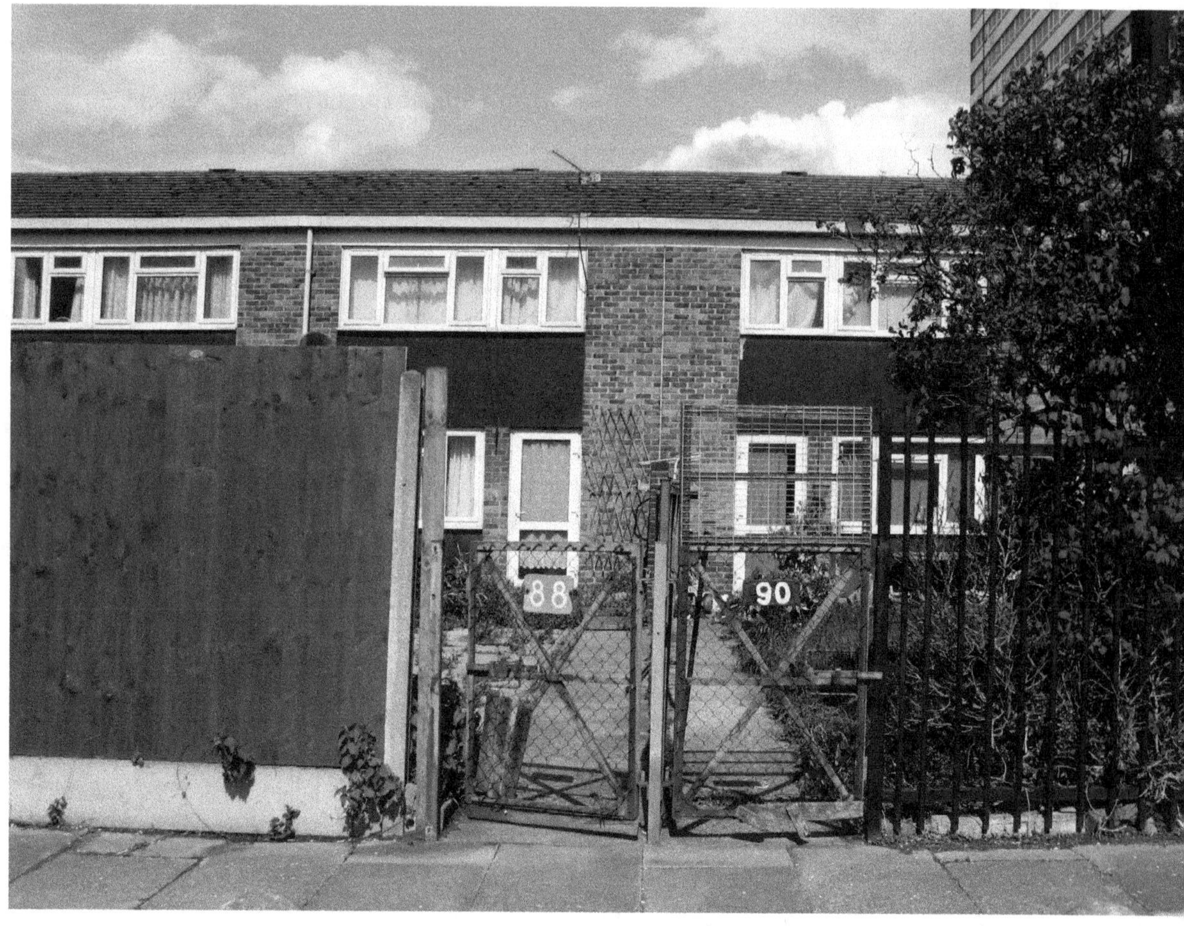

from Kings Cross station to Stratford; from the elegant squares of Bentham and Keynes, over to the depleted (but surely well hidden) empty expanses which lie heavily between the Carpenters Estate blocks; from fete to fate. The Camden Council enactment of their 2007 'strategic vision' amount *in toto* to the second Hausmannisation of Bloomsbury, the processes of 19th century resurfacing. It is of little wonder then that Russell Square is to be fenced off, so that access to the universities can only be made from the North; that the whole of Malet Street, running down the West border of the campus, will be taken up by VIP lanes for media transport.

This also fits in with UCL's strategies to continue its upwards capital trajectory. It is quite clear to anyone even glancing up at the dazzling plate glass of Nido blocks that student housing blocks are now built as vehicles for this seasonal hotel industry. The student population and infrastructure of the modern university can also be put to use in the name of the Olympic spectacle. Bloomsbury, central and well furnished with upmarket cafés and fast food joints, plentiful hotel rooms and luxurious penthouses, situates itself in the out-of-term market as a perfect area for conferences and temporary accommodation. All those student blocks, so well funded and maintained by the university, are being given over throughout Summer 2012 to the hordes of paparazzi and broadcasters covering the season's activities, replete with its battalions of advertising technologies and souped-up multimedia stardust.

The methods of development by which Bloomsbury has been built up and repurposed in recent years visits itself back on the structures of Stratford, but in reverse. The student blocks are not erected to one day be hotels, but the hotels to one day be student blocks. The interchangeability of students and tourists, both now firmly wedged into the class of the nomadic moneyed consumer in the eyes of the bourgeoisie, can be counted on as a vital element of the metropolis and its architecture. The corporate and university forms approach each other ever more closely; the hotel and the student housing block blur as much as the academic and corporate conference – and the shell mutates the organism.

Not being able to build *up*, and limited in the extent to which they can burrow *down*, the universities have opted for two other remaining options: the recapitalisation of housing described above, re-mechanisation, and colonisation.

MACHINES

UCL clearly represents the kind of university which the 1960s USA student movement declared a collaborator in the 'military-industrial complex'. Wealth creation from biomedical sciences is becoming a priority for UCL and its sister organisation, UCL Partners. Malcolm Grant (UCL's President and Provost) has been named Deteriorator-in-Chief of the NHS, overseer of the national project of biomed growth, and the creation of the 'London-Cambridge pharma-corridor' as a government report enthuses. The Systems Engineering Department boasts of its links with Ultra Electronics and BAE Systems, and offers an MSc module in 'defence systems'. This runs in parallel with the Department of Space and Climate Physics, incorporating the Mullard Space Science Laboratory, which has been central to the UK's satellite programme for over 40 years.

It is around such projects as these, eloquently mollified under the acronym STEM (Science, Technology, Engineering and Medicine) that university policy has been

The technologies of the modern university spin bio-chemical and petro-military armaments into the world

nurtured through the crisis. The Carpenters' Company of the 19th century gave its money to UCL for technical education, naively believing it to be a place where craft and masonry could be propagated. The technologies of the modern university spin bio-chemical and petro-military armaments into the world, not ogies and rib vaults.

Meanwhile, waste labour (the unemployed and all the forms of 'bad labour' that creates) is converted into the basic ground for regeneration, and thus supports the dreams of the financiers backing the wasteland projects. The recent King's Cross and Euston developments are showing what happens when you continue to gentrify a neighbourhood beyond the point where gentrification could have already been said to have occurred. UCL's problem is not how to simply increase its class standing but, to borrow Bordiga's phrasing, how to suck more young blood from the dead labour within it. The administrators of Bloomsbury's crisis management are responsible not only for the riches of their masonry, but also the impoverishment of London's workforce. The 50,000 security guards who will cover London this Summer will all be employed through the technics of sub-contraction, a mode of employment which UCL is determinedly rolling out across its estates. University College London sees the unemployed and envisions an army of coffee workers, security guards and cleaners – God forbid, even *teachers* – to service its high-end consumer market.

COLONIES

Bloomsbury knows that it will always need its laborious base and a working class to service it; but it knows too that it can move into that class and reform it in the image of its own capital composition: repackaged, refinanced, privatised – but only so long as a new working class is found to serve it. So the question remains: for Bloomsbury to grow, it must exploit. It has no option but the imposition of technology and forced relocation. Those currently relocated by the Olympic neopolis include the Clays Lane Estate, as well as the residents of Newham's statutory traveller sites.

Adjacent to Newham, the Hackney marshes have been trespassed by the heaving curves of the Media Centre, one of the most fought over toys of the regeneration frenzy. The main competitor for the kitted out village is the Rothschild backed iCity, aiming to be a corridor of pumping techno-fizzle stretching out across the marshes. With promises of mass-scale educational partnerships, the glittering website is like a hundred other Olympic visions: warm sunrises over glass towers, and swarming digitised figurines playing joyfully between elephantine screens and retail palaces. We know the glass towers of the Olympic visions well; and the interiors they hide. In such utopias, there are critical realities which are divorced from the mind. Utopia, with all its glass panelling, is already present – it bounces off the students of Bloomsbury, reflecting their image as they glide through its sweep. But one glance away from the mirrors and the alienating truths stare back: the labour that breathes underground, in the maintenance sheds and engineering laboratories.

The question remains however, that once Stratford has been mechanised, where will the automated, impoverished residents live? The answer of course is further out of London: to Leyton and Walthamstow, Croydon, Mitcham and Thornton Heath. But these are the very areas where, following the mass criminality of August 2011, business and development finance is being bolstered next. This is to be calibrated under the aegis of Sir Stuart Lipton, one time chairman of the Commission for Architecture and the Built Environment (CABE), the vanguard of PFI aesthetics and skyline recompostition, who was forced to resign after it was revealed that he was essentially giving government design awards to buildings he had himself financed; and Julian Metcalfe, founder of Pret, the manicured hand of McDonald's desperate grasp over every high street and concurrent forms of bad labour. As East Londoners are chased further towards exurbia, the developers follow suit.

The situation in East London then, for all its

glorification of renewal and - the industrialist salivating into his calcifying spreadsheets - *growth*, is the result of two kinds of waste colliding: wastelands and waste labour. On the one hand, waste land repackaged and sold as a new product. Artificially manoeuvred into a new price band by the very fact that the radioactive detritus can be safely ignored by developers managing the otherwise celestial habitations of future citizens, the marshlands now present a tidy profit. On the other, the forms of bad labour enacted by the current mechanisms of global capital, with Bloomsbury as one of its most pristine axes.

The Olympic site will, of course, deteriorate. Beneath the buildings, marketed as a new utopia, the accumulated dead labour will be killed off yet again so that more living labour can be sucked from the working classes which will be pulled in from exurbia to service it. The radioactive dust distributed through the soil will become more and more radioactive until, a thousand years hence, its effects will finally start to show and - social turn-arounds notwithstanding - capital will find a mechanism of extracting value from the waste and disaster which entails.

Richard B <richardb@riseup.net> lives in London and organises with Bloomsbury Fightback!

FOOTNOTES

1 'UCL looks east towards Newham for additional university campus', http://www.ucl.ac.uk/news/news-articles/1111/111123-newham-additional-campus

2 The financial revolution of the 18th century forced land owning corporations, including the guilds and livery companies, to turn their assets into security for the new technologies of financial instruments. This not only had the effect of shifting their focus away from employment control and into asset management, but also into some of the foundational sources of cash flow for the expanding global aspirations of the nation state.

3 An unexploded bomb was still waiting at Sugar Hill Lane just down the road, when it was unearthed a few years ago. Another was found on Leyton marshes the other day.

4 The area of Ham, situated between the Thames, the Lea and the surrounding marshes, has been through numerous reallocations of administration and nomenclature. At the end of the 19th century it divided into the Essex county boroughs of East and West Ham, but in 1965 the two were incorporated into the new London Borough of Newham. Carbuncular and marginal, it fell outside of the London County Council remit and instead the council housing was overseen by the Ministry of Housing and Local Government (MOHLG) Development Group, as well as the Newham Council Planning and Architecture division.

5 'Affordable housing', of course, falls victim to the usual government double speak, in which affordable denotes the ability for the members of the most admired social strata (the 'middle' class) to devote oblational mortgages at the domestic altar, while those on the lowest wages must be content with the sub-layer titled 'social housing' constructed by those same rentier boddhisatvas. The irony is that *society* is invoked to entirely conceal the obliteration of social magnanimity this trophic economising entails. See http://www.metamute.org/editorial/articles/regeneration-games and http://www.communities.gov.uk/housing/housingresearch/housingstatistics/housingstatisticsby/affordablehousingsupply/affordablehousingnotes/

PROUD TO BE FLESH:

A MUTE MAGAZINE ANTHOLOGY OF CULTURAL POLITICS AFTER THE NET

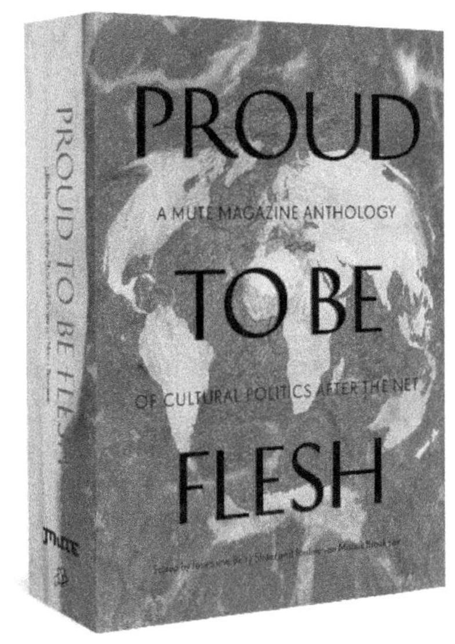

Edited by Josephine Berry Slater and Pauline van Mourik Broekman with Michael Corris, Anthony Iles, Benedict Seymour, and Simon Worthington

Compiling 15 years of *Mute* content, *Proud to be Flesh* offers 624 pages of some of the magazine's best writing, including interviews, essays, polemics and more. Divided into nine chronologically arranged chapters treating key themes associated with the 'digital revolution', *Proud to be Flesh* provides a unique history of a turbulent era and an excellent teaching tool.

Hardcover **£44.99** Softcover **£24.99**
Now available on Kindle **£7.81**

Proud to be Flesh can be purchased at all good bookshops, or previewed and ordered online at **metamute.org/proudtobeflesh**

To make a credit card order call
+44 (0)20 3287 9005

For further enquiries, contact Howard Slater **<howard@metamute.org>**

Published by Mute Publishing in association with Autonomedia

Softcover ISBN 978-1-906496-28-9
Hardcover ISBN 978-1-906496-27-2
Kindle ASIN - B0085WV7WU

'This collection of articles from the many incarnations of the *Mute* project is a great read, and a summation of that remarkable period of recent British history running from 1994 to 2009.'
-James Heartfield,
Spiked Review of Books

'Essential reading for anyone interested in the ways in which evolving technology and business practices transform our culture - and how we might oppose such influences.'
-David Barrett, *Art Monthly*

'At a time when recent advances in digital technologies are still considered innovative yet remain an unexplored field for many of us, *Mute* can already claim scholarship in this area. I think *Proud to be Flesh* is an invaluable reference tool for researchers and it should be on the desks of all digital media curators and educationalists.'
-Nayia Yiakoumaki, Archive Curator, Whitechapel Gallery

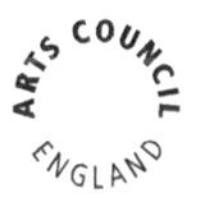

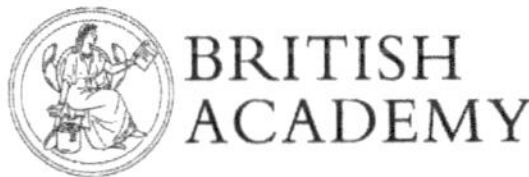

Supported by Arts Council England and The British Academy

BACK CATALOGUE: OPENMUTE PRESS AND MUTE BOOKS

Since 2005, OpenMute Press has been helping artists, writers and other independent producers bring their book ideas to fruition using Print On Demand, Short Run Press (which is also used to make our magazine) and, more recently, eBooks. Our back-catalogue also includes the first titles from Mute Books and Mute Publishing's anthology, *Proud To Be Flesh*. In addition to all the usual online retailers, these diverse publications are made available through **Metamute.org/shop**

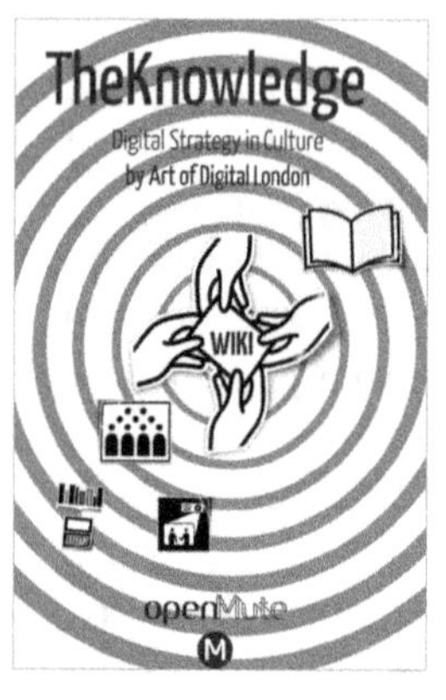

OpenMute

TheKnowledge - peer learning for digital strategy in culture

(April 2012)

The Art of Digital London (AoDL) is a digital strategy network for cultural organisations. its programme encompasses digital salons and surgeries, online resources and monthly meetups.

Alongside a series of specially commissioned articles, TheKnowledge compiles and synthesises all the information and experiences generated by AoDL and offers key digital strategies and guides for the creative and organisational dimensions of all cultural production.

ISBN - 978-1-906496-68-5 / £4.49

Kindle ASIN - B007SB3RM2 / £2.56

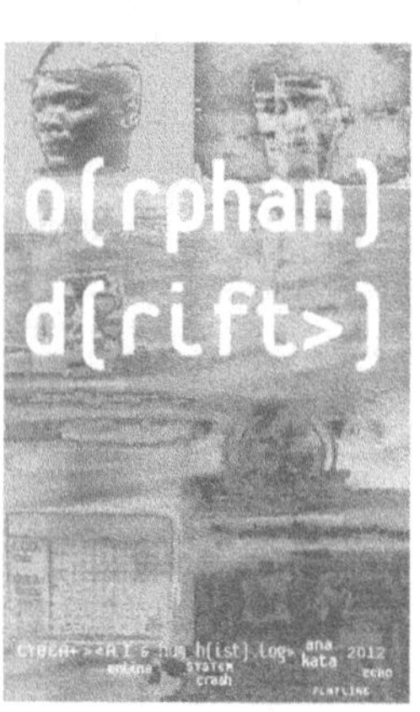

Various

O(rphan) D(rift>)

(April 2012 - 2nd edition)

Second edition published by Cabinet Editions / OpenMute London. Originally Published in 1995 by o(rphan)d(rift>) / Cabinet Editions 978-1-9064968-07

Drift. Adrift. Not simply leaving a shore, but diverting a course, a fluidity. where it goes, we are not planning to go... the shore of the ocean, displaces itself along with it.

ISBN - 978-1-906496-80-7 / £9.99

Sniff, Scrape, Crawl...
{on privacy, surveillance and our shadowy data-double}

Renée Turner

Sniff, Scrape, Crawl... {on Privacy, Surveillance and Our Shadowy Data-double}

(May 2012)

Crawling and scraping, the ambient social network creates a portrait of who we are, and maps our demographic character. Where once surveillance technologies were associated with the government and military, the web has fostered a participatory and less optically driven means of monitoring and monetizing our lived experiences. This book explores current debates on privacy and surveillance in the digital age.

ISBN – 978-1-906496-81-4 / £10.00

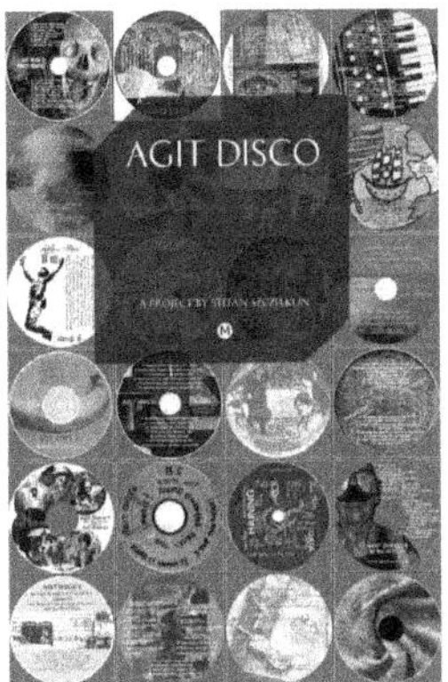

Stefan Szczelkun and Anthony Iles (Eds.)

Agit Disco

(Jan 2012)

Agit Disco collects the playlists of its 23 writers to tell the story of how music has influenced and inspired them politically. The book provides a multi-genre survey of political musics from a wide range of viewpoints, that goes beyond protest songs into the darker hinterlands of musical meaning. Each playlist is annotated and illustrated. The collection grew organically with an exchange of homemade CDs and images. These images, with their DIY graphics, are used to give the playlists a visual materiality.

ISBN – 978-1-906496-51-7 / £11.99

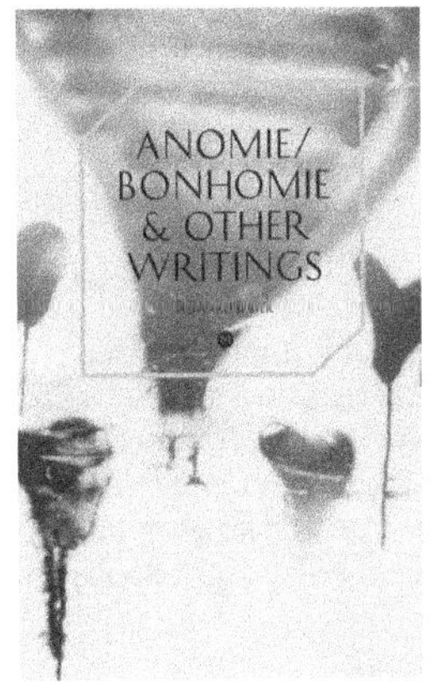

Howard Slater

Anomie/Bonhomie & Other Writings

(Jan 2012)

In this collection of writings, Howard Slater improvises around what Walter Benjamin could have meant by the phrase 'affective classes'. This 'messianic shard' and its possible implications leads Slater to develop a therapeutic micro-politics by way of a mourning for the Workers' Movement and a grappling with the 'becomings of capital'.

ISBN – 978-1-906496-72-2 / £9.99
Now available on Kindle, ASIN - B007KO5NP6 / £6.99

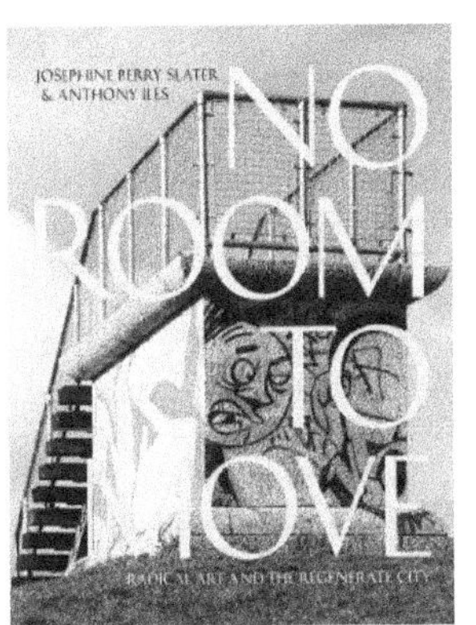

Josephine Berry Slater and Anthony Iles (Eds.)

No Room to Move: Radical Art and the Regenerate City

(Sep 2010)

As the Creative City model for urban regeneration founders, Anthony Iles and Josephine Berry Slater take stock of an era of highly instrumentalised public art making. Focusing on artists and consultants who have engaged critically with the exclusionary politics of urban regeneration, their analysis locates such practice within a schematic history of urban development's neoliberal mode. Featuring projects and interviews with Alberto Duman, Freee, Nils Norman, Laura Oldfield Ford and Roman Vasseur.

ISBN – 9781906496425 / £14.95
Now available on Kindle, AISN - B0085WV9AK / £6.41

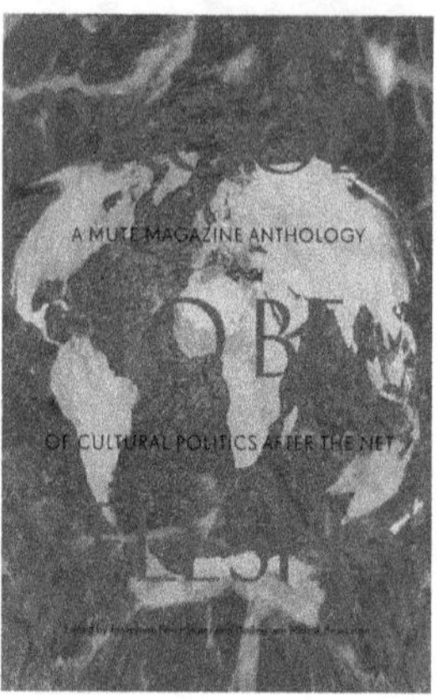

Josephine Berry Slater and Pauline van Mourik Broekman (Eds.) with Michael Corris, Anthony Iles, Benedict Seymour and Simon Worthington

Proud to be Flesh: A Mute Magazine Anthology of Cultural Politics After the Net

(Nov 2009)

Proud To Be Flesh offers an expansive collection of some of *Mute*'s finest articles and is thematically organised around key contemporary issues: Direct Democracy and its Demons; Net Art
to Conceptual Art and Back; I, Cyborg; Reinventing the Human; Of Commoners and Criminals; Organising Horizontally; Art and/against Business; Under the Net - the City and the Camp; Class and Immaterial Labour; The Open Work.

Softback, ISBN – 9781906496289 / £24.95

Hardback, ISBN – 9781906496272 / £44.99

Now available on Kindle, ASIN - B0085WV7WU Price - £7.81

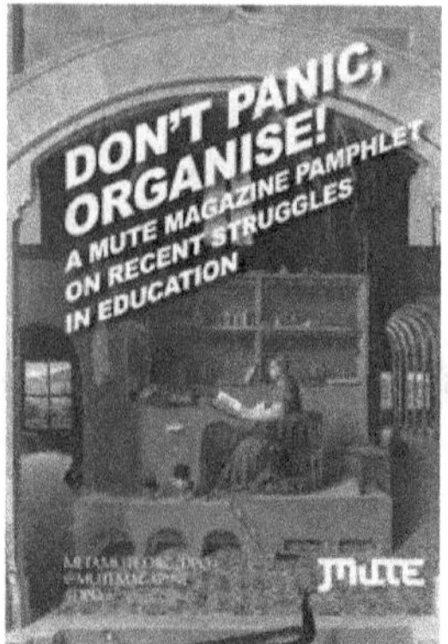

Don't Panic, Organise! A Mute Magazine Pamphlet on Recent Struggles in Education

(Dec 2010)

From the introduction: 'They should be understood as part of the more gradual process of what George Caffentzis, in his analysis of the international situation, calls the "breakdown of the edu-deal"; the inability for capital, and therefore the state, to pay for the costs of producing a well educated workforce or to guarantee that investment in education will result in a more vigorous economy and increased living standards for those with qualifications.'

ISBN – 9781906496548 / £2.99

eBook ISBN – 9781906496555 / Free

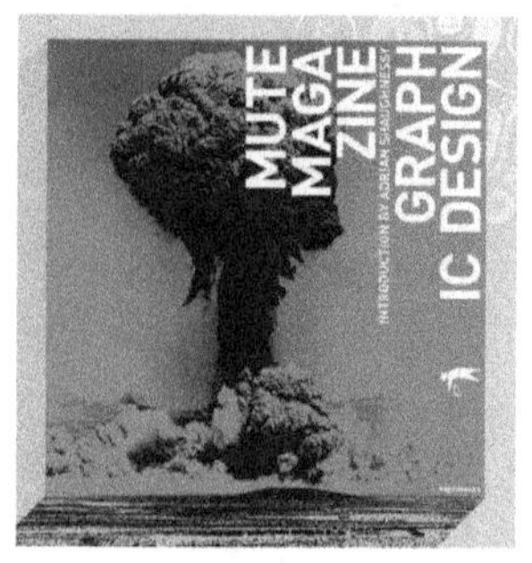

Damian Jaques, Pauline van Mourik Broekman, Adrian Shaughnessy and Simon Worthington (Eds.)

Mute Magazine Graphic Design

(May 2008)

In the early 1990s, long before the Internet became an integral part of life, a handful of pioneering magazines took it upon themselves to imagine the Internet into existence using fiction, interviews, speculative theory and experimental graphic design. Founded by artists Simon Worthington and Pauline van Mourik Broekman, London based *Mute* occupied a central position. *Mute Magazine Graphic Design* presents and contextualises its graphic output. [Published by Eight Books]

ISBN – 9780955432224 / £19.95

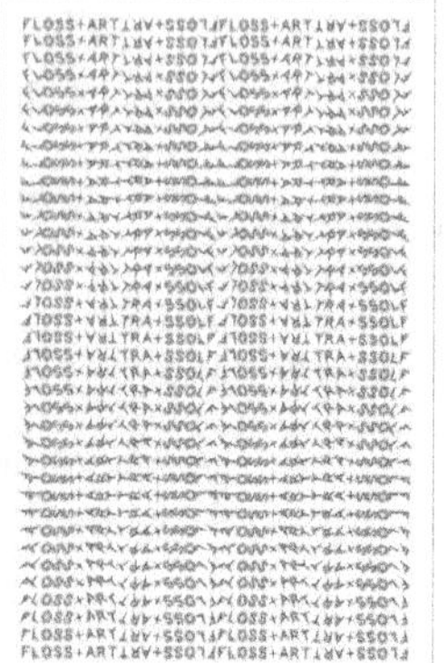

Aymeric Mansoux and Marloes de Valk (Eds.)

FLOSS + Art

(Aug 2008)

FLOSS+Art reflects critically on the growing relationship between Free Software ideology, open content and digital art. It provides a view onto the social, political and economic myths and realities linked to this phenomenon. Contributors: Fabianne Balvedi, Florian Cramer, Sher Doruff, Nancy Mauro Flude, Olga Goriunova, Dave Griffiths, Ross Harley, Martin Howse, Shahee Ilyas, Ricardo Lafuente, Ivan Monroy Lopez, Thor Magnusson, Alex McLean, Rob Myers, Alejandra Maria Perez Nuñez, Eleonora Oreggia, oRx-qX, Julien Ottavi, Michael van Schaik, Femke Snelting, Pedro Soler, Hans Christoph Steiner, Prodromos Tsiavos, Simon Yuill.

ISBN – 9781906496180 / £18.50

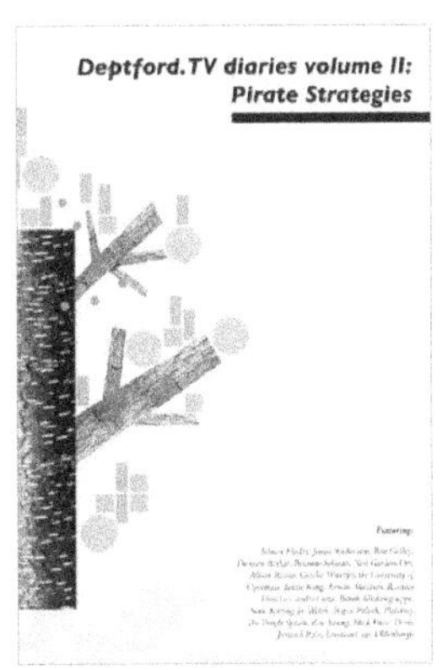

Deptford.TV

Deptford.tv Diaries II – Pirate Strategies

(Apr 2008)

This reader problematises the notion of 'tactical media' – calling for a more strategic approach. Contributors: Adnan Hadzi, Jonas Andersson, Ben Gidley, Duncan Reekie, Brianne Selman, Neil Gordon-Orr, Alison Rooke, Gesche Wuerfel, the University of Openness, Jamie King, Armin Medosch, Rasmus Fleischer, andrea rota, Bitnik Mediengruppe, Sven Koenig Jo Walsh, Rufus Pollock, Platoniq, The People Speak, Zoe Young, Mick Fuzz, Denis Jaromil Rojo, Lennaart van Oldenborgh'.

ISBN – 9781906496111 / £5

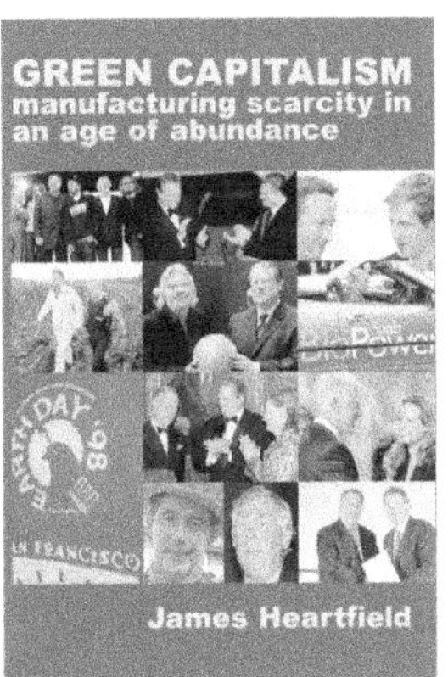

James Heartfield

Green Capitalism: Manufacturing Scarcity in an Age of Abundance

(Feb 2008)

A polemic against 'Green Capitalism' which James Heartfield accuses of profiteering from climate change and other environmental scares. Green capitalists like Zac Goldsmith and Al Gore are manufacturing scarcity to boost prices. The technological revolution has removed scarcity from most of our lives, but the green capitalists are trying to re-invent it.

ISBN – 9781906496104 / £7.50

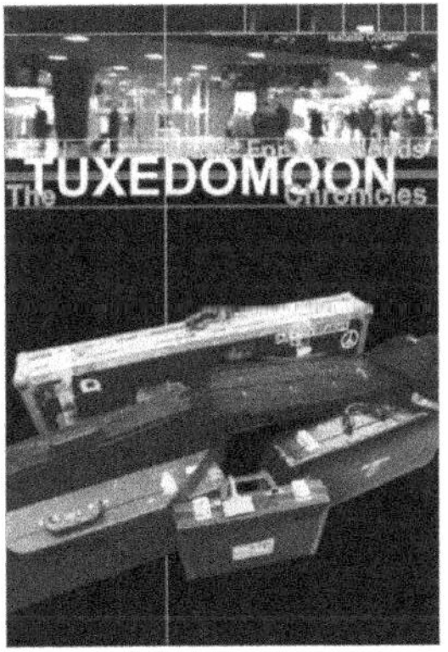

Isabelle Corbisier

Music for Vagabonds: the Tuxedomoon Chronicles

(Jan 2008)

Tuxedomoon is a group of musicians and performers that was formed in San Francisco in 1977. Their identity is as elusive as their geographical location. Tuxedomoon have attracted followers and gained cult status, never ceasing their quest for a permanently elusive and lost 'home' – some other America or the quaint Europe of their fantasies. From 2001 onwards, the author of this book found herself sucked into Tuxedomoon's spiral of vagrancy and travelled the world to meet the actors in this ongoing 30-year-old story.

ISBN – 9781906496081 / £19

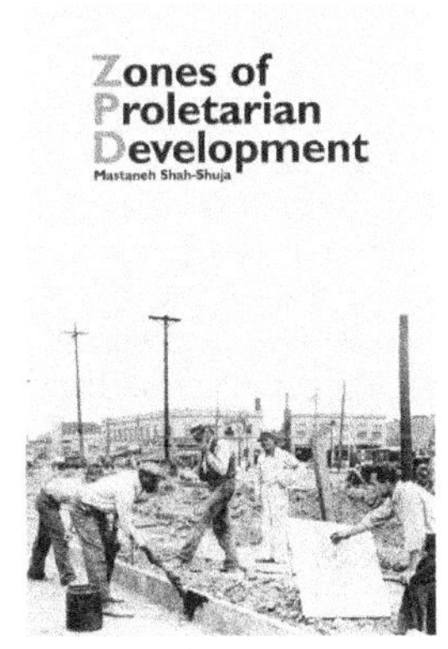

Mastaneh Shah-Shuja

Zones of Proletarian Development

(Jan 2008)

Zones of Proletarian Development is an attempt to theorise the anti-capitalist movement from a neo-Vygotskian perspective. Using Marx, Vygotsky, Bakhtin and Activity Theory, it analyses a series of proletarian activities including incendary May Day celebrations in London, carnivalesque football riots in Iran, the anti-poll-tax rebellion and the anti-war movement. It concludes by looking at past and current proletarian organisations and makes a number of proposals for future modes of organising conducive to radical consciousness and autonomous activity.

ISBN – 9781906496067 / £15

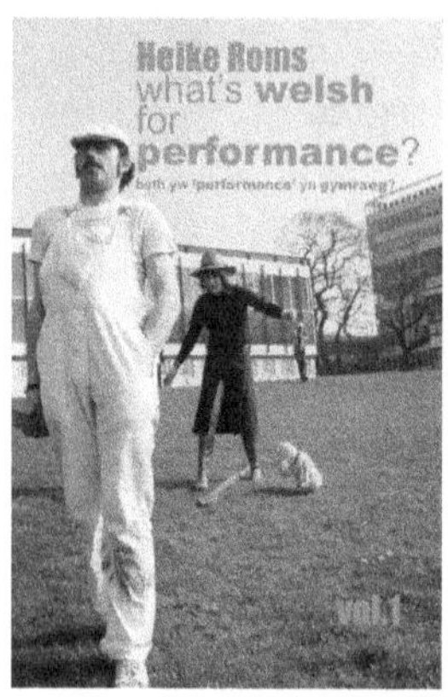

Heike Roms

What's Welsh for Performance?

(Dec 2007)

For more than forty years artists have been creating performances, happenings and other time-based art in Wales, yet their work remains largely confined to half-remembered anecdotes, rumours and hearsay. *What's Welsh for Performance?* tries to uncover Wales' hidden history of performance in conversations with key artists who have shaped this history since 1968. With: Shirley Cameron, Ivor Davies, Anthony Howell, John Chris Jones, Timothy Emlyn Jones, Andrew Knight, Roland Miller. Dr. Heike Roms is lecturer in Performance Studies at Aberystwyth University, Wales.

ISBN – 9780955392726 / £10

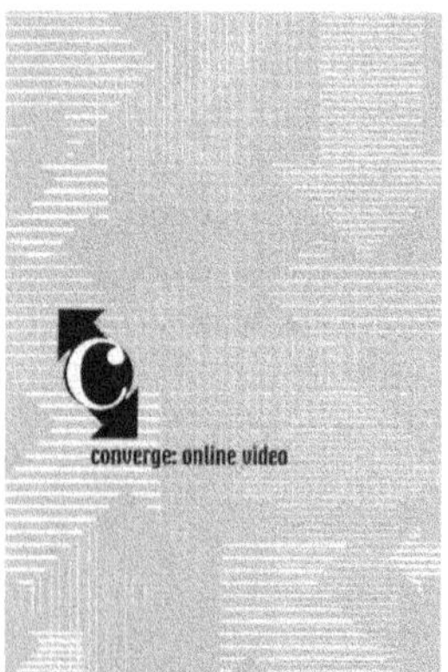

Converge – Online Video

(Oct 2007)

Using media as a means of working with, and empowering marginalised people in their communities is a practice that has emerged strongly in recent years, nurtured by the extraordinary growth of digital media and the Web. These developments have enabled a participatory culture – particularly online – in which young people are now more able to represent themselves and their concerns. This book offers first hand accounts of work across and beyond Inclusion Through Media, alongside critical analysis of many of the processes involved, and the policy issues it raises. The book includes an accompanying DVD.

ISBN – 9781906496005 / £9.99

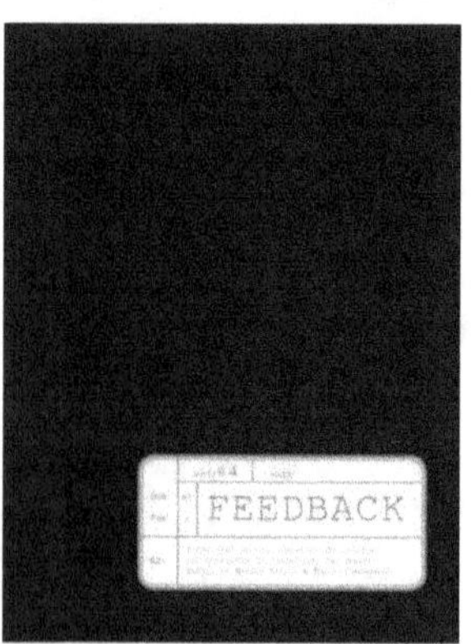

E. Karaba (Ed.)

Feedback 4: Ideas that Inform, Construct and Concern the Production of Exhibitions and Events

(Sep 2007)

FeedBack 4 focuses on participatory art events and examines them from the point of view of the artist, the curator and the participant. It brings together contributions from many authors interested in curatorial debates.

ISBN – 9780955479687 / £6.50

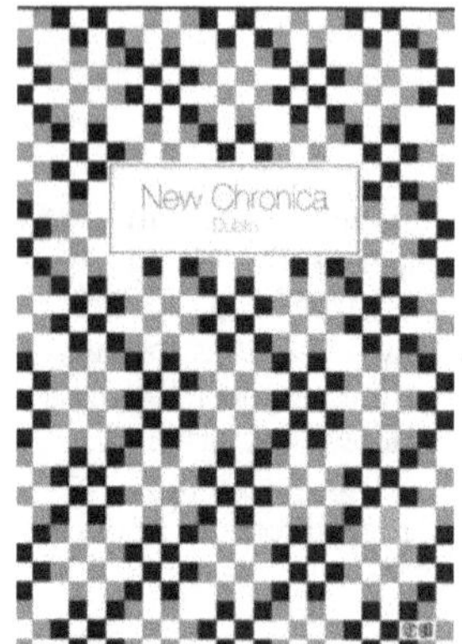

Steven Dickie

New Chronica Dublin

(Jul 2007)

New Chronica Dublin is a graphic novel and musical album download, based on a collection of contemporary folklore from the Irish capital. The dilution of identity and the inevitable displacement of population which the rebranding of economic and social areas brings, may result in this being the last opportunity to witness the community's galvanised common identity as it negotiates a position within the new Dublin.

ISBN – 9780955479663 / £10

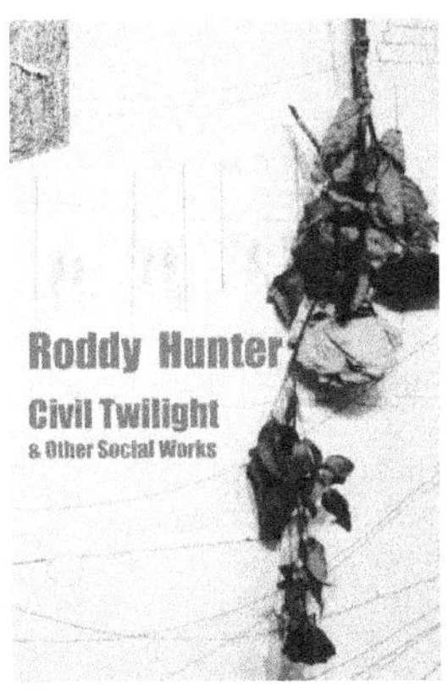

Roddy Hunter

Civil Twilight & Other Social Works

(Feb 2007)

Civil Twilight & Other Social Works explores the performance artwork of provocative Scots artist Roddy Hunter. Through the artist's own texts and archival documentation, Hunter introduces us to his methodology of research into the idea of urban civic centres as places where collective identity is formed.

ISBN – 9780955392719 / £10

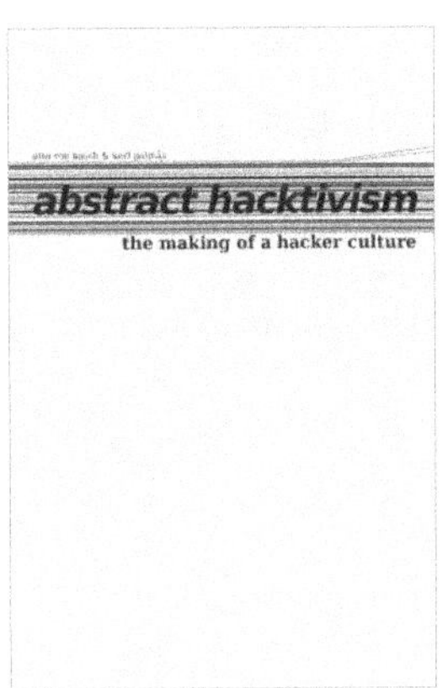

Otto von Busch & Karl Palmås

Abstract Hacktivism: The Making of a Hacker Culture

(Dec 2006)

In recent years, designers, activists and business people have started to navigate their social worlds on the basis of concepts derived from the world of computers and new media technologies. According to Otto von Busch and Karl Palmås, this represents a fundamental cultural shift. In the 19th century, the motor replaced the clockwork as the universal model of knowledge; new media technologies are currently replacing the motor as the dominant 'conceptual technology' of contemporary social thought.

ISBN – 0955479622 / £5

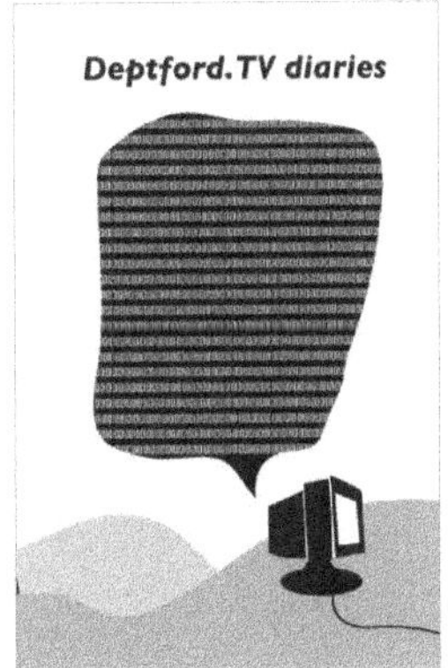

Deptford TV

Deptford.tv Diaries

(Dec 2006)

Deptford.TV is an audio-visual documentation of the regeneration process of Deptford (south-east London) in collaboration with SPC.org media lab, Bitnik.org, Boundless.coop, Liquid Culture and Goldsmiths College. Contributors: Adnan Hadzi, Maria X, Heidi Seetzen, James Stevens, Erol Ziya, Bitnik media collective, Andrea Pozzi, Andrea Rota and Jonas Andersson, alongside selected public license texts from Hakim Bey, Jaromil and Guy Debord.

ISBN – 0955479606 / £5

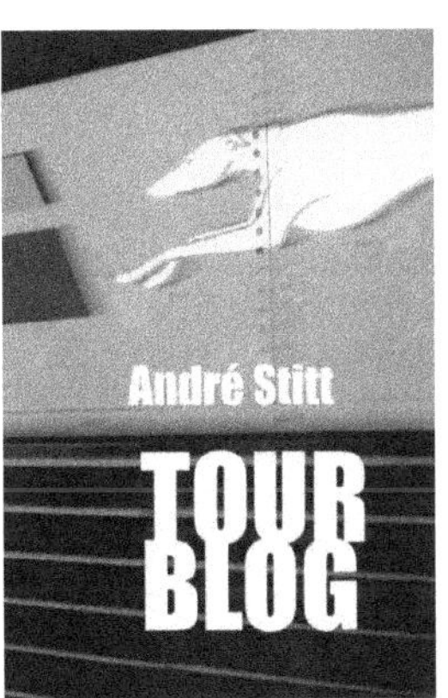

André Stitt

Tour Blog 2006: On Tour with Panacea Society USA

(Sep 2006)

No Sex, No Drugs, No Rock 'n' Roll. Just freak-beat, psyche-garage, prog-techno and artyness. Who do they think they are, these performance artists who want to be the new Golden Gods of Art-Rock? Find out as you join The Panacea Society on their 2006 North American tour. When asked by one of his students what he would be doing during the Easter break, performance artist André Stitt decided to write a tour diary.

ISBN – 0955392705 / £10

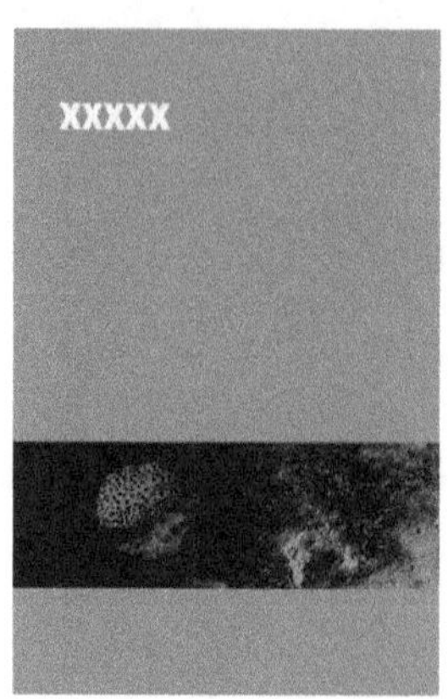

XXXXX

(Sep 2006)

[The] xxxxx [reader] proposes a radical, new space for artistic exploration, with essential contributions from a diverse range of artists, theorists, and scientists. Combining intense background material, code listings, screenshots, new translations, [the] xxxxx [reader] functions as both guide and manifesto for a thought movement which is radically opposed to entropic contemporary economies. xxxxx traces a clear line across eccentric and wide ranging texts under the rubric of life coding which can well be contrasted with the death drive of cynical economy with roots in rationalism and enlightenment thought.

ISBN – 0955066441 / £15

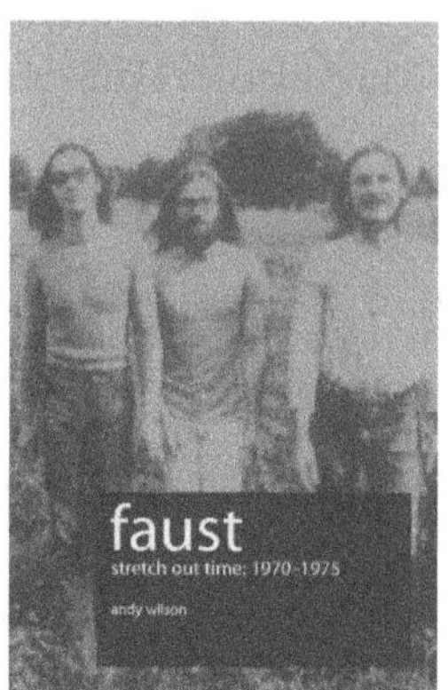

Andy Wilson

Faust: Stretch Out Time 1970-1975

(Jun 2007)

In 1970 Polydor Records funded an unusual experiment. They gave some unknown German musicians a retreat in the countryside near Hamburg, equipped it with a studio and their best engineer, then left them free to do as they liked. This is the story of Faust and the music they made between 1970 and 1975, music which continues to inspire and confound listeners to this day.

ISBN – 095506645X / £10.99

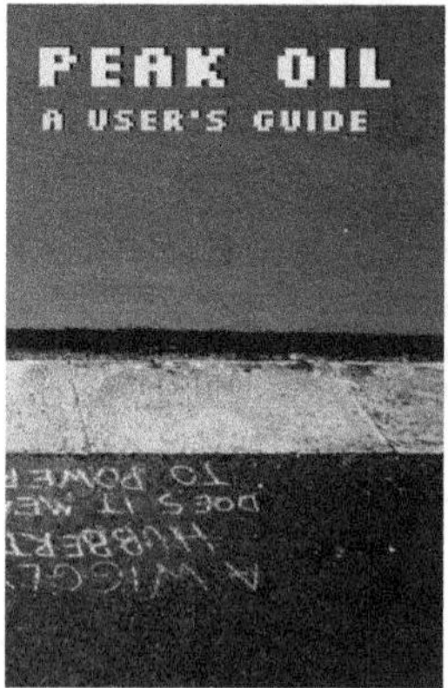

Popex

Peak Oil: A User's Guide

(July 2006)

This book is composed of two parts. The first part is the manual for the Peak Oil Olympics, a happening which took place on the 1st and 2nd July 2006 in Bristol, UK. This has been updated with documentation from the event, and expanded by the second part which is a look at Peak Oil from a more critical angle incorporating texts by George Caffentzis and Iain Boal which provide a more systematic analysis of what Peak Oil might mean.

ISBN – 0955066468 / £4

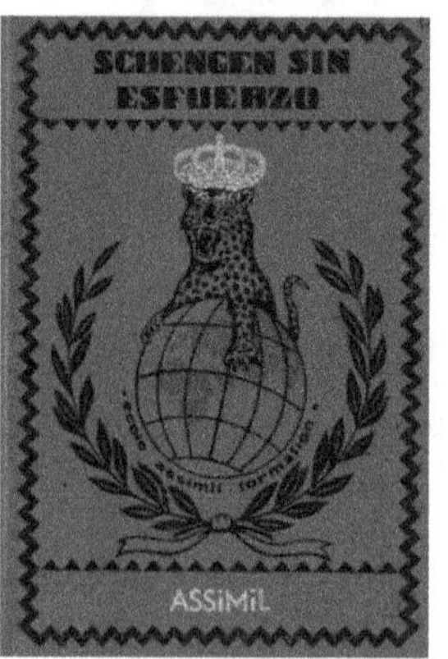

Vahida Ramujkic

Schengen with Ease

(Feb 2007)

'Extra-comunitarios', or citizens of non-European countries, have the 'extra' bureaucratic task of changing their status, to one that will allow them to move and work 'freely' within the European Union. The length and complexity of this process can vary depending on the type of 'extra-comunitario' in question. Almost everyone agrees that bureaucracy is the most boring thing in the world. *Schengen with Ease* is a compilation of material from a variety of official and non-official sources, brought together to explain how daily practices are affected by the application of the EU Foreign Legislation and the Schengen Agreement in the territory of the European Union.

ISBN – 0955066484 / £8.29

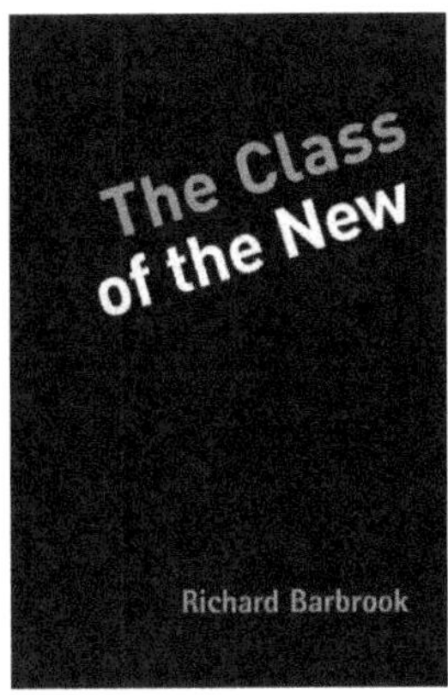

Richard Barbrook

Class of the New

(May 2006)

Netizens, elancers, cognitarians, swarm-capitalists, hackers, produsumers, knowledge workers, pro-ams... these are just a few of the monikers that have been applied to the new social class emerging from the networked workplace. In this short book, Richard Barbrook presents a collection of quotations from authors who in different ways attempt to identify an innovative element within society - 'the class of the new'. Announcing a new economic and social paradigm, this class constitutes a 'social prophecy' of the shape of work to come.

ISBN -0955066476 / £4

NODE.London

A NODE.London Reader - A Survey of Media Arts, Technologies and Politics

(Feb 2006)

The NODE.London reader, *Media Mutandis*, projects a critical context around the Season of Media Arts in London March 2006 and provides another discursive dimension to the events of October 2005's Open Season. It engages debates in FLOSS (Free/Libre and Open Source Software), media arts and activism, collaborative practices and the political economy of cultural production in the present day. Contributions from Sabeth Buchmann, Toni Prug, Armin Medosch, Simon Yuill, Chad McCail, Critical Art Ensemble, Jo Walsh, Richard Barbrook, Michael Corris, Harwood, Kate Rich, Agnese Trocchi, Matthew Fuller, Rasmus Fleischer and Palle Torsson, Brett Neilson and Ned Rossiter, Matteo Pasquinelli and Francis McKee.

ISBN - 0955243505 / £5

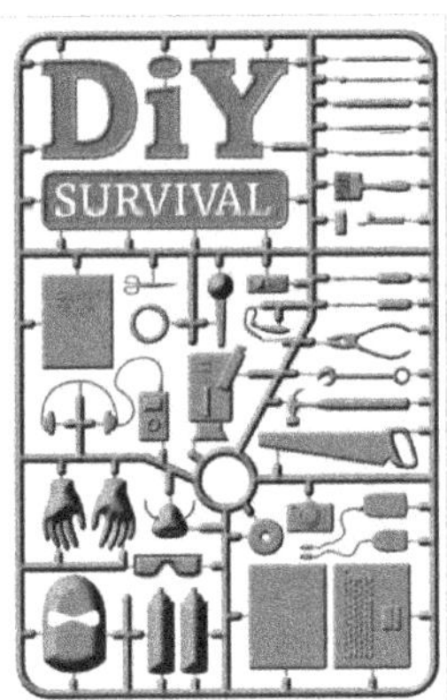

C6

DiY Survival

(Oct 2005)

DiY Survival There is no subculture, only subversion. DiY or do-it-yourself survival is a collection of essays, tips and case studies collated from an online call for participation by the maverick art group C6. The eclectic mix presented within these pages shows the breadth and diversity of art/activism practice today. Whether that is creating wireless networks, pissing on national monuments or building cardboard friends, it is certain that these submissions show that practitioners are taking their work to new spaces and audiences, redefining, through the engagement with the community, what we have considered to be 'art'.

ISBN -0955066492 / £4.99

WWW.METAMUTE.ORG/SHOP

Please get in touch with us on **mute@metamute.org** with any queries about producing your book through OpenMute.

Further information and pricing is also available at **www.metamute.org/services**

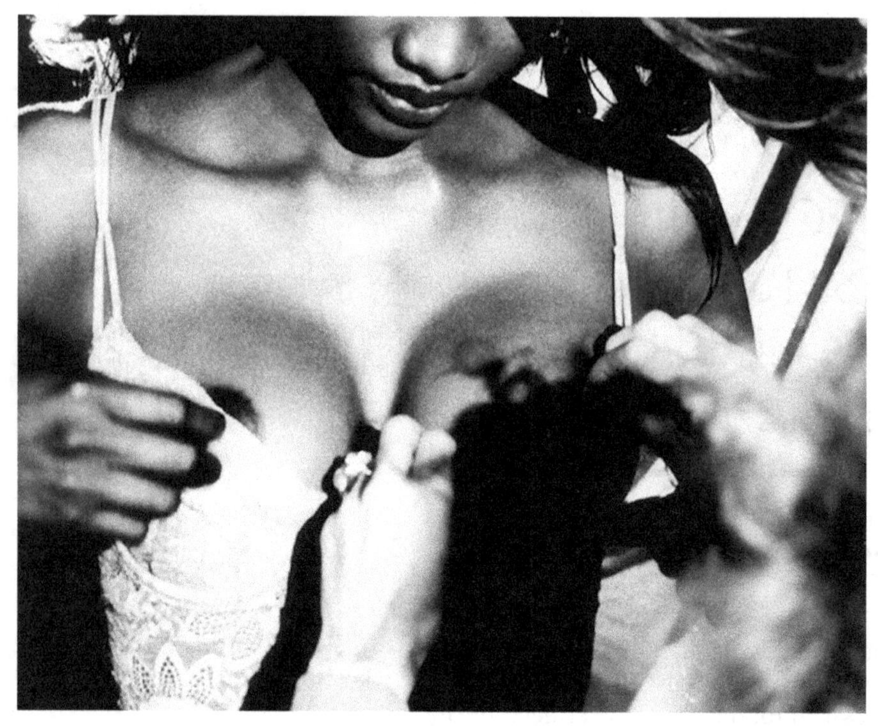

www.ingramcontent.com/pod-product-compliance
Lightning Source LLC
LaVergne TN
LVHW080331110826
845155LV00024B/146